from publisher

Jane Apt

June 16, 1970

SEXUAL ADVENTURE
IN
MARRIAGE

SEXUAL ADVENTURE IN MARRIAGE

by

JEROME AND JULIA RAINER

INTRODUCTION BY
HAROLD THOMAS HYMAN, M.D.

SIMON AND SCHUSTER
New York

CONTENTS

———•———

INTRODUCTION

———•—•———

A RECENT ADVERTISING CAMPAIGN, WAGED ON BEHALF OF organized religions of various persuasions, took as its slogan *the family that prays together stays together*. By the same token the general practitioner, who doubles as family confidant, learns that the husband and wife who enjoy a pleasurable sexual rapport also stay together. Not for them the analyst's couch or the divorce court if, in the sanctity of their bedroom, they can dispel the usual spate of marital trials and discords.

By contrast, the couple whose coital experiences are unsatisfactory, whether for one or both, do not readily or easily arrive at an accommodation when confronted with the differences that arise in any and every connubium. Indeed, as the differences, however petty at first, widen and intensify, the sexual relationship worsens and may even come to a halt. And with a worsening sexual relationship, the foundations of the marriage appear to crumble until the threat of separation, annulment or divorce darkens the home and its inhabitants, including the non-combatant children.

As when a stone is thrown into a pool of clear water, a domestic conflict spreads in ever-widening circles. Either or both partners seek the solace of a friend of the opposite sex, a search that all too often has an act of infidelity as a by-product. Or either or both develop some symptomatic complaint or psychosomatic disturbance that re-

quires intensive and expensive investigation and treatment. And so the miseries mount.

The authors of this informative book have set themselves the task of revitalizing the sexual relationship that
can bind a couple together against the divisive stresses of
daily living. Their marriage manual, which is also a book
of social criticism, speaks vigorously in behalf of unspoiled
sex and levels a just charge at contemporary culture. In
their view, the sexual instinct is easily debased, certainly
attenuated, by forces that daily exploit it for selfish or
material gain, or that use its power to win advantage over
a fellow human being.

And so, as a counterbalance to what they deem is a
growing cynicism and callousness toward sex in our society, the authors recommend a return to enjoyment, a
psychophysical gift with which we were all born but later
deprived of by sexual maleducation. The only proviso is
that married couples, as they recultivate a capacity for joy,
follow this single rule: No harm, psychic or physical, must
be visited by either one upon the other.

In the light of their central concept, there is a natural
place in married life for the many postural variations and
teachings in the book. And the swift panoramic view, in
the form of excerpts from literary classics revealing man-
kind's quest for joy throughout the centuries, should help
to dissipate whatever ghosts of sexual inhibition still haunt
the married.

This book is a fascinating sequel to the authors' earlier
work which received both national and international attention. It may prove the lifeline that saves many marriages on the verge of shipwreck.

—HAROLD THOMAS HYMAN, M.D.

AUTHORS' NOTE TO THE READER

A SOVIET CITIZEN WHO ALL HIS LIFE HAD ADMIRED THE UNITED States finally received permission to visit this country. After his arrival he went directly from the airport to what he had been schooled to believe was the very nerve center and soul of American life, Times Square. He wandered from street to street, stopping before store windows, movie marquees, newsstand displays and apparel shops. Wherever he paused to look, the omnipresence of sex stunned him: the banal photographic nudity of the girlie magazines, the lurid sex illustrations of the paperbacks, the busty fashion manikins in filmy lingerie, the leering postcards and sexual novelties. To add insult to injury, in the dimming light on the way to his hotel, he was accosted by a male prostitute.

When he faced his American host that evening, he exploded with righteous indignation. "How can this be possible!" he groaned. "And in a country with such a high culture!"

Patiently his American host attempted to explain that the attainment of a high culture came at a price, oftentimes a painfully high price, and that the suppression of printed matter, however contemptible, often tended to pose a threat to our freedom of speech. And that, as for prostitution, it ranked among the smallest of our social problems. But the Russian visitor's outrage was only partially ap-

11

peased. The multiple forms of female nudity brazenly displayed in print, virtually unknown in his native land, still offended him. He would have the police confiscate all such matter lest American youth become contaminated.

The latter danger was admitted to be a real one, but police censorship his American host would not endorse. To illustrate his point, he showed his Soviet guest a reproduction of a French painting. It was a nude seated on a stool, her legs dangling, in a pose that might be considered lightly but not blatantly erotic. "Would you have the police confiscate her?" the Russian was asked. He hesitated, then tersely replied: "Yes—I don't approve," and he turned away.

It became immediately apparent that this Soviet paragon was the modern equivalent of that almost extinct species, the American Puritan, who roamed this country circa 1620 to 1900. The nude he rejected as unsuitable for display was a painting by Matisse, the original of which hangs today in the great Hermitage Museum in Leningrad.

Nudity is one of the least consequential symptoms of the current sexual revolution. Whenever it becomes extreme, or lapses into bad taste, we somehow manage to deal with it. Actually our problems are not the obvious external ones. Where our Soviet visitor missed the mark was in his failure to apprehend the real difficulties that our new sexual freedom has generated.

We may have banished the Puritan and the Victorian from our society, but we are not set free from our internal tensions. We may be free as the pagans in our articulate attitudes toward sex, but guilt feelings still cling in the recesses of the personality. The signs of sexual liberation are everywhere, but its accent has been on extramarital and premarital sex. It has not greatly enhanced the pleasures of sex within marriage. When we finally learn to experience total sexual joy, we do not often succeed in harnessing it to the service of the marital relationship.

Perhaps one of the reasons the present authors' earlier book, *Sexual Pleasure in Marriage,* became a nationwide bestseller and has been translated into ten foreign languages is that it offered the hope of achieving a natural and uncomplicated attitude toward sex while learning to experience one's full potential for sexual joy. Most of the letters we have received since its publication expressed gratitude for a new and refreshing outlook upon marital sex.

Some appreciative letters suggested, however, that something more was needed to sustain sexual pleasure throughout the fluctuating climate of most marriages. As a number of readers expressed it:

"You have helped us discover pleasure in our marriage. But when monotony develops, what alternative does one have? Some of our friends, we know, have found escape from monotony through petty infidelities. We can't accept that as a solution. . . ."

". . . Can you tell us, as concretely and as helpfully as you did in your book, how sexual happiness can be prolonged? We both understand that marriage is for life and are pledged to our commitment."

"We think we have a very good relationship. Yet my wife and I both admit that we have not quite reached a stage of total sexual freedom with each other. Now that you have brought us at least to the threshold of freedom, where do we go from here? Is there such a thing as a sense of adventure that we can bring into our marriage? . . ."

There is, and this book proposes to explore it. Yet it is

important to recognize that for sexual love within marriage to remain an enduring excitement, for erotic joy in each other to be approximately as keen at the twenty-fifth anniversary as at the fifth, something more than erotic competence is needed. A basic compatibility of personality must be present before the greater heights of Eros can be scaled. It will be stated many times in this book that the dissonances of marriage, when they are brought about by the immaturity of one or both partners, cannot be removed merely by expertise in the erotic arts. Advanced sexual knowledge cannot help disorders of the personality nor accelerate the growth of retarded emotional life.

This book will take issue with many of the forms of sex that masquerade today as eroticism. It will expose the shoddy substitutes for real sensuality that somehow come to be woven into a commercial culture. But principally it will present to the emotionally well-adjusted the prospect of tasting all the delights of hedonistic sex as it might have been practiced in pagan Greece, in Scheherazade's Baghdad or Pompadour's France—with one's own husband or wife.

As medical writers and authors, individually or together, of some twenty books, we have found our sources for this book in the knowledge provided by modern physicians and social scientists, in the wisdom of century-old erotic writings and in the experience of marriage and family living for more than twenty-five years.

SEXUAL ADVENTURE
IN
MARRIAGE

1

———·•·———

SEXUAL ADVENTURE:
COUNTERFEIT AND REAL

SEXUAL ADVENTURE—WHAT IMAGE DOES IT CALL TO MIND?
Don Juan, leaping from boudoir to boudoir, in a repetitious round of perpetual seduction? Or his modern counterpart, the bachelor playboy, luring one sleek beauty after another to his penurious pad or his luxurious penthouse? Is sexual adventure the snatched moment of illicit love with another man's wife in a motel? Or the expensive hour with a call girl between meetings of the business convention in a city away from home?

These are the stereotyped images of sexual adventure. But many of us are too sophisticated today to be deluded by them. We know that Don Juan flitted from love to love because he could neither give nor find sexual satisfaction with any of them. As for the sexual playboy, despite the attempt to make him an American institution, he is nothing but a cartoon character; his bosomy girls are the pin-ups of adolescent imagination, his pad or penthouse a Hollywood film fantasy. And the furtive adultery, whether in a cheap motel or an expense account hotel suite, is usually drunken, tawdry and banished from memory as soon afterward as possible.

None of these is sexual adventure. None of them refreshes the senses and expands the spirit. As a sexual way of life, every one of these fancied adventures in sex, no matter how exciting in anticipation, ends in boredom and discontent. They represent a counterfeit species of sex.

The only genuine sexual adventurers are the well married.

This categorical statement seems to defy common knowledge. But common knowledge has swallowed a cliché. Without question or challenge, American belief today is that sex within marriage is by definition less exultant, less charged with electric emotion and generally inferior to the kind of sex that occurs outside of the connubial establishment. The myth persists that marital intercourse is little more than a pleasing biological habit producing at best a second-class emotion. Sex within marriage is thought of as a tame domestic brand, somewhat plodding and humdrum, for which apologies have to be made.

We need only consider how that vast reflecting mirror of our society—our modern literature, films, plays, periodicals—confirms and reinforces the image. How often are married lovers chosen as the protagonists, that is, lovers married to each other? In the sex-drenched passages of our modern novels, how often is conjugal passion dealt with, unless on the wedding night? How often are the lovers, licit or illicit, past the age of forty?

Is conjugal sex really such dull stuff that authors and readers will have none of it?

Often, alas, it is. We tend to be convinced by the fictions around us that once we take the marriage vows we must say farewell to adventure in sex and settle for convenience. So powerful and ubiquitous is the cliché that many well and happily married spouses accept its dictum, and thereby deprive themselves of one of the high privileges of married love.

Literature has its own reason for avoiding conjugal sex and painting illicit sex as perennially purple with passion. The writers and film makers have to keep the true lovers apart; without frustration there can be no tension. Once they are in each other's arms, the play is over. Married lovers attract us only when they are in trouble; otherwise there is no story. About happy lovers there is nothing to tell except that they are happy.

We become conditioned to imitating the myths of our mass media, and today these reflect an age that is at the same time sex-ridden and sexually anesthetized. Modern sex seems to need the added charge of the illicit before it can entice. Poor tame domestic sex, bound to the selfsame partner, will not do. This is, after all, the supersonic age! In a technological revolution such as ours, we may soon be tempted to redesign, repackage and automate marital sex like cans of soup, all of uniform quality. To make it attractive we may even have to add a perfumed touch of fashionable sinfulness.

Many young marrieds are confused by this public picture of sex. They see their peers and their elders separating love from sex with cool detachment. They watch as marital commitments are almost casually sundered. They hear around them the echoes of marital discord as therapists and counselors try to put together again the relationships shattered by sexual strife. The young people look in vain for guidelines in the free-for-all arena where games are played with the most profound of human relationships, the sexual love of man for woman.

Sexual boredom is so taken for granted, is so much the

expected pattern within marriage, that it is all too often
accepted without a struggle. There is, oftentimes, more
lively interest exerted in buying a new model of car or in
refurnishing a home than in refurbishing and renewing
an erotically deteriorating relationship.

Sexual boredom frequently invades the decent lives of
husbands and wives who in all other respects are well
mated and solidly committed to marriage. It is a factor in
divorce, although attorneys' briefs may describe it as sexual
incompatibility.

What has happened to connubial sex in this second half
of the twentieth century? Has it in fact lost its sheen, its
vitality, its spontaneity and delight? Was it more adventurous in some past century? Literature, we have said,
rarely treats of marital sex either now or in the past. But
occasionally we have glimpses from a living record. In the
uninhibited diary of one William Byrd, a gentleman and
plantation owner of Colonial Virginia, we may see how a
waning afternoon of a bygone era was brightened by a
spark of spontaneity. In his diary for July 30, 1710, he
made this brief entry:

"In the afternoon my wife and I had a little quarrel
which I reconciled with a flourish. Then she read a sermon
in Dr. Tillotson to me. It is to be observed that the flourish was performed on the billiard table."

It would be a sad commentary on American marriage to
admit that today's married lovers are incapable of such
lusty pleasure in each other. To be sure, few of us have
private billiard tables. But far sadder is the loss of a spirit
that approaches sex as an impulsive and joyous expression
of love and gives to intercourse the high-hearted name of
"a flourish."

We come back to the question: what is sexual adventure?

We know what adventure means in other contexts of human life. It is man's pact with himself to taste the new and the untried, to relish the unexpected, to savor surprise. To Robert Louis Stevenson it meant "to go flashing from one end of the world to the other both in mind and body; to try the manners of different nations; to hear the chimes at midnight; to see sunrise in town and country; to be converted at a revival; to circumnavigate metaphysics; to write halting verses, run a mile to see a fire, and wait all day long in the theatre to applaud a play."

In the marital context, sexual adventure is love erotically expressed between man and wife in the widest possible range of pleasure and delight, on an advanced and sophisticated level. Its essence is variety and surprise.

Adventure has always been a sophisticated taste. Primitive peoples were not adventurous; they had to struggle too fiercely for survival. Only when security came to man, when the urgent needs for shelter, food and comfort were met, were there sufficient energy and curiosity to set forth on adventure.

The great age of cultural and sexual adventure, the Renaissance, came after the long medieval centuries of struggle for survival against poverty and plague. With abundance and security came the flowering of the arts and the sophistication of sex.

Similarly, when husbands and wives become secure in their love, and the survival of their marriage is no longer in doubt, they become adventurous in the sexual expression of their love.

Today's sexual adventurers, freed from problems of survival, can view their erotic life together as a continuing voyage of discovery that seeks ever widening vistas of sensory enjoyment. In their conjugal lovemaking, they have broken loose from the moorings of routine and conformity. Like connoisseurs, they cultivate a taste for sensuality, exploring the delights of new ways, new settings, new times of day or night for lovemaking. They welcome the impulsive and spontaneous. They plan and prepare for pleasure. They fashion sexual love into a joyful art, drawing upon a treasury of erotic knowledge that is limitless.

Only as joint adventurers, bound to each other by the ties of commitment and mature love, can husband and wife learn to escape the sexual boredom that so often threatens modern marriages.

Sexual boredom is a subtle phenomenon. It does not strike suddenly like disease or accident. Often the marital partners themselves are barely aware of it as a specific process. It occurs as imperceptibly as winds erode a cliff, until a pattern is formed. The partners become mysteriously unhappy, vaguely disturbed, restless. They desperately seek escape in faddist interests, in passing thrills, in casual infidelities. Like all boredom, sexual boredom is a form of low-burning rage that may bring the partners close to the brink of emotional separation or divorce.

Sometimes, sexual boredom is so suppressed that it goes underground and reappears in various puzzling masquerades. This happened to a young architect and his socially prominent and very beautiful wife. Throughout the six years of their marriage their sexual life might have been depicted as a gray monotone: correct, conventional, biologically normal. At the proper statistical interval there was male desire followed by female acquiescence. Intercourse always took place in a darkened room and only after the wife had made doubly certain that the children were fast asleep. Often she interrupted lovemaking if she imagined one of the children was wakeful. They never made love in any but the standard posture, and almost invariably on weekend nights. The husband, in all of their married life, had never seen his wife fully nude in the light, excepting once in a bathhouse in Italy.

To his therapist, the husband reported feelings of panic that his creative capacity was declining. He feared that he was about to be replaced in his job. After several more sessions he revealed another underlayer of his personal life. He spoke of hostility that he felt toward his wife's family and of resentment of their social status. He had suspicions that they considered him socially inferior, that his wife had come to regret that she had married a man of no social distinction. He admitted also that in recent years he had engaged in sexual affairs with other women—waitresses, nightclub attachés, the daughter of a charwoman and, finally, quasi-prostitutes.

He could offer no rational ground for his feelings of social inferiority; he had never been snubbed or slighted. At the same time he admitted that he had never thought of trying to change his wife's sexual responses, which were indeed less than robust, or of introducing more variety and color in their lovemaking. He had passively accepted the monotony of conjugal sex and permitted his suppressed rage to be directed at an imaginary target, his wife's social eminence.

His wife, who had also sought professional help, complained of being trapped by her marriage to a degree that bordered on physical suffocation. For relief, she fanatically buried herself in the study of child rearing, stridently endorsing one school, then another. Her agonizing about infant toilet training and regression stopped short of burning in public the books of the Child Study Association.

She admitted to a deep personal misery and to anxieties about her husband's fidelity.

Both partners were unaware of their sexual boredom with each other; both had sought to repair their misery with unsatisfactory devices. Neither had imagined marriage as the beginning of sexual adventure. They had accepted instead the cliché that marriage was the end of the road for sexual joy, dooming themselves to wear masquerades that brought pain and frustration into their lives.

In an era of counterfeit sex, genuine sexual adventure does not come easily to every marriage. Its crux lies in that much abused word, love, which in its modern psychiatric sense is the open door to mature sexuality and thence to erotic freedom. This kind of love is not simply an emotion. It is a relationship that engages the whole personality of each—the heart and soul and mind and total strength. Part of this strength is channeled in an outgoing concern for the other, a sympathy that is at the same time erotic and responsible, physical and spiritual.

This sensitized concern for the welfare of the sexual partner is the core of mature love, and it takes time to achieve. That is why sexual adventure is not for the newly married or the neurotically married, but for the well married. Sexual adventure is not compatible with infantile love which, like the squalling demands of a child, expects to receive all and to give nothing. The infantile lover uses the loved one for satisfactions of his own, without thought of the other. This is not love, but a form of unconscious exploitation, the instrumental use of another human being for greedy self-satisfaction or the titillation of one's own feelings.

Unfortunately, infantile love is the motivation of many youthful marriages today. The resulting pleasure is often ephemeral. Immature sex may be of high voltage, but it seldom reaches a high degree of erotic development. And partners who use each other exploitatively, simply for the relief of sexual tension, are destined over the long run to end in a quagmire of boredom, their senses erotically dulled.

Not only are newlyweds who have not learned the secret of mature love ineligible for the privileges of sexual adventure. Equally unfitted are those who make a game of sex, the playboys and the playgirls, who are poor in love and for that reason poor in sensuality.

Only married lovers who truly know each other in the Biblical sense, and love each other in the mature emotional sense, are the prime candidates for sexual adventure.

These candidates need only remember one simple but crucial principle: that in the sexual union of two persons who regard each other not merely as bodies, but as two priceless personalities, there is nothing sinful, wayward or perverse about any form of behavior that is productive of pleasure, provided only that it is invested with mutual respect and mature love.

The wayward ones in our Western society are the ones who have lost the way to high erotic adventure, those who invest sex, not with sensuality, but with negative values that are not inherent in sexual love. They are the anti-lovers of modern times, the counterfeiters of sex who abuse nature's gift of genuine sexual pleasure.

2

———•·•———

SEX WITHOUT SENSUALITY

TO ACHIEVE SEXUAL ADVENTURE, AND THUS TO RECOVER THE lost art of lovemaking that has always been one of the graces of civilized societies, husbands and wives will need to cultivate a new attitude toward sensuality. The tendency of our times is to debase healthy sensuality. We are under constant threat of being manipulated, cajoled and seduced into accepting as genuine healthy sex a sterile, desensualized substitute.

Part of this process of debasement can be attributed to the anti-lovers. The anti-lovers have brought something new into modern sex life, something as cool and unruffled as the hum of a computing machine. It is the soothing, germ-free, unemotional voice of reason. This new intelligence, spawned by the age of technology, takes its sex straight, without the bother of love or pain or striving. This reasoned sex comes cellophane wrapped; no heart has ever touched it. It is fast as a freeway, efficient as a diaphragm, balanced as an equation. There is no arguing with its logic.

An outstanding novelist and observer of the American scene revealed the reasoning of one disciple of this cool school, a wife who was debating whether to have sexual intercourse with her divorced husband. Finally she concluded that "one screw more or less could not make much difference when she had already laid it on the line for him about five hundred times." Truly incontestable logic.

An embattled theologian, bemoaning the anti-erotic drift of American sex and its loss of emotion, not to mention heat, summarized the situation: "Sex used to be hot stuff, but now it smokes like a piece of dry ice. Instead of burning us, sex gives us frostbite."

To realize more sharply, if more sadly, the extent to which modern sex may be entering a new glacial age, the following instructions on the marriage art are noteworthy. Recently they were widely disseminated by a physician who presumably had thrown Ovid and Vatsyayana on the dustheap but who had not handed in his stethoscope to the American Medical Association. Called the *ice-spurred special,* his instructions are quoted in full:

> Before intercourse the wife places at the bedside a bowl of crushed ice or a handful of cracked ice wrapped in a wet towel. Both partners strip and enjoy sex in any face-to-face posture. As the husband starts his final surge to climax, the wife picks up a handful of crushed ice or the cold towel. Just as the paroxysms of orgasm start, she jams the ice-cold poultice against her husband's crotch and keeps it there throughout his conclusion.

Still another stanza of this touching love duet, titled *urinary passage pressure,* begins: "As the husband hits his absolute peak, the wife can press her bunched fingertips firmly into his flesh just at the back of his scrotum in a harsh goosing jiggle."

So much for science in the tender service of sex.

But the aseptic hand of logic, the ice bowl and the harsh

goosing jiggle are not the only means to shrivel the American sexual impulse.

Modern coitus is viewed with such a clinical eye, such a dry, hard look, that poets hardly dare to sing the praise of its excitements. The sexual drama is etched in acid, lampooned in outrageous burlesque, pulverized by the jargon of parlor psychiatry. Playwrights, practicing public self-therapy, harp on mother-maimed sons, on castration and sexual cannibalism. Who, any longer, dreams of holding hands with his beloved, of inhaling her breath in perfumed gardens, of walking in the woods for amorous dalliance? That is nineteenth-century stuff and for squares!

Violence and venom are present, too. The sexual act is used as a mirror of social injustice. Thus a writer of stature describes a scene of miscegenation:

> Under his breath he cursed the milk-white bitch and groaned and rode his weapon between her thighs. She began to cry. I told you, he moaned, I'd give you something to cry about, and, at once, he felt himself strangling, about to explode or die. A moan and a curse tore through him while he beat her with all the strength he had and felt the venom shoot out of him.

This devaluation of sexual experience is part of a general social malaise. Joyless sex implies a disorder of the spirit, a breakdown of morale. Even sex without love is preferable to sex without sensuality. Deeply disturbing is a study reporting that 42 per cent of husbands between ages of twenty-one and twenty-five engage in masturbation. These young men engage in spiritless, solitary sex not because they are deprived. Falsely educated to believe that sex is shameful and practiced only by "bad girls," they are emotially unprepared for the sensual joy of intercourse with their own wives, who ostensibly are "good girls."

Erotic pleasure, or sensuality, still carries a burden of disapprobation. This is understandable; sensuality has had a bad history. After the sexual excesses of the Roman empire, medieval churchmen for centuries decreed against sexual pleasure even if taken in the conjugal bed. It required centuries to obliterate the memory of decadent emperors who used children to inflame their flagging senses and who made of sexual intercourse a public entertainment as spectacular as their gladiatorial displays.

The dehumanization of sex is not all. There is another influence, specific to this country, that confuses and distorts a healthy adult approach to sensuality and hence to sexual adventure. It is the false glamour that is attached to the sexuality of youth.

Because we are a nation that has made a cult of youth, enshrining it as if it were the quintessence of total desirability, we have come to emulate and to adore the sexual traits of youth. We have swallowed the bait of advertising and popular literature which alternately charms us with the sexual cuteness of youth and its phony elations, and disarms us with its flippant and cynical sexual manners.

If they are to attain healthy sensuality, adult husbands and wives cannot afford to be influenced or bemused by youthful sex which is so casually accepted as a staple of our society. Not only is youthful sex overrated and overadvertised. It is underfed, and under its windblown and sunburned exterior, it is actually fearful, mistrustful of its own sexual impulses and deeply ashamed. Too often, its sexual biography has been written tawdrily in the back seats of automobiles, in neon-lighted beer taverns and the nightmare setting of the modern superhighway.

A famous choreographer has come to a similar conclusion by observing how youth dances today. Modern teenagers spurn the American square dance, a communal socio-sexual experience in which male and female link arms, watch each other, touch each other and move together to the rhythm of music. But modern youth has invented its own dances—the twist, the pony, the slop, the mashed potato—in which they dance separately, eyes averted from partners, rotating like zombies on a disembodied self-centered axis. Primitive peoples danced this way. It was the civilized who touched and clasped each other as, over the decades, they performed their courtship dances: the waltz, the polka, the tango, the black bottom. Even in its recreation, our modern youth reveals an aspect of alienation and distrust.

Another enemy of healthy sensuality is the highly developed practice of sexual innuendo, in all of its faddish, leering guises. It is a by-product of many of our mass media, and a specialty of the college-age magazines that trade on the sexual impoverishment of their readers. Thanks to our amplifying methods, the volume and frequency of sexual innuendo have been stepped up today to a point never equaled in the history of the human race.

Far from furthering erotic sensibility, sexual innuendo depresses and degrades it, and tends to become its substitute. It is the erotic shadow, without the substance of mature sexual competence. Its limited objective is titillation, often on the brink of vulgarity. Healthy sensuality, on the other hand, ranges over the full erotic uninhibited spectrum. The physical expression of love binds husband and wife into a closer emotional union and often ennobles it.

Married couples who would cultivate sexual adventure

face other deterrents. Despite our growing affluence and comfort, there are many husbands and wives who find their healthy sensuality inhibited rather than stimulated in our modern glass and steel environment. The growth of cities and their turgid populations, their hurry, noise and jittery pace, are factors in clogging the avenues to sensual delight. Especially to city dwellers, living constantly with speed and ceaseless motion, sensuality is becoming a vanished rhapsody.

There is a limit to the stimuli the senses can deal with. Under the insistent aggressive assault of sensory impressions, simply in order to escape being overwhelmed we automatically turn off our senses. Or rather our brain short-circuits them for us. This is a kind of anesthesia, and it spells the decline, if not the death, of sensuality. We tend to lapse into air-conditioned languor and toy with sex routinely like an invalid with a jaded appetite.

Many of us have experienced this paralysis of the senses when we have been suddenly transported from the country to the city. Sounds and sights, taste and touch, are never more sensitively experienced than in a quiet and isolated setting of nature. Here we can handle the orderly flow of stimuli; after a few days, our senses begin to regain a pristine zest and sharpness. And not incidentally, we develop a keen erotic appetite.

But transferred abruptly to urban jangle, danger and incessant cacophony, we switch off, in sheer self-preservation, the currents of sensory perception. As a result, our natural eroticism, far from being whipped up by the wicked city, is actually rendered torporous; what we regard as sensuality is merely physiological desire, and sometimes only the memory of desire.

Man has just begun to suspect the dangers to human

health and welfare inherent in a highly machined society. It is not merely for fun and recreation that the conservation movement, which would preserve more forest land, seashore and wildlife, is doing battle against the bulldozer. The ultimate purpose of this trend is to ease the drain and pressure upon the human psyche and nervous system, which cannot indefinitely withstand the bludgeonings of city and suburban living. Nature is a master healer and soother of the frazzled psyche. And, as will be shown in the next chapter, nature has the power to refresh the senses and revive the sensuality of those exhausted, not by overindulgence, but by the routine and regimentation of their immediate family environment.

With a little exercise of ingenuity, we can change our attitudes both toward sex and toward the physical arrangements that promote sensuality. Sexual adventure becomes a lively possibility when husband and wife, with a joint lust for life and for each other, are willing to attack the forces of monotony and conformity and to introduce measures of novelty within the privacy of the home.

If frenetic city and suburban life is often inescapable, the home can still be a sanctum for sensuality. The children need not dominate the entire preserve; in most American families children get more material comfort than is good for them. This excessive, pervasive concern for the physical well-being of children often is exercised at the expense of the sexual joy and freedom of the parents.

Sensuality thrives in the appropriate setting. What, for example, has happened to the boudoir? That exceptional pleasure place, for three hundred years, adjoined the European bedroom. Among its silken divans and couches and draperies, the lady of fashion received her husband. Redolent with perfume, its mirrors gleaming with candlelight, the boudoir was designed for lazy repose and luxurious languor. Preening herself at her toilette, milady welcomed her visitor, exchanged sly jokes and intimate gossip. Here, the husband might watch her dress and bathe, "seduction seemed to rise, beauty to be reborn"; so wrote an eighteenth-century chronicler. In the soft, flickering light and warmth of the hearth, intercourse took place. Here were privacy, peace and total passion.

In the average American home, what are the consciously planned arrangements for privacy, peace and passion? Wherein have its designers taken into account the sensual ingredients of healthy lovemaking? Children's quarters overrun and coalesce with adults'; partitions are so thin that a cough or the flush of a toilet reverberates like gunfire.

The assumption is plain: sexual intercourse, like burglary, must take place in stealth and at scheduled times, preferably when the children are dead asleep or away from home. Sexual courtship is obviously an anachronism that belongs back in the courts of the Louis. Sexual spontaneity is for teen-agers; you're grown-up married folks! Architect-philosopher Lewis Mumford states the case for biology and building:

> Lovemaking and homemaking, eroticism and domesticity, sexual delight and the assiduous nurture of children—these are among the highest goals . . . Good design means going back to fundamentals; a child at work in a stable, reassuring world; a pair of lovers at play in a room where the scent of lilacs may creep through the window, or the shrill piping of crickets be heard in the garden below.

One can, of course, do without a rococo boudoir; there are modern equivalents to produce an equal result. But the erotic ingredient needs to be kept in mind and not forgotten for other purposes scarcely so vital. One adventurous couple designed a living room among whose various uses is included the one for lovemaking. Distantly separated from the children's quarters and other areas by solid, soundproof sliding doors, it offered visual and aural privacy. Muted red draperies covered the glass walls overseeing a woodland garden.

From the room's wide and high Colonial fireplace came a caressing warmth that can be equaled by no source other than the sun for eroticizing the skin. In front of the hearth lay a soft sheepskin rug, flanked by assorted couches and chaises. Tuned-down hi-fi music, the smell of wine mingling with whiffs of wood smoke and traces of feminine perfume completed the milieu for love.

There was one more detail which Madame Pompadour would have envied: an electric dimmer. This ingenious and not too expensive installation, by a turn of the knob, could vary the room's lighting and provide visual moods of many effects, from vivacious evening to mysterious twilight to glimmering dawn. In the dusky glow the nude female form bestowed extra sensual delight; the quality of light even sensitized the end organs of touch.

Another illustration of homemaking with a built-in sensual feature, especially in warm climates, is the private patio that opens out from the bedroom and brings the lovemaking area closer to nature. One such bedroom patio, formerly a children's play-yard, was made into a quaint and lush Victorian bower, with plantings of shrubs, vines and flowers and a plot of grass which, when freshly cut, blended its aromas with those of night-blooming flowers. Screened on all sides, with roll-down canvas shades for added privacy, the patio was a modern version of the summer house, or temple of love, of earlier centuries. Chaise, hammock, even a wide-seated swing, hung from the limb of an intruding tree, gave an air of indulgent ease and subtle sensual suggestion.

In past eras the swing has contributed its part to experimentation. In antiquity, male and female sometimes enjoyed coitus sitting and being slowly wafted in a swing, the woman astride with her legs extended on the opposite side. In a later Chinese period, the wife sat alone on the swing while the husband stood in front and entered; the slight motion of the swing undoubtedly added erotic interest. In our own nineteenth century the slatted lawn-swing was used in courtship but seldom allowed close contact. In various times and cultures, the garden surrounded by a high wall or dense hedgerow, with its verdure, soft turf, nooks and cool fountains, invited lovers to dally in the privacy and quiet of nature.

There are countless ways of transcending our anti-erotic environment, of circumventing the threat of conformism which would routinize conjugal coitus, and these will be described later. Many earlier cultures considered erotic enjoyment an art worthy of delicately detailed perparation. This is how a Hindu husband of long ago was told to embellish the scene of his lovemaking:

> Choose the largest, and finest, and the most airy room in the house, purify it thoroughly with whitewash, and decorate its spacious and beautiful walls with pictures and other objects upon which the eye may dwell with delight. Scatter about this apartment musical instruments, especially the pipe and the lute, refreshments such as cocoanut, betel-leaf and milk, which is so useful for retaining and restoring vigor, bottles of rose water and various

essences, fans for cooling the air, and books containing amorous songs, and gladdening the glance with illustrations of love-postures.

Splendid wall lights should gleam around the hall, reflected by a hundred mirrors, whilst both man and woman should contend against any reserve, or false shame, giving themselves up in complete nakedness to unrestrained voluptuousness, upon a high and handsome bedstead, raised on tall legs, furnished with many pillows and covered by a rich canopy, the sheets besprinkled with flowers and the coverlet scented by incense such as aloes and other fragrant woods. In such a place let the man ascend the throne of love, enjoy the woman in ease and comfort, gratifying his and her every wish and every whim.

Modern wives and husbands will note that the passage of centuries has not changed substantially the stage setting for amorous drama. If the laws governing interstate commerce have shielded the gaze of lovers from illustrated love-postures, there are still love-songs to murmur from the hi-fi set, fans that cool the air electrically, bottled perfumes in abundant variety, protein-enriched milk for cellular restoration, mirrors to the ceiling to reflect nakedness. The Hindu's high and handsome bedstead, whose practical value in enhancing lovemaking was known throughout Greco-Roman times, has now reappeared, probably unbeknownst to its manufacturers, in the form of a mechanically controlled bed that can be raised or angled for a variety of love-postures.

Healthy sensuality in married sex is possible when attitudes toward sex have been freed of shame and guilt, of prurience and modesty. The more one makes an effort to understand the sources of such attitudes, the greater the insight into them and the sooner total freedom from them can be won. The hedonistic or pleasure-loving approach to lovemaking has not been an American tradition and it was not so long ago that the Puritan footprint led directly into the conjugal chamber. The sexual revolution has come, and with it problems of imbalance in our sexual mores. Not the least of them is the commercialization of sex by the product hucksters. But they, too, can be driven from the temple.

It would be incorrect to equate the sensualist in marital lovemaking with the voluptuary. The voluptuary dotes on sex to the exclusion of human values. Sex can be a rich enjoyment, yes, but if it is no more than a titillation of the senses it ends only in dullness and weariness. Sensuality is the full use of the senses in love, not their exploitation to exhaustion.

It is not the contention of this book that the sole key to conjugal felicity is higher education in erotic practices. The enhancement of the sexual repertory with extra incitements to Eros will not transform crashing temperamental dissonances into dulcet marital harmony. Nor will neurotic disturbances vanish overnight with the use of new and exotic coital postures.

Sex is not a prescription for nervous tension nor a solution for neurotic conflict. Let the insomniac take a pill and the neurotic consult his analyst. Sexual adventure and delight are the privilege of healthy lovers within a healthy marriage.

Sex, of course, is easily accessible in marriage. There will always be intercourse and babies and the pleasures of both. The sexual instinct, if not always love, will find a way. But that alone is not the goal. Sex should not be permitted to dissipate its essential sensuality through either the faults of our environment or the errors of our own attitudes. The aim is that sensuality remain in the service of love, be kept refreshed, for as long a time as nature permits, as one of the glories of married life.

3

———•———

THE SENSES REFRESHED

ALMOST SINCE THE DAY THEY STOPPED FIGHTING THE CAVE
bear, men have been looking for ways to vary their sexual
pleasure. The procession of hip-swinging female sex objects
undulates through history: slave girls, concubines, hetaerae,
odalisques, right down to the modern stripper and call girl.
Even today, many a modern man's dream of Paradise is the
life of an Oriental potentate, with so many and various
beauties in his harem that his only problem would be
which to choose for his pleasure each night.

But even this male version of Eden had its flaw. A nephew
of the famous Saladin appealed to the Jewish savant
Maimonides for advice. His problem was that he had
acquired an addition of female slaves to his harem, and
he was unable to maintain his sexual powers, wearying
under such a surfeit of sexual partners. Maimonides pointed
out the folly of turning sex into a dutiful performance for
which appetite was lacking.

So it appears that even in a harem of houris, a man could
become entrapped in the plodding dullness of routine. No
wonder the wise men of those cultures counseled variety,
not of women, but of ways; a thousand and one nights
could be best enjoyed not with a thousand and one women
but with one woman in a constantly varying pattern of

occasions, settings, postures and sensual experience. Make love to your wife, they counseled, as though she were thirty-two different women.

Some specious modern advisers suggest a return to polygamy to revive the American husband's pleasure in sex. If these advisers knew their history, they would know that polygamy made a man's life not a dream of delight but the routine of a stallion put to stud. What the husband needs who complains of a lack of variety of sexual partners is not more women but more imagination with the woman he has.

An unmistakable aura illuminates two people who have attained maximum sexual pleasure with each other. In his memoirs of his boyhood, Carl Sandburg recalled the radiance that suffused the family breakfast after his parents had experienced the pleasures of intercourse. Only long afterward, in retrospect, did he understand the source of this familial happiness. The memory of it still glowed in his later years, giving evidence that the sexual joy of parents, too, is visited upon the children, no less than their errors.

It is a physiological fact that the senses become dulled with repetition. The same piece of music that delighted the ear on first or second or third hearing loses the listener's attention on the tenth or twelfth consecutive performance. The most exquisite perfume, costing many dollars an ounce, makes its first delicious impact, and after a few seconds we no longer smell it at all. People who are addicted to a monotonous dinner menu find themselves adding more salt, more pepper, more spices, finally drenching the dish in tomato ketchup, just in order to taste something. Yet let them go on a vacation abroad, and live on pasta or sukiyaki for a while, and then how delectable seems the American hamburger or hot dog!

The lesson is obvious: the senses are dulled by routine, refreshed by change. It is not the sense organs themselves that weary of sending the same message of pleasure. It is the mind that wearies of receiving it. There is a brain mechanism that filters out the meaningful from the meaningless. Without this we should never be able to concentrate on either work or pleasure.

Science thus explains what wise men and poets have always known. The tedium of sexual routine can creep into the healthiest marriage, once the first ecstatic period is past. Yet there is no need for this to happen. There are ways to cultivate new erotic gardens within the conjugal relationship. Only, as a Persian sage once said, the garden must be planted before it can be brought into blossom. Conjugal partners can courageously face, without disrespect toward each other, the fact that their lovemaking has begun to lose savor.

The ways to refresh the senses are nothing more than ways to vary their experience. Why, for example, does lovemaking always have to take place on a bed? Granted that this is a traditional symbol, and that it can be very comfortable. But need it be exclusive? Even veteran marital partners can reproduce a piquant atmosphere of seduction by a simple change of furniture. Adventurous modern couples have proven to their satisfaction that this adds extra erotic dividends.

Unblushingly, they have taken their cue from some French eighteenth-century engravings describing coital encounters that were clearly illicit. In one scene, the female partner, her voluminous skirts billowing above her waist, was perched on a richly adorned console in what appeared to be a parlor or music room, and in this position she was receiving the erotic attention of her lover, who stood facing her. Not accidentally, perhaps, the console was of just the height so that the genitals of both were in precise apposition. Her silk-stockinged legs encircled her lover's waist, and she swooned rapturously against a painting of cavorting wood nymphs and satyrs. The seduction was depicted at that moment in foreplay before the lover had made entrance but not before an irate husband had made his entrance into the room.

Another illustration showed the female partner leaning over the back of a luxurious sofa in relaxed comfort, her rounded buttocks and spread stance appearing through a cloud of petticoats and inviting her lover, who stood nearby, to hasten entrance; here, too, genital apposition was precise. Obviously the artist intended these to be scenes of stolen coition, for a rakish hat was still poised on the lover's head, and although loins and thighs were bared, the partners were otherwise decorously dressed.

Modern couples need not put on eighteenth-century masquerade to find such measures of erotic diversity. Nor do they need period furniture to achieve the same effect. In any home there is likely to be a chest of drawers, desk or table of proper height for coitus, upon which a wife may be lifted. The illusion of seduction is not the only added touch, for in this posture the husband, standing in front of his wife, has both his hands free for a full range of caressing foreplay.

Love can be transplanted not only from the bed but from the bedroom. When a wife is taking a leisurely bath or shower, a husband might well join her there. Some charming medieval woodcuts, dating from the thirteenth century in Europe when the sexes bathed together, show the pleasures of languorous coitus in a bathtub for two. The smoothness of wet bodies and the warmth of the skin add a new erotic dimension, and the pleasant relaxation of the bath slows the pace and lengthens the pleasure of erotic play. The novelty of the setting can be exploited to conclusion, with coitus in the bath itself, provided, of course, that the tub is of ample size for two. Or the partners can emerge wrapped in a large bath towel, or one of the enveloping terry cloth robes that are widely advertised, and pursue their adventure on the bed, a chair or the carpeted floor.

Almost wholly neglected, and denied a genuine role in the sexual experience of American married couples, is lovemaking in the outdoors in surroundings of natural beauty and privacy. Nature, free of charge, bountifully provides adventurous mates with sites galore and varied, where coitus may be enjoyed and its pleasures refreshed. These sites, whether beaches, inland woods, riverbanks, lake dunes, mountain eminences or fresh cut hayricks, need no other requirement than that they be entirely deserted. While bulldozers may have leveled some of these lovesites, they still exist in abundance if one cares and dares to search them out with an unembarrassed mind and a taste for the changeable moods of nature. Says the Chinese proverb: "Once in the field or along the road, amid the tranquillity of nature, is equivalent to a thousand times in bed."

Consider the lonely beach along the miles of America's coastlines, the sheltered nooks of its countless lakes, the grassy slopes near meandering waterways, where mass recreation has not yet penetrated. To reach them, one often need not walk more than a mile after parking a car in the vicinity. Young lovers since time immemorial have contrived to find these places; why not healthy spouses?

Marriages have been known to grow stale indoors, not merely because of the unvaried repetition of intercourse, but from the psychological constraint of rooms that are too small or too cluttered or too aseptic. The human figure is viewed out of scale, against backgrounds that are hackneyed and unflattering. In nature's outdoor mansion, rent-free and tax-exempt, the human nude is transformed. Against leafy boughs or briny boulders, racing along woodland paths or the surf's edge, the naked figure becomes a sprite or satyr; the sensual and the sensuous are joined, the body and spirit liberated.

A couple married twenty years had reached such a low ebb of sexual interest that acts of intercourse were seldom remembered a moment after orgasm. Their marriage was not so much shaky as it was emotionally barren, and an ailing son was perhaps the only bond that held it together. One summer they took their son to a health camp in one of our mountain states. Instead of stopping at a nearby hotel, to save money they hit upon the happy inspiration of camping on the shores of a virtually deserted glacial lake miles distant from tourist haunts. The forest floor where they spread their tent was springy with pine needles; they fished for food, cooked among the boulders, sunbathed and braved the icy water in the nude, until their bodies glistened like sandalwood, and incidentally produced some excellent nude photography. In the cold evening, they dressed for bed before the campfire; reversing the custom, they made love during the day, with a zest and abandon they had never known. Their dormant sensuality was re-aroused, and under the healing influence of unspoiled

THE SENSES REFRESHED 45

nature they turned a new leaf in their sexual and emotional history.

Love-postures may be adapted to the topography of the outdoors. While these will be treated in detail in forthcoming chapters, a few may be mentioned here. The husband, sitting on the ground, his back against a tree and slightly crouched, receives his wife astride his loins. After entrance she may remain in squatting position or stretch her legs forward, bracketing both her partner's flanks and the tree. Leaning backward, her weight on hands or elbows, she may strengthen her pelvic thrust, since all astride positions somewhat limit the husband's movements.

For the athletically inclined, standing coitus may be effected while the husband leans against tree or boulder, his wife also upright and facing him. To bring the genitals in apposition, it may be necessary for one partner to stand on a sturdy box or flat stone; entrance is made as the wife lifts one leg from the hip, obliquely and forward. If the wife is slightly built she may, instead of standing, curl her legs around her spouse's hips in tight embrace.

When bodies are naked, wet and relaxed after a swim, and the sun is warm, outdoor coitus has its own exquisite rewards. Since long before builders sheltered us in rabbit warrens and automobile makers hobbled us with lazy legs, lovemaking in the open has been a recreative pursuit. During the Athenian supremacy in ancient Greece, along its countless islets and coves, not only the gods cavorted with mortals in amorous play. In the shimmering sun or waning light of their Mediterranean paradise, Greek men enfolded their maids in simple sensual delight.

Love in the outdoors need not wait, however, for a vacation or a weekend away from home. All the adventurous partners need may be within reach of their own back door, a terrace or a strip of lawn shielded by hedge or garden wall from prying windows. Nothing is more magical than to make love on the grass in the velvet darkness of a soft summer night.

What man may enjoy on land he may also enjoy on the sea and even under the sea, as mates have discovered who share a taste for the lake and ocean. Couples who like sailing have made love under the sun or the stars, in the cockpit of sloop or schooner; and others who have had a pool or pond with a float on it, and enough privacy, have made love on that.

Still more adventurous are the underwater lovers. Those who swim under the surface with snorkles have discovered that the weight of the human body is such that they can float standing or sitting, the whole of the body underwater except the top of the head and the snorkel, and thus they could make love as they pleased.

Skin divers have a further advantage. Carrying their air tanks on their backs, they can make love among the undersea coral gardens, at any depth that is comfortable, safe and private. They have a unique setting, and they have, besides, a unique sensation: they are weightless, and can take any love-posture they like without the interference of gravity. This has all the elements of a magical erotic experience; Undine could have shared it with her lover, had he not been earthbound. It will probably not be matched in sensuous wonder until the first conjugal astronauts take off in their space capsule for two, en route to the next galaxy. But the advantage of skin-diving love is that when you come up you are not wandering in space, but safe on the pleasant green earth.

Privacy is an indispensable ally of sensuality, and its loss is constantly threatened. Some lack of it is unavoidable.

Parents and children live in a tight environmental embrace. Lovemaking often faces interruption by the bedside telephone, the unexpected demands of business or profession. Many homes have ceased to be man's inviolate castle. In swarming suburbia it is often a way station along a seething social conduit. We pay a price for our love of friends and people, our easy hospitality, our devotion to children and our tolerance for impromptu visitors and door-to-door solicitors. Spontaneous sex often gives way to scheduled sex.

The privacy of the bedroom can usually be maintained, if not by a latch, then by carefully nurturing in children, from an early age, a respect for privacy, their own and others'. Yet even a well-reared teen-age girl can burst impulsively into the parental bedroom to announce some news of great emotional import to her.

Unhappily, sensuality between husband and wife thrives poorly in an atmosphere of threatened intrusion. Overnight visitors can be borne, and sex deferred if necessary. But the chronic or long-term visitor should be stanchly resisted, especially if there is limited house room. Whether blood relatives or not, they spell the death of sexual spontaneity if visiting is stretched beyond a decent interval. The best way to dislodge the sluggish or thoughtless wayfarer is to tell the truth bluntly: that sexual privacy is being invaded.

Often, to enjoy an erotic holiday free of the threat of intrusion, marriage partners can arrange for the responsible care of the children and manage to make a clean break with their immediate marital surroundings. For half a day, a day, a weekend or longer, they can put to profitable use the enormous mobility provided by the automobile. In a matter of a few hours or less of driving, they can arrive at a rural hotel or motel and achieve not only sexual privacy but the added stimulation of making love in a new setting. This does not amount to sexual spontaneity, to be sure, but it does break the pattern of routined and often hurried lovemaking in the familiar bedroom.

Yet even at home, once the imagination has been stirred to seek new settings for sexual adventure, it will also devise ways of assuring privacy. Or, with the sense of adventure kindled, familiar situations which offer privacy will be rediscovered in a new light as opportunities for undisturbed enjoyment.

Not only the routine of a familiar setting can be broken, but also the routine of a familiar time. In an era when the working week included Saturday, and the working day was longer than it is today, Saturday night sex was almost inevitable; there was little leisure for an alternative choice. But today working hours are shorter and leisure longer, and a particular time for sex is not enforced by anything except habit, that deadly enemy of pleasure.

Why only one time for lovemaking? Twilight is as fine as midnight, dawn as suitable as darkness. In the private haven of marriage, any moment is the moment for lovemaking, whether dressing for breakfast or dressing for dinner—it is easy enough to undress again. What of love in the afternoon? Ovid describes the witching effect of afternoon light upon an amorous encounter:

> In summer's heat, and mid-time of the day
> To rest my limbs upon the bed I lay;
> One window shut, the other open stood,
> Which gave such light as twinkles in a wood
>   Like twilight glimpsed at setting of the sun
>   Or night being past and yet not day begun . . .

Then, continuing with his rhapsody on afternoon love,

> How smooth a belly under her waist saw I,
> How large a leg, and what a lusty thigh!
> To leave the rest, all liked me passing well;
> I clinged her naked body, down she fell;
>> Judge you the rest, being tired she bade me kiss.
>> Jove send me more such afternoons as this!

4

<hr/>

WHAT HUSBANDS ENJOY

HUSBANDS ENJOY AN ACTIVE SEXUAL PARTNER. ANY WIFE who loves her husband and has a normal response to sexual pleasure may be schooled to become a more active, participating companion than she believes herself capable of being. Without compromising her conscience or principles, she may learn to enlarge and embellish her erotic repertoire and remain serene in the knowledge that neither society nor her husband will protest.

Yet even a husband who is ready and eager for adventurous sex with his wife may hesitate to approach her with a novel or unexpected form of lovemaking. He feels restrained, inhibited. He is unsure how she will receive novelty. After years of a familiar pattern of sex, he actually has little idea of how she feels about his lovemaking.

A good and loving wife usually accepts without comment or criticism or further suggestion whatever kind of lovemaking her husband offers. If she is inexperienced, if indeed this is the only lover she has ever known, she may have little idea of other ways of making love. In our society she has not been educated in lovemaking as were brides in older societies; erotic literature has not been part of her preparation for womanhood.

What has happened, in many loving marriages, is that

in this most intimate aspect of their relationship they have actually lost true intimacy, true communication. By accepting, week after week and year after year, one single ritual of lovemaking, one time and setting and manner of intercourse, they have set their sexual expression in a rigid mold which actually precludes any further communication.

Falling into the same familiar pattern each time, they need say nothing more, feel nothing more for each other, than they have said and felt before. It is as though they had limited their speech with each other to a vocabulary of ten words. There is not much people can say to each other in ten words, whether the speech is verbal or the physical language of love. All the more reason why adventure in sex—an expansion of the physical language of love —is essential to full and enduring happiness in marriage.

But adventure cannot be a solo performance. It takes two to explore this intimate world of lovemaking. A husband can initiate; he can lead the way. But he cannot lead far unless his wife will follow. And mere compliance will not encourage him. He needs a partner who will go with him with the same adventurous spirit as his own.

Many husbands miss this sense of joint adventure in sex. But they are vague, often, about ways to set it in motion. There is no reason why a man cannot spend at least as much time developing an understanding of coital finesse as he does studying the finesse of golf, bridge, skiing or cabinet-making.

Even the most loving and willing wife needs an erotically knowledgeable husband. Without an adventurous teacher who will expand her erotic experience, her sexual interest will wander and dissipate itself either in other interests or in rummaging aimlessly among fantasies of ideal masculinity.

In the past, husbands have had to compete with phantom images that unconsciously engaged at least part of their wives' sexual ardor. These ideal images ran in fashions. Not long ago it was the tall, broad-shouldered, slim-hipped, strong and silent man. If he was a bit gangling he was all the more lovable. What he had to possess, above all, was integrity and unostentatious courage, and if his clean-cut face gave out a frank and boyish gaze, he became utterly irresistible. Casanova was a fragile eighteenth-century fellow of almost feminine build. During the romantic era, a Byronic profile with flowing hair and pale esthetic mien was the rage. Rudolph Valentino was a panther whose glowing eyes consumed the female.

A male type that seems to be popular in contemporary America is neither svelte, slim nor particularly strong-looking. Husbands feel more comfortable and less competitive about him. He is real, not a phantom, and more like themselves. This type is a craggy man of short stature, rough beard and intensely formed facial features that are striking in photographic close-up but would hardly be noticed in a crowd. One famed anthropologist is of the opinion that this type not only is endowed with extraordinary sexual capacity but is also likely to possess those solid virtues that make a fine, reliable husband.

The emergence of this new realistic lover image may mean that today wives are getting more sensual pleasure with their own husband-lovers and no longer have to fantasy an ideal, if hollow, cinema lover.

A husband's sexual capacity is only as good as his ability to take his wife along with him into realms of pleasurable adventure. His potency, if it only leads him to a hit-or-miss system in coitus, is not likely to produce the joyful, active participation in sex that he really seeks.

The modern husband tries to guarantee that his wife will share his full orgastic potency and pleasure. Yet, even in the most considerate husband—as wives should recognize—there remains a very substantial, and probably built-in, male pride in his sexual prowess. This has been true throughout history. Long before Kinsey, in the Pullman smokers of yesteryear, men regaled each other with preposterous stories of sexual athleticism.

This has not changed. In a recent poll, students of a class in psychology, all males, were asked to cast their votes for the hero in history whom they would most like to resemble. They voted unanimously, not for hearth-loving Thomas Jefferson or some wholesome smiling astronaut, but for that international champion of sexual license, Don Juan. According to Mozart's librettist, Don Juan seduced 643 women in Italy, 231 in Germany, 100 in France, 91 in Turkey, and 1003 in the land of his legendary birth, Spain.

Few mature husbands view sex in such numerical terms. Nor do they dream of emulating the eighteenth-century French nobleman who was so impressed with his ability to have intercourse with his lady twelve times in one night that he had imprinted on every article of his wardrobe and on all his pistols, swords and dinnerware, the number twelve, thus making certain that history would be mindful of his achievement.

Generalizations about sexual types are perilous, especially today when myths can travel with the speed of light. The mass media can convey myths about sex that are damaging to the whole process of mate selection and to marriage itself. Wives can be entrapped by such myths and pass on to their daughters delusions that men with much hair on their bodies or heavy-set bald men or men of Latin origin are good lovers, while men with small hands, feet or penis, or of fair smooth skin, make poor lovers.

One very young and possibly unstable wife told her psychiatrist of her clandestine affair with a burly, two-fisted state trooper. In her talks she gave the impression that her husband was a pale, fluttery, shy man. She complained that never during their marriage had he "taken me by storm." She believed implicitly in the cliché that all barrel-chested, rough-talking, dark-haired males were the epitome of virility. It became clear to her therapist that throughout her adolescence she had battened on swashbuckling movies and emotionally bankrupt fiction. When finally he met his patient's husband he was surprised to observe that the man was neither shy, nervous, fluttery nor pale. He also learned that the husband was as potent sexually as the Neanderthal lover.

The wise wife would do well to ignore myths about sex and look at some of the facts. Many of them she knows from experience. She knows that the rate of her husband's arousal is more rapid than her own, that his urgency, once triggered, is not easily deflected. She has seen this universal male trait illustrated in caricatures: the convalescent male in hot pursuit of his nurse along the hospital corridor, the pompous executive dizzily chasing his secretary around a desk. The classical Greeks did not caricature, but they painted, on their exquisite vases and amphora, scenes of nymphs pursued by laughing satyrs in full erection.

The male's irrepressible urgency may be a legitimate source of public laughter but privately it may cause psychological pain. One troubled husband complained bitterly of a wife who tittered when he approached her sexually. That he made his approach without prelude or foreplay, before his wife had become aroused, never occurred to him as one reason for her unseemly response. Nevertheless, a key to his discomfiture lay in the fact that the male tends to find in his performance of the sexual act a source of pride not to be made fun of.

Men derive not only pleasure but also support for self-esteem through sexual conquest. This is especially true for men who have doubts about themselves, and in a society that puts a premium on competitive achievement at all levels, most men suffer some doubts. A considerable number of men suffer rebuff, rejection or disappointment in the course of their everyday pursuits. They seek to re-establish status by proving their sexual prowess, either within marriage or outside it. A husband's need for self-verification cannot be taken lightly. A wife would do well to react with sympathy and tolerance and even with deliberate erotic enticements. To be merely submissive is not enough.

Husbands enjoy wantonness in the private sexual conduct of a wife. They tend to be impatient with prohibitions or strictures based on some real or imagined moral code. The male's sexual desire is directed frankly and uncomplicatedly toward penetration and ejaculation. Everything he adds to this in his sexual behavior, every act of delicacy, considerateness and tenderness toward his partner, is acquired, developed, learned.

The sexual directness of the male is often worrisome to wives who mistake it for coarseness or lack of sensibility. They judge from their own pattern, which is channeled along different pathways. In the male, sexual desire has no other objective than the vaginal goal, while in the human female, sexual desire takes various detours, along such routes as a sense of security, a need to be valued for herself and, most importantly for many women, the wish to be a mother of children.

This last distinction was recently proven by scientific test. Somewhere in the brain's computer mechanism is a link to the nervous pathways that control the opening of the eye's iris. The pupils increase up to 17 per cent when an interesting object is identified. Women viewing a picture of a mother and baby responded with the maximum opening of the pupil, while males viewing the same picture barely responded at all. On the other hand, pictures of nude females produced the maximum opening of the pupil among the males.

Husbands enjoy uninhibited sex, no strings attached and no holds barred. One of the reasons why so many otherwise dependable husbands are found among the steady customers of call girls today is that these purveyors of commercial sex know what a man wants, erotically speaking. What professionals may lack in genuine passion they make up in expert technique and sometimes in an understanding of male sexual psychology. Many a courtesan of classical antiquity won popularity, even immortality in poetry, not alone for her skill in assuming a variety of postures in coitus but for the tremulous motion of her buttocks.

But not only is it the responsive thrust of his wife's buttocks that he enjoys. A husband is grateful for a psychological climate of freedom in his sexual relations with his wife. He is irked by reticence, by unspoken taboos, by female embarrassment or by any attitude that is restrictive or critical of his erotic behavior. He decries the placing of any curtain between them that would suggest that one is a sexual liberal and the other a sexual conservative. He prefers to approach sex as an intensely absorbing entertainment in which his wife engages with ardor, delight and lustfulness to equal his own.

A husband enjoys having his partner occasionally take the initiating role in lovemaking. Not too often, however, and not as a matter of habit. The molds of social conditioning, which for millennia decreed that the male is the pursuer and the female the pursued, may be cracking in the heat of social change but they have not yet crumbled.

Yet although shyness and coquetry may still have a place in premarital courtship or the early months of marriage, they are likely to irk the seasoned husband. Usually he prefers his wife to be entirely honest and bold in the pursuit of sensual enjoyment. Some of the standard marriage manuals, still in the grip of Victorian reticence, recommend that a wife respond to the sexual advances of her husband with delaying actions and coy retreat. Most modern husbands might prefer their mates to be better informed concerning the erogenous zones of the male, rather than play the role of the unravished bride.

Husbands enjoy being voyeurs, not in the perverse sense, which is compulsive, but as interested observers of the partially or entirely nude female body. Modern woman has not forgotten for a moment this characteristic male penchant. But few remember that she has begun to undress herself only within the past few decades. The Cretan women of Knossos thirty-five hundred years ago wore long flounced skirts with tight bodices and bared their breasts but not their ankles. Upper-class Athenian women had their party gowns made of silk so translucent they might have been wearing a film of water.

Excepting the women of preliterate societies, secrecy cloaked the Western female form for more than a thousand years, in both public and private display. European women submitted their bodies to a husband's embrace under cover of bedclothes, in pitch darkness. In the great feudal castles, the huge canopied bed stood openly in the great hall, and intercourse took place behind its curtains in the presence, if not the view, of servants and retainers. Nudity in lovemaking is a modern luxury regained after a long drought in sensuality, and it is welcome.

Nudity is welcome because it is a major stimulant, among many others, to male sexual interest within the connubial establishment, and it can be rewarding to the sexual relationship. The husband is rare who will object if his spouse goes through her cosmetic ritual before her dressing table clad in panties and bare to the waist, or emerges nude from her bath within his gaze. If his wife can present her nudity to him without shame or brashness, the modern husband need only fear the builder of housing developments who seems to design dwellings on the premise that American couples are sexually neuter and have their children by test tube.

While he rarely requires special enticements to desire coitus with his wife, the healthy husband enjoys her enthusiastic response to his advances. Nothing can be more calculated to curdle the male's amorous disposition, and to corrode his ego, than a wife who reacts to his amorous intention with a "What, again?" attitude. A wife who participates in the sexual act as if she were conferring a favor of great price on her mate should not be surprised if it were sometime to be conferred for less, by another.

In today's world, female submissiveness is an anachronism. Passivity is anti-erotic. What a husband enjoys is participation. While there exists a wide variability of sexual response in both males and females, the mutually happy coital encounter is a highly charged, exultant experience that ends in euphoria; for a time, at least, neither partner has a trouble left in the world.

Husbands enjoy a mood of adventure in their conjugal sex. The male is aggressive, direct, inventive, blatant and boisterous, compared with the female who is soft, subtle, stable, modest and supportive, and thus he may be the one to set the stage for surprise. In joining with her husband in erotic adventure, a wife need not fear that she is abandoning her feminine role. On the contrary, she is adding joy to her life and stability to her marriage.

A hard crust of misinformation and fear still mars the sexual world of adults. It was only yesterday that the fear of pregnancy tarnished the sexual act for many wives and discouraged their spouse's ardor. The patient, considerate husband who can see beyond his own auto-eroticized horizon is not yet the general reality. And there are wives who consider themselves so sexually sophisticated that they would not stoop to reading a good marriage manual. It is possible to be intellectually sophisticated about sex and yet to be erotically illiterate. The puritan streak still haunts many marriages no matter how sexually frank and thoroughly modern we believe ourselves to be.

One wife illustrated, to her chagrin, that one can be intellectually advanced and erotically backward. Before the failure of her marriage she had always thought of herself as an articulate modern woman, keen in her understanding of world affairs, progressive in child-rearing and homecraft. She had two very brief premarital affairs, followed by the swift and ardent courtship of a rising government official, whom she married. She was an accomplished hostess, a loving mother and a stimulating companion on her husband's many trips to distant parts of the world. In every way she was her husband's social and intellectual match. She grew as he grew.

She called upon professional experts for all family contingencies as they arose: internist, dentist, obstetrician, pediatrician, gastroenterologist, ophthalmologist, attorney, tax consultant, language teacher, ballet mistress. Taking full advantage of this age of specialization, she left no expert unturned.

Once on board a ship with her husband bound for India, she noticed something alien to his customary conduct. He seemed to swagger and to talk too volubly. At bridge games he paid elaborate attention to a rather vivid divorcée of uncertain age. Later she grimly recalled that her husband behaved as a youth does when he is sexually stimulated. On the night before the ship's arrival, she espied him in amorous embrace with the flamboyant divorcée.

On their return to Washington, before the separation agreement, she added another expert to her list, a psychologist specializing in sexual counsel. This is a fragment of one question and answer session dealing with the couple's sexual history over the eighteen-year span of the marriage:

Q. Was the episode on shipboard the only one?

A. No, there were others in the past few years. The reprehensible thing was that I was with him on the boat.

Q. Did you have intercourse with him on the boat?

A. No, I was unwinding. We left in a terrible rush. I was bushed.

Q. Excluding pregnancies, menstruation or illness, how often have you refused your husband?

A. Refused? I don't think I ever refused.

Q. Excepting on the boat . . .

A.   That was not a refusal. I was in no frame of mind, as I said.

Q.   Were there other instances when, because you were not in a frame of mind, you discouraged intercourse by implication?

A.   Only when he wished it in some unusual way. Such as entrance from the rear.

Q.   You objected to that?

A.   Yes, simply on personal esthetic grounds. It smacked of the barnyard. After all, he is a distinguished man, you might say, in an important office. Such animal behavior is not—well, it's just a bit ludicrous.

Q.   And you laughed him out of it?

A.   My husband has an excellent sense of humor.

Q.   Would you say that both of you were sexually happy with each other?

A.   I have been perfectly satisfied, and I assume that my husband has been too.

Q.   Until, as it turned out, he looked for satisfaction with other women.

A.   That, I suppose, is the beast in the male, but I'll have no part of it.

To many wives, like this one, the philandering husband is intolerable. A few wives of resilient and tolerant nature manage to withstand the occasional dalliance of their mates. But even the most understanding woman finds a husband's infidelity, however lighthearted, a worry and a threat.

It is a worry because, as most spouses know intuitively, some imbalance in the marital relationship is at the root of most infidelities. This is so even when we exclude neurotic disturbances. The relationship of marriage has the greatest chance to remain unmarred by infidelity when there is social, intellectual and sexual equality between the partners.

In Periclean Greece, wives were not worried when their husbands sought the company of glamorous prostitutes or yielded to the blandishments of beautiful lute players at their stag banquets. Greek wives were not the social or intellectual equals of their husbands. The upper-class Greek male had his pleasure with hetaerae, and also kept concubines for daily enjoyment. Domestic sex, often without benefit of pleasure, served merely the national goal of procreation. In Epicurean Rome women feared not their husbands' philandering with other women but their infatuation with slender youths available either commercially or socially for pederastic purposes.

In modern Tokyo there are signs of social or intellectual imbalance in marriage. After their day at the office, husbands are reported to "take the long way home," meaning that they dally at one of the many thousands of nightclubs, bars and cabarets where charming hostesses entertain them for a fee. Apparently a wife is not the sole source of male sexual pleasures, and a billion-dollar entertainment industry has taken up the slack.

But in the Western world today, and outstandingly in the United States, a wife expects and is expected to be her husband's full partner, sexually and in every other way. If she suspects that he is looking elsewhere for his sexual enjoyments, she would be wise also to suspect the quality of her own contribution to their sexual life together. He will not need to seek sexual adventure abroad if he has an enthusiastic fellow adventurer at home.

The government official's wife had neither time nor inclination for erotic development. Her concept of the male was that of a sexually inflamed quadruped whose "animal behavior" was something to be guarded against by the respectable wife and mother. In her attitude toward sex she resembled, as Ovid described it, a frozen pump. Of the real sexual characteristics of the male she displayed dire ignorance.

It is not enough for a husband to have social and intellectual rapport with his wife. He wants her to understand and to accept him sexually. As he gains knowledge and finesse from experience and from such chapters as follow, he wants his wife to join him in erotic adventuring. He wants the closest contact with his wife in all spheres of living, as male and female members of the human family.

"It is in the living touch between us and other people, other lives, other phenomena that we move and have our being," wrote D. H. Lawrence. "Strip us of our human contacts and of our contact with the living earth and sun, and we are almost bladders of emptiness. Our individuality means nothing."

Certainly intercourse between man and wife represents the most profound human contact there is. To enrich this contact, to obtain full value in pleasure, is a purposeful goal in marriage.

Does the female member of the partnership have erotic interests which differ in kind and degree from those of the male? What actually does she enjoy?

5

---·•·---

WHAT WIVES ENJOY

AMERICAN WIVES TODAY ARE THE MOST PROMISING CANDI-
dates for a life of adventurous sex with their husbands
that history has produced in a long time.

If she were able to see herself in one of those rare and
blindingly clear moments of self-illumination, the healthy
midcentury wife would rejoice most of all in one single
revelation: that she is happy to be a female. She would
hope, furthermore, that her femaleness suffers no liabili-
ties from the cultural past, no psychic damage from parental mismanagement, no constriction or personal anxiety
from living in an insecure world, no pangs of discontent
that she is not as beautiful as Aphrodite, as rich as Croesus'
wife, nor as sexy as the reigning femme fatale of the films.

In her rendezvous with reality, she has reason to be
pleased, in fact quietly delighted, with herself. The axis
of her life seems to spin on her sexuality, yet she is not sex-
ridden. She deals with problems, the tough intractable ones
as well as the petty little ones, with a resiliency that is
sometimes the envy of men who meet them with taut guts
and gnashed teeth. The goal of the midcentury wife is to
be the epitome of femininity. She is not competing with
men. She never gives a moment's wistful thought to being
anything but vitally and joyously female.

She is likely to be bored with the entire contemporary mystique about female orgasm. She sometimes wonders whether it might not have been better for modern woman if Kinsey's monumental works had been kept on medical bookshelves, and if some psychiatrists did not bear down so heavily on the problem of female frigidity. She is puzzled by the fuzz around the phrase "sexual fulfillment," and wonders why so many sex manuals like to call sexual intercourse "communion," a word that suggests sacrament and not sex. For herself, she has a fine time in bed with her husband whom she adores with all his moles, and who adores her with all her moles. She accepts coitus whenever he offers it, in whatever way he asks it, and never pauses to judge whether she is perverted or he is inverted, or to guess what the latest paperback might have to say about it all.

The midcentury wife is well on the way to being a woman truly free. Part animal, part prescient mind, she launches her children like a mother cat, holding them firmly and lovingly by the scruff. Watchfully, but with little need for the purring reassurances of gentle Dr. Spock, she allows her young to strike out into the dangerous world without holding a crippling leash on them after they are able to stand by themselves.

She is in fact what a woman may be today, one who never felt the clammy hand of Victorian prudery, who was never jarred loose from her feminine role by the rash and raucous jazz age of the twenties, who has rejected the sexual counter-reformation of today's *avant garde* with its cool aseptic probing of sex and its denial of honest sensuality.

The healthy midcentury wife enjoys the spontaneity and deep sensuality of her sexual life. She did not apply these from the outside, like a veneer. She learned very early that these precious qualities could come to the surface only after inner growth. She put her own emotional household in order first before meshing her life with another. It was no simple chore. The concept of a fully realized personality eludes many wives. An inward strength of self, capable of forming relationships with other individuals on a level of mature and rich emotion, is the core of a woman's sexuality. This cannot be bought in a store or found in a recipe. We all recognize this woman of confident self-identity when we meet her. The personality seems made of whole cloth; there are no rents or seams of indecision, veils of self-doubt, masks of false self-esteem.

She enjoys her own sensuality and her husband's, knowing at the same time that marriage alone does not answer all her needs. Her goal was never to be completely independent of the rest of humankind. To be human is to need other human beings. The difference is not that one no longer needs other human beings, but what one needs them for. The paradox is that a really strong ego is no longer ego-centered. Egocentricity is the prime characteristic of childhood, and the purest egocentric of all is the infant, who knows only her own needs. The wife who demands attention, comfort, care, things, who regards other human beings in terms of what they can do for her, who when she is unhappy sees herself as victimized by others—that is an infant in disguise. Many an infantile woman has hidden her immaturity in marriage, as has many a man, and everyone has witnessed marriages that have gone afoul because of it.

She need not accept substitutes for true sensuality. Having cultivated, through learning and loving, sexual sensitivity in herself and her husband, she can spurn all the commercial institutions that capitalize on a people's sexual insecurities to sell merchandise; these sniveling forms of erotic suggestion—whether in certain kinds of magazines or fiction, in ads for cigarettes or for toreador pants—are beneath her notice. A recent best-selling book addressed to single girls allegedly taught them how to look sexy, to drive sexy cars and furnish sexy apartments, so that men would wine and dine them and give them expensive presents. This bankrupt brand of sexuality never enticed our modern wife. She has no need to be sexy in this shallow, exterior sense. She is sexuality itself.

She enjoys candor in sex, but not the kind that confuses shock with sensuality. She engages in coitus with her husband uninhibitedly and with wantonness, and is under no compulsion to prove anything, to exchange anything, to fulfill any duty, to break any icons, to defy any convention. She knows that the sexual impulse cannot be cheapened or subverted so long as its control and release are willed by the emotions. This is why she is pained to learn from a responsible novelist and critic that there exists in this country a practice known as "the key game." Any number of married couples can, and do, play it. Total titillation, without emotional purpose, is its goal. The wives throw their house keys into a grab bag, each husband picks one blindly and, provided it is not his own, escorts the owner to her home and has intercourse with her.

The healthy wife enjoys her exuberantly erotic role, feels free and comfortable in it, because she knows that her sexual conduct and that of her husband are emotionally based. She feels no need to be constantly reminded that he loves her, and that she loves him. That is why, in their intercourse, they have never drawn a line between modesty and immodesty, made rules or regulations, or cared about decorum or protocol. She remembers what a wise gynecologist told her about partners in intercourse: "Let them play, frolic, hang from the chandeliers if that is what they wish, provided only that they do not harm each other, or do harm to others, and provided also that in their total nudity they find some garment to cover themselves with, which I would hope is the garment of emotion."

She enjoys the indulgence of a few physical and psychological comforts. She likes to dress for intercourse, not literally to be sure, or on every occasion. But sometimes she enjoys preening herself at the first drop of an amorous hint, bathing and adorning and perfuming herself as women have done since the dawn of civilized sex. She finds in such preparations a measure of erotic arousal.

She enjoys the total freedom to request of her husband a more extended period of foreplay if she feels that she needs it, or none at all if she wants quick, deep and vigorous genital union. She enjoys intercourse in a dim half-light because she knows that it enhances her nudity which her husband loves to see, and if a mirror is nearby, she will enjoy with her husband the extra stimulation of observing their own action.

She enjoys the minor necessities of erotic engineering: a proper pillow for her so that she can more comfortably absorb and enjoy the pressure of her husband's weight and thrust; the arrangement of an armless chair for coitus while sitting; a comforter or soft rug on the floor when extra space is required for certain postures. She enjoys the sight of her husband's erection and is excited by it because it promises pleasure for her. And if they are fortunate enough to possess erotic literature of worth or erotic illustrations of intrinsic beauty, she enjoys these too because over the years she has developed a taste for them, and now they are a source of highly joyful erotic stimulation.

One of the reasons why the healthy midcentury wife can invest her erotic life with such total sensuality is that she has never examined it with microscope, slide rule, computer or any analytical device. She does not count her husband's orgasms, much less her own. She is aware that the male always has an orgasm in coitus and that the female does not always have one, that there are ways for her to seek and perfect the conditions that will give her orgasm more often. She knows that orgasm is not an integral part of woman's sexual response and that, like much of her behavior in intercourse, orgasm must be learned.

She takes no part in the curious debate that has been going on over this learning process. Some psychiatrists say that there are two kinds of orgasm that a woman can experience, a clitoral orgasm and a vaginal orgasm. The first occurs and is sensed in the region of the clitoris, the second takes place deep in the vaginal canal. The clitoral orgasm, they say, is the kind that adolescent girls experience by masturbation, and hence is of an immature variety. The vaginal orgasm is said to be the hallmark of full sexual maturity.

We have a right to inquire into how the distinction is made. Women describe their sensations in orgasm to their professional counselors. They do so in the only way possible, in subjective terms. Most women seek professional help when they are having difficulties of an emotional nature. Subjective evidence is not the best kind of evidence, especially when it is offered by a person who is emotionally upset. The consensus of these patients is that a clitoral orgasm is a purely local sensation of pleasure, while a vaginal orgasm pervades the entire body with pleasure. They draw largely upon metaphors to describe their orgasms. The clitoral climax is like a sputtering fuse, they say, while the vaginal one is like an explosion or cataclysm. One woman told her psychiatrist that her orgasm was like going over Niagara Falls in a barrel. She did not mention whether she had ever made such a descent.

The similes become even more elaborate. One likens the vaginal orgasm to golden bombs bursting, another to blazing pinwheels; almost invariably the convulsion is said to extend from the roots of the hair to the toes.

Such sexual literacy is, of course, admirable, were it not for the temptation to establish a caste system of the haves and the have-nots. Already two castes have sprung up: clitoral woman and vaginal woman. It would seem to be merely a matter of time before articulate wives will gather in knots discussing their orgasms. "How went it last night on the launching pad?" one might be heard to ask. "Perfectly celestial—a heavenly aurora borealis! And you?" "Soaring, like a cadenza in Mahler's Ninth!" Mere clitoral woman stands by, her head hanging: "I'm afraid I—fizzled out."

One has every right to question the grounds on which some women are to be relegated to second-class sexual citizenship. In fact these grounds have been challenged by objective investigation. Dr. Kinsey employed a team of five qualified gynecologists who tested 879 women for genital sensitivity. An overwhelming majority felt no sensation whatever in the vaginal canal. Virtually all subjects displayed keen clitoral sensitivity. It may be seriously doubted, therefore, whether such a phenomenon as vaginal orgasm exists at all, excepting as a rhetorical symbol to express a high peak of pervasive erotic pleasure that is suddenly released.

If the healthy midcentury wife wishes to be certain that she is experiencing orgastic success of high degree, she need only observe her own state of mind after coitus. Does she feel totally calm, relaxed, all her tension spent, at peace with the world, grateful to her husband and satisfied with herself? After rest or sleep, does she feel ready to attack her work with energy and optimism? Or does she feel impelled to claw her husband, to climb up walls? On the day after coitus, when she gazes in the mirror, does she look like the wracked woman on the television screen who has mislaid her aspirin? Plainly, she need not go over Niagara Falls in a barrel to decide whether she has had a warm and loving erotic experience with her husband.

Nor does the healthy modern wife, in her sexual attitudes, allow herself to be saddled with that numbing, chilling, anti-sensual concept that, in recent years, has been labeled sexual responsibility. In our age of joint adventuring, has she not assumed enough responsibilities? Sexual joy and sexual responsibility, by definition, would seem to be mutually exclusive. How frustrating for a husband, after disrobing his wife, to find her still swaddled in awesome layers of responsibility!

If anything, she needs lighter and less cumbersome baggage on her erotic journeying. Some of it, to be sure, is subsurface. She is not always aware of influences that cause her to be more slowly eroticized than her husband and to require more stimulation before reaching orgasm. But she can be confident that she will throw off these restraints as she gains insight and experience in coitus. Her slightly slower rate of arousal does not disqualify her from offering her husband a high erotic return, especially since his sexual advances are neither brusque nor routine nor demanding, but move her to feel that she is the one, the unique female whom he devoutly desires. She knows of her husband's capacity to fantasize and to become erectile in a matter of seconds. But she is aware also that she possesses a built-in aphrodisiac that is not merely genital, but an inborn, instinctual desire to receive his sperm, to conceive and tend his offspring, to be a lifelong companion and sharer of his sexual ecstasies.

Nor is she intimidated at the word frigidity, which is sometimes given the valency of a fatal disease. It exists, of course, but popular literature and loose jargon filched from psychiatry have given it such careless currency and so stretched it beyond its original and limited meaning that it has assumed the proportions of an epithet.

Much that is described as frigidity is no more than reticence or inhibition, stamped in a woman's psychic biography during childhood. It may have been put there accidentally or by design, impressed by parents or teacher, or even playmates, and made her feel that sex was wicked, shameful or violent or fearsome or darkly mysterious.

Scientists find great difficulty in describing frigidity with precision. A man's impotence is apparent; one can see that he has no erection. But a woman who is frigid, or thinks she is, can only report certain subjective symptoms about feelings she experiences in coitus. She says that she does not experience very much erotic excitement or attain orgasm, despite tests that reveal no genital anesthesia. Only psychiatry can determine the extent of a difficulty which may be situational, and quickly resolved, or something profound in which psychic wires have become crossed, and require disentanglement under treatment.

Suppose the modern wife cannot bring herself to be free, sensual and uninhibited in her sexual relations? It is a reasonable question to ask. She belongs, after all, to the twentieth century, not to an Indian or Arab or other culture where the erotic arts were woven into the texture of a very different kind of society. She did not marry to be the erotic plaything of some powerful rajah, caliph, or Arabian Nights prince, whose major interest was the enjoyment of wealth and sensual delights.

Yet it may be argued that American wives, more than ever before in Western history, are bent on enjoying the arts of living with unparalleled gusto, taste and energy. Most of these arts are enjoyed by the exercise of the five basic senses. Women's appreciation and expertness in cookery, fashions, interior decoration, entertainment and travel have been developed to a point of high sophistication. Modern husbands are undoubtedly happy to play a part in this ascending scale of material living. But has the American wife progressed to as high a degree of knowledgeability in that crucial area of married life, sexual pleasure? During our postwar boom in living standards, how much has she improved the quality of her sexual life? How many wives can honestly say that they know as much about refinements in erotic enjoyment as they know about refinements in salad mixing, gardening, child care, cosmetics and weekend entertaining?

Ideally, as we have said, the midcentury wife is as interested in a richly pleasurable sex life as she is in all these other arts of living. Indeed, she is more interested in it, because she recognizes its value in enhancing the core of her life, which is her relationship with her husband. About this she is in no doubt.

What she may doubt is her ability to develop this art. It was not part of her girlhood education; it was not sanctioned by society, as it has been sanctioned in other times and cultures. The hetaera of Greece and the odalisque of Islam were schooled in the erotic arts from childhood on, as training for their future vocation. The Japanese bride took her bride's book as a textbook on marriage. In the American way, we have allowed this essential learning to slip into a girl's education by the back door—or, rather, via the back seat of the automobile. Most wives today learned all they know of the refinements of sexual pleasure from these youthful, secretive and often inept experiences.

But this, happily, is an art that it is not too late to learn. The capacity for sexual pleasure is built into the human female, as it is in the human male. She may have some feelings of strangeness to overcome at first; some shreds may still cling of the girlhood feeling that this is forbidden fruit. Once she accepts her right to full enjoyment of the pleasure function as wife and lover, she will find that she can shed her restraints and with them her tensions. She can go on with her husband to explore the whole range of adventuresome sexual experience.

6

———•———

ADVENTURE IS NOT
PERVERSION

ONE OF THE RESTRAINTS THAT KEEP SOME CONJUGAL LOVERS
from an adventurous approach to their lovemaking is a
specific fear, the fear of perversion.

Usually this fear is not named or expressed in words. It
may even be unrecognized as anything more than a vague
uneasiness, a disinclination to depart from the standard
and familiar form of coitus, with or without preliminary
play.

Husbands seem less often troubled by this fear than
wives, perhaps because—as we like to think—the male is
by nature an adventurer and the female, by nature or by
social conditioning, a conservative. In one respect at least,
wives contradict this pat theory, for they show more dar-
ing than their husbands in articulating this particular fear.
It is the wife, usually, who asks her doctor whether one or
another sexual practice is a sign of perversion.

The source of this fear is a confusion; the confusion is
quite simple and understandable. Some of the erotic enjoyments of healthy, normal sex are also part of the patterns of some kinds of deviant sex. But similarities between
two things do not make them the same thing.

That is like assuming that because pathological gamblers bet on horse races, every one who puts down a two-dollar bet at a parimutuel window is a pathological gambler. Or that because some unfortunates who drink are alcoholics, everyone who takes a cocktail before dinner is a drunkard.

If the source of confusion is simple and understandable, so is the difference. The healthy bettor at the race track and the healthy partaker of a drink both have a choice. They can bet or not, drink or not, as they please. The pathological bettor and drinker have no choice. It is the very nature of their sickness that they cannot do otherwise than gamble or drink, even to depriving their families or risking the loss of their jobs.

The analogy in sex is obvious.

Perversion is psychosexual enslavement. Adventure is freedom.

The freedom to choose, to vary, to explore and adventure in their lovemaking is inherent in a healthy sexual partnership. We might even call it a right that they acquire in making the total commitment of themselves to the relationship of marriage. We may say without hesitation that the fullest use of this freedom is a sign of the health and vitality of the relationship rather than the reverse.

The glory of human beings is precisely this capacity for variety, for change, for adventure. A cow is like other cows; the farmer who knows his herd may discern individual differences, but still each animal's behavior is predictably cowlike, or sheeplike, or doglike. We can say that human behavior is also predictable to a degree, but then we must add endless qualifications.

Each one of us, man, woman and child, is a collection

of individual differences. Each one of us is a living history of our own individuality, of our particular environment and experience acting upon the particular inheritance with which each of us is born. No two of us are alike; even identical twins manage to develop separate identities.

Yet we do accept conformity of many sorts; we do repress our individuality in certain defined areas, as a condition of living together in a human society. We restrict behavior by means of laws and customs; we accept standards of propriety in dress and public conduct; we obey inner precepts of morality and ethics. Many such restraints are essential to our common safety and well-being. Learning to conform to one's society is part—and a most significant part—of growing from infancy to adulthood.

How far must these conformities go?

It is a provocative fact that the most rigidly conformist societies are the most primitive ones. In a community of Australian aborigines or African bushmen there is very little margin for individual differences or nonconformist behavior; every aspect of life is conducted by prescribed, ritualistic tradition. The farther we advance in civilization, the broader the area that is left to each member to decide for himself.

Our freedom to adventure, in sex as in other activities, is our human heritage, endorsed by our society, which accepts individual freedom as a basic right. And so, when conformity follows us into the privacy of the conjugal bedroom, and is enforced there by an uneasiness akin to or stemming from fear, we have reason to look into it further. Against fear, or confusion, knowledge is the best weapon.

The sexual deviant, we have said, is the slave of his particular deviation. He cannot achieve orgasm by any other route. Yet some of the deviant ways of arriving at orgasm occur to normal lovers, too, as part of their repertoire of courtship and arousal on the way to orgasm.

The peeping Tom, or voyeur, may haunt a neighborhood, seeking a lighted window with shades undrawn where he may watch a woman undressing or hope to catch a glimpse of her body nude. Only then can he release his sexual tension by masturbation to orgasm.

But every normal, healthy husband also has a bit of the voyeur in him. He delights in catching a glimpse of his wife nude or semi-nude; he is pleased and aroused by the sight of her bare breasts or buttocks. If the circumstances allow, he may then and there pursue this pleasure further and draw her into a coital embrace. This is very far from the unhappy deviant peering furtively through a strange woman's window.

Another kind of deviant finds his release in exposing his genitals in public, within the view of a woman or more often a young girl. This is exhibitionism in a pathological form. Much rarer, and usually much sicker, is the female exhibitionist who takes her clothes off in public, sometimes under the inhibition-loosening effect of alcohol.

Yet most normal, healthy women have a normal and healthy degree of exhibitionism. They take pleasure, and give pleasure as well, in exhibiting a shapely pair of breasts in a becoming decolletage; they fuss over the precise length of a skirt to reveal their legs to best advantage. On the beach or at a swimming pool they push exhibitionism as far as decorum and shapeliness permit; hardly anything could be more exhibitionistic than a Bikini swim suit.

What is wrong with that? It is part of the natural interplay of the sexes. If the male takes pleasure in seeing and desiring, the female takes pleasure in being seen and desired. The same mechanism works in reverse, although to a lesser degree. Men like to show their muscles, if they have them, and women like to see them. In an earlier society it was the male who showed a well-turned leg in his doublet and hose, and the female who appreciated it. A little exhibitionism of this kind adds to the enjoyment we take in each other's society. In conjugal privacy a wife takes all the more enjoyment in her husband's pleasure in her nudity, and it would be a sad deprivation for both if she did not.

The fetishist cannot enjoy a woman in the flesh but must take his sexual release a step removed. In the symbolic embrace of some part of a woman's clothing, he achieves his physical outlet by masturbating. A tender custom of Japanese lovers long ago was to exchange intimate garments when they were to be parted for a while. Romantic lovers in literature cherished a glove or a handkerchief belonging to the beloved, and even purloined some article of hers to stroke and kiss if she were absent or perhaps unresponsive. A healthy husband may also take pleasure in the look and texture and special fragrance of his wife's nightgown or undergarments; if this were not so, the entire lingerie trade would be wasting time and money in making its products so alluring. No one would confuse any of this with fetishism.

Sadists and masochists derive their orgastic outlet by beating or being beaten, usually over the buttocks; they cannot reach sexual climax except through pain. Sometimes this is not physical but psychological pain, in insults and harsh or threatening words. A psychiatric explanation is that the masochist pays in suffering for the pleasure he dare not otherwise enjoy, while the sadist takes pleasure in inflicting pain because for him the sexual act has been reduced to an act of hostility and aggression. Sometimes these two reciprocal patterns are combined in a single individual, in the form called sadomasochism.

Some normal, healthy sexual partners also play rough. They bite, pinch, squeeze. Undoubtedly there is, as Freud pointed out, some kernel of aggression in the sexual encounter. Erotic literature often describes coitus in terms of mock combat. There is also a kind of puppyish, childish vitality in this kind of play, like the rough play of young animals.

Vigorous physical contact is a normal and pleasurable release of energy for many people, and we recognize the normality of it in many of our sports. Athletes play football, box and wrestle, some for fame, some for money, but they might choose any of a number of other ways to achieve these ends if they did not enjoy the roughness of the sport. And so in sex, if both partners enjoy their rough play, and no one really gets hurt, there is no reason for them not to throw off restraints and enjoy each other as vigorously as they like, without fear or hint of anything abnormal in their play.

Most familiar and widespread, and therefore probably most troubling in the thoughts of conjugal lovers about their own practices, are the practices of homosexuals. Men and women who can achieve sexual satisfaction only with members of their own sex, or sometimes with either their own or the opposite sex, engage in many of the erotic activities that are enjoyed as foreplay by normally sexed partners. Manual and mouth-genital caresses are part of the healthy lovers' repertoire of mutual arousal. The fact that homosexuals also engage in these activities need not concern the conjugal partners at all. It is not these practices that make the homosexual a deviant. What makes him a deviant is his inability to form a lasting and exclusive relationship with a member of the opposite sex. It is actually as simple as that.

What has happened to the sexual deviant, that he or she is not able to enjoy the freedom and variety of a normal sexual relationship but is compelled to find sexual release only through one rigidly exclusive means?

In the case of any individual deviant the whole answer might be hard to come by. Psychiatrists have sought through endless case histories to find, for example, a single differentiating factor that leads to homosexuality. The human being is too complex. Anything that goes wrong with his development, anything that, unlike measles or the common cold, cannot be traced to an infectious agent visible under the electron microscope, is likely to be the result of many factors. There is no single factor to which we can trace delinquency or mental illness. In sexual deviation, also, there appears to be no single factor on which we can lay the blame.

But we can safely make one generalization, and it is illuminating for normal as well as deviant sex. Human sexuality develops from birth, and it develops in clearly marked stages.

Sigmund Freud make this clarifying discovery, and shocked many of his contemporaries when he first wrote about infant sexuality. We know today, and accept as a truism, that we are born either male or female and that we are sexual creatures from the day of our birth.

The stages of sexual development are quite well marked. The infant nursing at his mother's breast derives many kinds of comfort and satisfaction. His hunger is appeased, his inborn sucking instinct is satisfied, and his need for warm and gentle contact, for the sensation of being closely and tenderly held, is also fed. This is why pediatricians recommend that even if a mother does not breast-feed her baby, she should hold him while she gives him his bottle. Automatic bottle-holding, whether by human or mechanical means, may fill a baby's stomach but it will not fill these other needs, which have to do with his whole development, including the emotional and even—as we have discovered—the intellectual. And, of course, the sexual.

Comes the day when the young child discovers pleasure in moving his bowels, and then in touching himself, especially in touching his genitals. He is an auto-erotic creature; his sexuality is still at a primitive level where he can satisfy it himself. Masturbation is now generally recognized as a normal stage in childhood's sexual development; not all children pass through it but most do, girls as well as boys, and it is widely accepted that this is a stage in which eroticism becomes focused on the genital organs.

This is also the time of what has been described as the family romance, although more accurately it might be called the family triangle, the age when small boys fall in love with their mothers and dream of supplanting their fathers, and small girls coquette with their fathers and fancy themselves in competition with their mothers. It is the first infantile flowering of heterosexual love, which must go through several further metamorphoses before it becomes functionally and securely adult.

It must—and generally it does—survive the homosexual "crush" of early adolescence, when a teacher or a club leader, or perhaps a more sophisticated friend, becomes the ideal and the model; this is the first step in love outside the family, and a step toward emotional independence of parents. It must also survive the first heterosexual gropings of calf love, or teen-age going steady, and perhaps some early disappointing experiments with adult sex as well as various degrees of petting. And it must survive the long economic and artificial adolescence, as differentiated from biological adolescence, which modern culture imposes on our young.

Most boys and girls do survive all these stages with their sexuality intact; the true and incurable deviants, despite all the attention we pay to them, are in fact a small minority. They are the ones who, the laws of probability being what they are, fail to progress past one or another of these immature stages of sexuality.

Usually they are held back by a fortuitous combination of inborn and environmental factors. A delicate or sickly childhood, an overprotective or dominating or unconsciously seductive mother, an unassertive or passive or perhaps absent father—these are some of many factors, far too many to list, that may turn a youth toward a homosexual adulthood. Reverse a few of the same factors—a vigorous athletic girl, a weak or unsympathetic or perhaps competitive mother, and a dominating or too appealing father—and we may have a young woman uncertain of her femininity.

Some of these outcomes are reversible, given once more a set of favoring circumstances. Some are not. What is revealing is that the sexual deviants are those who have not developed into full adult heterosexuality; they are fixed at some earlier stage of sexual development. They may have appeared to be going from one stage to the next, but when the full flood of adult sexual freedom washes over them, they lose their insecure footing in maturity and slip back to a more comfortable, less demanding form of sexuality, that is, an infantile form.

Yet the individual is not, after all, an infant. He is of

adult stature, adult intellect, and in other ways he may be emotionally adult. At the very least, he is likely to have sexual appetites of adult strength, and in his effort to satisfy them he cannot literally go back to infantile or childish behavior. And so he finds, or is forced into, deviant sexual patterns.

It is revealing that the homosexual outcome, at least, has been recognized in societies other than our own. The Greco-Roman world encouraged the attachment between an adolescent youth and an older man, on the grounds that the youth had much to gain in education and culture; when he came of age, he married and reared a family, and later took youthful protégés in his turn. Persian and Arab custom also accepted homosexuality.

Whatever the special circumstances of an individual's growing up, most in our society come safely to adulthood and adult sexuality, as we have said. But we bring with us into adulthood all the stages through which we have gone along the way. Each human being is a walking documentary, a living, feeling, acting record of his own past. We recapitulate infancy, childhood and adolescence in all our most important adult experiences. We are full of physical and emotional memories, and every one of them enriches—and sometimes confuses—our experience of the present.

We bring with us into adulthood also our sexual memories. Sexual play between adult lovers calls upon all those memories of infant and childhood erotic experience, and is enriched by them. It is no surprise that some kinds of play resemble the practices of deviants. Adult lovers enjoy the full range of erotic pleasure, childish as well as adult. The sexual deviant is fixed and compulsive in his special pattern, but healthy lovers are free to adventure among them all.

If individual freedom is a privilege of healthy lovers, so is another concept, the concept of privacy. Until quite recently in history, privacy was unknown even to members of the privileged classes. People lived, ate, slept and made love, all in one room; the poor had a room barely large enough to hold the family, and the rich had a baronial hall spacious enough for all their retainers. Today privacy is still limited to privileged societies, but in those it is every man's right and it is protected by law.

Privacy is a condition of individual freedom, and it is especially a condition of the sexual freedom of conjugal lovers. In privacy and intimacy, they can adventure as their fancy leads them. In privacy, nothing two people do who love each other need ever be taboo.

There is more to fear from shame and shyness than from perversion. Modesty, propriety, decorum—all these are public virtues, but they are private faults. Within the shelter of a loving relationship, there is no need and no reason to draw back from any form of shared and mutual erotic enjoyment. Marriage can be blighted by bedroom taboos. Inhibition, not perversion, is the real enemy to lovemaking.

Conjugal lovers enjoy a sexual freedom that is like no other; in their closeness and intimacy there is no room for shame or fear. They are free to enjoy variety and change of pace, to play and to experiment. They need never settle for monotony. They can range without restraint through the whole spectrum of adventure in erotic enjoyment of each other.

7

———•———

PRELUDES TO PLEASURE

THERE ARE TIMES WHEN INTERCOURSE WITHOUT PRELUDE OR elaboration of any kind seems precisely right. Neither husband nor wife is in a mood of playful suspense, neither wishes a change of pace or surprise. Any preliminaries that might delay coitus are bypassed; the act of love is shared immediately, impetuously and urgently.

This is often the way well-mated couples enjoy intercourse after an absence from each other, when there is accrued hunger. Desire rises at equal tempo and coitus occurs as suddenly as a summer storm. Pleasure is telescoped into a few brief moments, and sometimes they may yield as much satisfaction as an elaborately erotic and sophisticated encounter.

Such quickly flaring, quickly ended lovemaking may be right as rain, especially if a repeat performance allows more leisurely enjoyment. But it is not sexual adventure in the sense we have used the term. No unexpected conditions surrounded the event, no promise of novelty, no diversified foreplay, however satisfying the result. Sexual and emotional tension were simply relieved in a climate of joyous reunion. This is as it should be.

It need not, however, be so always. One instance of sexual spontaneity, under unconventional conditions, may be cited here. A devoted young couple spent an exhausting winter month tending their brood of sick children, one of whom was dangerously ill. In their anxiety, they refrained from intercourse until the crisis was ended. Then, carefree, they headed for the ski slopes for a weekend of astringent exercise. Around the bend of a secluded valley, in deep dry snow and fading sunshine, these intrepid and desirous mates doffed their skis and enjoyed intercourse without a care for chilblains or the benefits of a heated bedroom.

Sexual courtship before intercourse has always been a mark of civilized, leisure cultures. Whatever form the preludes may take, they add social as well as sexual excitement, since both partners are aware of impending seduction. Yet there are undoubtedly countless couples who take their sex straight, without prelude or emotional preparation.

There is not much that can be said in praise or dispraise of healthy, honest, unadorned physiological sex within the frame of a good relationship. Those who live intense, absorbing everyday lives, with time at a premium, may find the preludes to adventurous sex extraneous if not impossible. But for most couples, some measure of erotic preparation provides a positive value. It enhances the frankly physical stimulation of foreplay and, most important, it offers an opportunity for constraints to be thrown off and for the cultivation of sensuality, that indispensable ally of healthy lovemaking.

Because the climactic moments of intercourse are all too brief, it is more desirable that erotic flirtation as well as foreplay be extensive, varied and, whenever possible, unpredictable. A wife may be permitted a sigh of boredom if, immediately the bedroom door is closed, her husband habitually encloses her in a smothering embrace. With an occasional touch of suspense, playfulness and ascending excitement he might find her an enthusiastic instead of a merely acquiescent partner.

The preludes to love may be played in differing keys. They may be mirthful and high-spirited, or silent in their total concentration. Western sexual partners, like the ancient Greeks, prefer to initiate intercourse in a mood of gaiety and lighthearted humor, especially after celebration or revelry. The spark that ignites lovemaking may be any event that is worth celebrating, beyond the usual birthdays and anniversaries: a long-awaited contract signed, some business or professional obstacle at last surmounted, any victory, large or small, in which both spouses have been emotionally involved. As history well knows, victory and love make ecstatic bedfellows.

The most trivial event is often worthy of sexual celebration. The husband, who abhors the smell of paint, telephones his wife to pack her bag and meet him at the baroque old hotel with the high ceilings and plush draperies, in the heart of the metropolis. Object: a weekend of lovemaking until their apartment is livable again. Another husband, who fought his boss and lost honorably, decides that a week of walking and loving in the mountain country where he first met his wife is a superior method of preparing for his next job.

Put together enough lighthearted pretexts, unexpected settings, unaccustomed modes of touching, kissing, embracing and entering, and over the years the custom of connubial sex need never become staled.

The road to sexual adventure has its hazards. Hurry is one of them. Too often in our wrathfully speedy age, we skip the preludes and rush toward the orgastic goal with the same anxiety that impels the automobile driver to gain ten yards over his neighbor on the expressway. The tendency to telescope the erotic preludes to coitus seems to be a symptom of the tense, mechanized kind of life we live.

Our automated age can confound the sexual impulse and drain it of all naturalness. A recent cartoon, describing the nightmare of automation, showed a single lonely man and a single lonely woman in a cavernous jungle of dials, switches and knobs; together they were operating, apparently with fingertip control, some vast industrial complex. He leaned toward her amorously, half-astonished at his own libido. She shrank from him, as if fearful of each accusing electronic eye. They were so utterly alone, yet she protested, "No, no, not here, John." In the awesome presence of the computer-god, sex indeed seems sacrilegious.

Hurry is not the only thief of erotic joy; there are others equally larcenous. A distracted or preoccupied mind yields only grudgingly to the sexual impulse. Tension, the jitters or other nervous side effects of the nuclear age not only reduce the profit in pleasure, they undercut incentives to have sexual pleasure at all. A wife who has put aside the day's harassments may be ready for joyful intercourse. But if she harbors anxieties about the household budget or an ailing child or her social status, she is as poorly qualified for a richly enjoyable sexual encounter as a husband who computes his tax deductibles while fondling his mate's thighs.

In setting the stage for sex, the considerate husband is aware that tender attentiveness has an aphrodisiac value. No matter that the compliments he pays his spouse have been uttered thousands of times before. To a wife they are true expressions of his feelings, a sign that he is putting aside all distractions and attending only to her. Familiar as they may be, to the responsive wife these age-old attentions are a sexual elixir, a gentle invitation that she also put aside all other concerns and arrange herself for the mood of making love.

Most every loving wife responds willingly. Still unapproached, she allows her normal voice to become muted, her posture to become lazily graceful, her limbs to relax into languor. A slipper drops to the floor, a naked thigh is revealed, sexual accessibility is written on her face, for the mask of the odalisque is no stranger to her.

Husbands receive these signals and transmit some of their own, adding to the erotic tension. The interchange may be interrupted and resumed. Delay generates its own excitement.

Petting may be begun, stopped and begun afresh. There is no reason for spouses to disdain petting simply because it happens to be a premarital custom. As distinguished from foreplay that immediately precedes intercourse, petting succeeds in keeping sexual interest in each other refreshed and youthful.

Sexual preludes may be continued sporadically throughout an afternoon or evening of gay social activity. No physiological harm will come to the couple who begin their embraces while dressing for a dinner party and discontinue such love play without a conclusion in coitus. A suspenseful erotic rapport between the married lovers is likely to glow throughout an otherwise uneventful evening. The erotic tension might even be occasionally renewed in stolen moments alone on lawn or terrace, in the kitchen or backyard, in the manner of lovers full of desire for each other. One couple, being driven home to the city from a party in the suburbs, admitted that they had broken the monotony of a long ride, and of the driver and his wife's dreary chatter, by rapturously petting under cover of a blanket in the back seat. They had been married eighteen years.

Predictability, the set pattern, the compulsive routine, are the enemies of sexual adventure. The nineteenth-century author of a marriage manual that is still influential today, although it is flecked with superstition, would have his readers believe that the sexual drama between man and his wife is like the figures of a formal dance, its precise sequences ordained by tradition. In the same archaic vein he suggests that it is unthinkable that a husband permit his wife any initiative in their lovemaking.

Granted that the problem of who takes the initiative is sometimes of sensitive concern in modern marriage. Sexual equality in Western society is a fact of life despite the mumbled objections of some males. The healthily sexed wife today who pulls her own weight in the marital boat can with justice argue that she should initiate sexual advances and seek intercourse with her spouse whenever her own desire urges it. She is no pampered doll or plaything of her husband's sexual whims. She has cycles of desire, and at their peak, just before and sometimes immediately after menstruation, she might wish coitus as ardently as any male. Riding home in a taxi, at any given time, her husband has no hesitation in initiating intimate erotic play. Why not she? Of what worth is her sexual freedom if she cannot have what she wants when she wants it?

The answer, of course, is that she can and does, using her own repertory of enticements, and few husbands reject the invitation. On some very rare occasion, perhaps, she might find him unready and without an erection. Should this be a frequent occurrence she might well wonder whether he is having a psychological difficulty or whether he is spending his store of energy elsewhere.

In a past Islamic culture, at a time when wives were indeed the sexual playthings, if not the slaves, of their husbands, it was considered praiseworthy for the wife to take the sexual initiative, according to this quaintly worded passage from a work on coitus:

> Arrived at the door of the house, and coming into the room, she lighteth a light, and unveiling her veil, calleth her husband, whom she addresseth with the softest of words. And sitting herself down upon his thighs, she presseth her bosom up close against his breast, until his heart beginneth to gladden and become merry, and his rod rigid. She thereupon uncovereth the lower part of her arms [an erogenous zone among early Arabs], and he getteth further excited and, losing his passion's control, his prizzle up-flameth clamouring to enter the rosebud vestibule of her garden. Which done, the husband will no longer listen to aught against his wife.

While the pattern familiar to us today is that of the active, pursuing, erectile male who takes the initiative in arousing his wife by his own tenderly sensual devices, there are times when her initiative is welcomed. This might come at a moment, perhaps, when his spouse's desire outran his own, after a period of highly exhausting labor or psychological doldrums. One wife confided to her husband that sometimes she awoke in the night, full of desire for him. But rather than wake him out of a sound sleep, she turned and composed herself and went back to sleep without solace. When he heard this he protested, with a genuine sense of loss.

The specific stimulants that are encouraging to lovemaking and add to its merriment are known to most. To active dancing, music, good food and drink might be added the art of paying intimate compliments, be it the spouse's new dress or hairdo, the curve of her breast or her buttock. Richly enhancing the sensual preludes to pleasure are erotic art and literature of esthetic worth which, when read or viewed together, provide an extra dividend of intellectual stimulation. As for music, the range is wide, from Richard Wagner to Dizzy Gillespie, both bathed nowadays in stereophonic grandeur. And since the earliest brewing of beer by the Egyptians five thousand years ago, alcohol has remained probably the most serviceable ally of sexual excitement, provided only that it is not taken in excess.

The proviso is important. Many couples take their sex straight, without prelude or play, while floating in an alcoholic daze. A commonplace today are weekend parties at homes, country clubs and nightclubs that seldom end before the celebrants have considerably dulled their ability to feel pain—or pleasure. Partially anesthetized, they fall numbly into bed, experiencing sex with all the nervous ecstacy of a rabbit or, more likely, muffing it entirely.

Perhaps because the bedroom is the habitual and conventional setting for lovemaking, and because it is where partners sleep, dress and undress, conduct cosmetic rites, strew clothes, bobbypins and small change, it has lost some of its original lure as a site for intercourse. A change of scenery to another room of the house adds piquancy, even a bathroom or kitchen. In a home where privacy is assured, lovemaking can escalate from room to room, ending in an armless chair or on a rug in some unaccustomed posture. Freedom to make love anywhere, and in any way, not only contributes to the gaiety of marriage; it frees the sexual relationship from those last, lingering traces of inhibition.

A varying and imaginative use of preliminary love play may serve, also, to allay anxiety in those who are unrealistically concerned with their sexual potency, especially husbands. The more lustful the preludes the less are the partners likely to fall victim to qualms about impotence.

The male's pride in his potency has been noted throughout man's history, although in early eras his concern was for fertility rather than his capacity for erection and orgasm. Today, sexual potency in both sexes has been given unprecedented emphasis because of the spread of psychoanalytic knowledge. Some of this concern is justified, and it will be discussed in a later chapter. But there remain in many males vestiges of superstition about potency, centering upon the use of aphrodisiacs for increasing sexual capacity.

The flaw in such thinking is not that aphrodisiacs, taken as food or folk medicine, are without value. It lies in the assumption that the quantity of sexual intercourse can possibly determine the quality of the sexual relationship in marriage. In times when a man had plural wives, concubines and harems to satisfy, his orgastic capacity was of some importance to him. Today, a husband's concern need be limited only to making the most profitable use—in terms of pleasure for both—of his inherent sexual capacity.

A better-informed use of his sexual assets, rather than the increase of those assets through futile and thoroughly discredited aphrodisiac substances, should be the aim of the modern healthy husband. A high sexual capacity can no more be equated with sexual delight than can the joys of gluttony with those of a gourmet.

Having chosen those measures from the repertory of love preludes most pleasing to both partners, the healthy husband may turn his attention to the initial phase of foreplay which, as the name suggests, is playful, spontaneous and no more planful than the petting of young lovers. The expectations advanced by romantic novelists and some sex guides, of a grandeur in coitus surpassing that of Niagara Falls and the Grand Canyon combined, had best be left to travel agents to describe; to expect more than keen, lustful, unashamed hedonism and a deepened relationship, after years of marriage, is to court disillusionment.

There are degrees of expertness in foreplay. These can be acquired. But as wise couples know, the emotional environment is primary, the technique secondary. Together they can transport the lovers and transform a marriage.

8

---·—·---

VARIETIES OF FOREPLAY

ONE OF THE UNCHALLENGED MYTHS ABOUT MODERN MARITAL sex is that the highest flights of erotic joy belong only to the youthful newlywed, that after the first exhilaration of early marital coitus, the only course is downhill or, at best, along a predictable and somewhat tame plateau. It is true, but only in purely quantitative terms, that youth holds the orgastic record, particularly the young male. But sexual love is not a race, and a record number of orgastic pole vaults cannot be equated with the depth and quality of truly erotic, truly sensual experience. For this, the sexual partnership needs not only experience but a widely ranging and mellowing intimacy that takes years to acquire.

Erotic sensitivity needs developing first, within a frame of sexual equality and a deepening relationship. A wife has much to learn; her husband, usually the initiator and the teacher, must himself learn from the vast treasury of love-making the knowledge that he will adapt to their individual taste. There are many and subtle variations of those mutually stimulating procedures that have come to be known in modern times as foreplay, and the conjugal lovers will draw upon them as their taste becomes cultivated and their responses more accurately attuned.

There have been fashions in sexual foreplay, and eras

when there seemed to be no erotic play at all. In some early Oriental cultures, foreplay amounted to little more than the mutual stroking of genitalia, almost immediate entrance, and the assumption of unusual postures, sometimes under such bizarre circumstances as riding in a donkey cart or on horseback.

Husbands in medieval India were told "to develop the desire of the weaker sex through embraces and kisses, unguiculations (scratching), morsications (biting), manipulating the hair, and other amorous blandishments; these divert the mind from coyness and coldness, after which tricks and toying the lover will proceed to take possession of the place."

Islamic teachers admonished husbands "not to forget kissing and cuddling and the interlocking of leg with leg, and to suck delicate lips, to bite with passion and rapturous kisses and then to pat and tap with swordlike weapon." The Arabic male also found stimulation in admiring a female vulva that was protuberant and curvaceous. The Greeks and Romans limited their foreplay to kissing and close bodily embraces, usually while nude; they also engaged in mutual mouth-genital play.

The great majority of spouses today engage in some form of foreplay before intercourse, lasting from a few minutes to half an hour or more. The deep kissing, stroking, pressing and caressing of erogenous zones which constitute the usual repertory of foreplay have, for their physiological purpose, the preparation of the sex organs for coitus. But the conscious goal is to lengthen the period of enjoyment by a gradual upward ascent from erotic peak to erotic peak until each partner is ready for entrance.

As is generally realized, the wife lags somewhat behind her husband in the upward erotic spiral, but only in the earlier

stages of foreplay. Once the husband has begun the tactile
stimulation of the vaginal area, and maintains pressure
manually or lingually upon the clitoris, the wife can attain
tumescent readiness at a speed equal to that of her husband. Healthy well-attuned lovers who seek quick arousal
in a matter of minutes have only to engage simultaneously
in deep kissing and manual fondling of the genitalia. Because the interior of the mouth and the genital surfaces
are the two erogenous zones most densely supplied with
nerves, their constant stimulation will hasten the moment
for entrance and orgasm. Some partners prefer this rapid
ascent when they desire immediate intercourse.

Wives need to understand that their slower rate of
arousal is no permanent, irreversible condition, nor is it
even a female liability. Throughout the period of foreplay,
with its refinements and bold improvisations, the husband
is enjoying deep sensual satisfactions. Added to his pleasure
of touching, caressing and pressing, are sensate psychological joys. He can enjoy the sight of his wife's total or
partial nudity, of her breasts and buttocks, the curve of her
naked hip and thighs, the line and sweep of her back. He
can fantasy, in characteristic male fashion, the special posture he has planned and into which he will shortly move
her, before he makes entrance. In his lovemaking, the experienced husband is a voyeur-esthete who can evoke
sequences of pleasurable chords as he plays upon his wife's
gradually eroticizing body.

And indeed his wife's responses will, in time, quicken
and match or even exceed his own. With experience in
coitus, in advanced procedures of foreplay, and within the
relaxed atmosphere of a ripened marital relationship, the
process of conditioning will take hold. This process is a
ceaseless one; it is a form of learning greatly shaped by

cultural factors. The pleasure a wife may experience in stimulating her husband's phallus manually or lingually, or in receiving from him lingual caresses of her vaginal area, is a pleasure that has been learned under the influence of changing cultural patterns. This mode of stimulation has today become customary in a substantial segment of Western peoples.

Thus, husband and wife, in their erotic play, are potentially capable of the same wide and colorful spectrum of sensual pleasure. What are some of these colors and shades?

A change in the locale for lovemaking, as stated in an earlier chapter, can be an added stimulus. The marital bed, as veteran lovemakers know, is not the only place to begin the amorous encounter or, for that matter, to complete coitus. It may sometimes pall. One husband, confiding to his attorney during a heated divorce wrangle, blurted out that he had had intercourse with his spouse one thousand times, in the same bedroom painted the same pink and beige, in the same old Colonial bed and in the same old position, and that for these and other reasons, it was time for a change. His special wrath at the bed was a symptom, of course, of other marital stresses. But had his imagination equaled his anger he might have known that a Colonial bed is often of such convenient height as to permit several of the more unusual postures in intercourse, and ones that were especially enjoyed in Europe's seventeenth and eighteenth centuries.

Before proceeding to an account of foreplay activity in its total diversity, one unusual beginning to sexual stimulation may be mentioned. Although the Hindus knew it long ago, and some modern Greeks are said to employ it today, the use of the bare feet as a source of arousal may be found to be erotically novel. The female foot is thought by some men to be a locus of pleasure, particularly when it happens to be beautifully formed. A wife might titillate her partner's genitalia with her toes as she might with her fingers, and a husband might follow suit. Ancient Hindu sculpture depicts a potentate being sexually served by five females at once; two of these he is stimulating with the toes of his foot at the vagina. In a recent foreign motion picture a pair of lovers were shown beginning a romance on the deck of a sloop; instead of caressing hands they were seen caressing feet in gentle stroking motions.

As well-attuned lovers know, foreplay may begin with the slightest subtle suggestion. Merely gazing intently at each other may be a harbinger of delight and produce genital moistening. The interlacing of fingers, mutual stroking of palms, light caressing of the hair and scalp, may evoke a tingling erotic response. The entire skin surface of the body is capable of eroticization, although certain specific areas are more thickly laced with sensory nerve ends than others.

There are no prescribed sequences, no programming in foreplay. However, a husband will try to be artful, tender and foresighted. He will know, for example, that it is wise to decide in advance what posture will be assumed in intercourse and where, specifically, it will take place, before he begins stimulating his wife's vaginal surfaces. Once he has begun persistently to stroke the clitoris and surrounding areas, it is best to maintain pressure there, without cessation, until entrance is made. If foreplay has taken place in bed, no problem is presented. But if it has been progressing on a sofa, chair or other article of furniture, with the intention of moving elsewhere, he would be wise to refrain from continuous vaginal stimulation until both are on the site where coitus will take place. A break in the rhythm of fondling the clitoris is disturbing to many wives and could make it difficult for the female partner to achieve orgasm.

As foreplay begins, some couples prefer to lapse into rapt silence, while others enjoy conversation that is playful, ribald or outright erotic. This, of course, is a matter of taste and temperament. Yet it is known that inhibition and tension, which may deter orgasm in the female or precipitate it in the male, are often eased by the spoken word. Also, a spouse may wish to tell her husband what kind of stimulation she prefers and where, according to her needs or whims. As partners seek total pleasure with each other, nothing should be withheld, not even remarks or exclamations connoting deep sensual enjoyment.

However, a dead silence is preferable to the advice suggested by the physician-author mentioned earlier who, it may be remembered, recommended cracked ice as a goad to passion. During the amorous encounter, he enjoins his readers, "Try calling your wife an A-1 tumblebun, or your husband a great big hunk of wonderful man." Some couples, rather than engage in such witty dialogue, might prefer instead to take vows of celibacy.

Classically, throughout the history of sex, the erotic stimulation that is most often mentioned is that of the lips and mouth, interior surfaces and tongue. When mouth stimulation occurs in public it is called kissing; when privately experienced it is properly termed mouth exploration or deep kissing. There are many gradations of pleasure in this activity, which may continue throughout foreplay and orgasm. Apart from the genitalia, the mouth is for most individuals the area of highest erotic sensitivity.

Adventuresome couples seeking to prolong pleasure may

choose to exhaust all the possibilites of mouth exploration before proceeding to other stimulations. The action may begin while bodies are not yet in embrace, with the light brushing movements of moistened lips from side to side. Then the surfaces of the lips may be engaged, first in vertical motions, then circularly. Thus far the teeth have remained closed, and the partners may enjoy the deep inhalation of each other's breath. This might constitute a first stage of deep kissing.

In a second stage, there might be mutual lip-play or the nibbling of the partner's underlip, especially; as more of the lip's inner surface is engaged, erotic sensation is heightened. The teeth are now parted and the tongue is introduced, probing and darting over all areas of the partner's mouth within reach, and joining with the other's tongue, which advances, retreats and enjoys mutual pressure. Saliva, which secretes rapidly in erotic excitement, is intermingled; from this action, poets have derived the metaphor of drinking the loved one's kisses and of tastes that recall wild berries.

The final or ultimate stage of mouth exploration is analogous to the insertion and clasping of the penis by the vagina in intercourse. The tongue is deeply inserted into the mouth of the partner, who envelops and sucks it vigorously; the active and passive roles are taken alternately by the partners. Spouses who omit this practice might prefer to employ only the tip of the tongue in teasing, titillating flicking movements over the other's lips and tongue tip. Some might enjoy a mock biting of the partner's lips. The love-bite has a long erotic history. Delicate and tender nipping of the other's ear lobes, or any part of the skin surface, provided that it is neither sharp nor painful, is also pleasurable; these are less intense than the bites that are sometimes bestowed, in almost atavistic fervor, during actual coitus.

Truly erotic deep kissing may approximate the vigor and blind excitement of intercourse itself once it reaches the stage of suction and tongue penetration. The three senses of touch, taste and smell are intensely involved in early sexual excitement. The husband's olfactory sense may be highly stimulated by the odor of his partner's natural body aroma, mingled with perfume, and the smell of her perspiration and genital secretions. And some wives also enjoy what they describe as man-smell, containing similar ingredients.

In lingering foreplay, the husband may wish to graze over his partner's body with his lips, bestowing pleasure and receiving it himself. If his wife enjoys the tactile stimulation of her breasts, he may dwell there, pressing and encircling the nipple with his moistened lips in tender suction. And if both spouses are so conditioned that no negative emotion results, he may approach with his lips and tongue the area of the vulva, impress a fleeting touch and then graze elsewhere.

The wife, meanwhile, having been erotically delighted, will wish to respond with her own active stimulations. If they are lying parallel, she may turn on her side and lock into tight embrace with her thighs her husband's erect penis. She may caress it with her hand, provided that he is still able to contain ejaculation and to receive this form of keen genital stimulation. She will caress her husband's penis quite lightly, encircling it with her palms and fingers, for as long as he desires it. The more lightly and teasingly she does this, the keener his erotic delight; by covering the glans with her own saliva, she will reduce friction and increase his pleasure.

So long as the husband has not yet approached the vulva and applied continuous stimulation there, the conjugal lovers may wish to graze in other erotic pastures before the final stages of foreplay that precede insertion. The hair and scalp, the ears and the armpits, the back of the neck, are places for erotic play. The tongue, moistly implanted upon the orifice of the ear, produces keen sensations; the back of the neck may be gently kneaded, also the base of the spine where nerve centers are bunched.

Sometimes, instead of proceeding directly to coitus, the lovers may wish to dally at intermediate stages, one of which might be the mutual massage of each other's body. Erotic massage appears in Roman and Oriental love-play; sometimes professional masseurs of either sex provided this sensual service. In our tense modern times, erotic massage combines therapy with sensuality; either husband or wife may alternately bestow it.

If it is to be the husband who bestows erotic massage, he may choose either of two comfortable positions: kneeling at the side of the bed, with his wife lying close to its edge; or straddling her on his knees while she lies at the center of the bed, on her stomach. With firm but not too vigorous kneading motions of both hands he first banishes tension in her shoulders and at the base of her neck. His hands glide with moderate pressure up and down the spine, increasing pressure and distributing it fanwise at the base of the spine. Then gradually he lowers the degree of pressure until his touch is light, titillating and definitely erotic. With subtle, fleeting motions, he traverses the buttocks, thighs and calves, dwelling lovingly at the anal and vulvar areas. When his wife's thighs part to admit his hand, he begins the gentle stroking of the inner surface of the thighs, the inner lips, clitoris and vaginal vestibule. But if there is to be an exchange of roles he will not continue vulvar stimulation; he will turn his wife on her back, bestow perhaps a lingering genital kiss, and himself stretch out on his stomach, with his wife playing the masseuse.

She may wish to kneel at his side or straddle him, whichever is more comfortable, and begin the vigorous kneading which her husband has done previously, then convert her strokes gradually to erotic grazing by fingers and palms, lingering at the sensitive perineal area between anus and scrotum, and finally encircling the phallus. When he turns on his back she, too, may apply the genital kiss, stroking the head of the penis with her moist lips and tongue, then encircling it with her lips as far as the cleft on its undersurface while she holds the shaft in her hand. There are some couples who prefer to omit this form of stimulation, at least in the early years of their marriage, or who use it sparingly. The sexual code and the sexual response which a partner brings to marriage need to be respected by each. If there is any variance, time and experience often eventually bridge the gap. Certainly there should be frank discussion about any sexual practice that is not mutually desired, or indeed enthusiastically welcomed.

Other considerations aside, there are practical conditions that may influence the circumstances when mouth-genital practices may be employed. A wife who is slow to be aroused may be more rapidly brought to orgastic pitch if her husband orally stimulates the vulvar area. The heat of lips and tongue as they are impressed by the husband upon inner labia and the clitoris, the heated breathing upon these areas and the exudation of saliva may quicken the wife's responses and hasten her orgasm when entrance is finally made.

Contrariwise, a husband who characteristically find it

difficult to contain ejaculation during intensive foreplay would be wise to eschew penile stimulation by his wife, either oral or manual. And there are a few wives so ready in their responses that they can experience orgasm merely by orally fondling the spouse's penis. For those couples without erotic disparities or objections of any kind, several comfortable postures for the practice of oral-genital stimulation will be described in a later chapter on postural variations.

When it has been planned that coitus will take place outside of the traditional bed, foreplay can be accommodated to the particular posture that will be employed. Before intercourse on an armless chair with the wife straddling and facing her husband, he may fondle her back and breasts with one hand, while the other gently stimulates the vulvar areas. If the husband is planning to make entrance from the rear, whether his wife stands and bends forward or kneels, he can stroke her abdomen and breasts with one hand, while stimulating the clitoris with the other. In the posture where the wife will be astride her husband, she need only move forward sufficiently to allow his hand to reach the vulva.

For the many wives who desire their husbands to stimulate their genitals manually, and not all do, the manner of stimulation is of some importance. With one or several fingers he will stroke the vaginal vestibule, that area on the anterior (or stomach) side from which the clitoris protrudes. His stroking will be rhythmic and at precisely the pressure his wife desires—usually this is gently but firmly. Part of the stroke should engage the clitoris which, as tumescence approaches, will become erectile. Once he has begun stroking, his wife will begin a gradual ascent to rising peaks of pleasure. And once this ascent has begun, he should not stop and occupy himself elsewhere, but continue until entrance is requested; from there the final ascent is made to orgasm.

While the husband is stimulating the clitoris, the wife may elect to stimulate the penis manually, as they lie side by side. Another position is possible, however, during mutual genital stimulation. The husband might lie on his side with his head toward his wife's feet, leaning on one elbow, or pillowing his head on his wife's thigh, a position which is exciting to men who are stimulated by the odor of female genital secretions or by the sight of the vulva itself. In this posture, the wife might either fondle his penis manually or, by turning her head slightly, caress the tip with tongue and lips. Should he feel too close to ejaculation the husband will disengage his penis from further stimulation, or ask his wife to delay it for a while.

As stated previously, there is no patterned order of erotic events in foreplay; choices are made according to the mood, the acuteness of desire and also the physical environment. All phases of foreplay can be entirely omitted and entrance made immediately. What has been missed in prolonged foreplay can be compensated for in prolonged coitus.

Since the husband is the leader in erotic play, and the wife is the active respondent, it is his role to introduce innovations and changes of custom whenever his erotic imagination suggests them. A wife may also ask for changes when all is not to her keenest satisfaction. Knowledge of each other's special erotic sensitivities and tastes comes with experience, but also with understanding. And understanding is possible only through free and unembarrassed discussion.

Some couples permit an irrational reticence to cloak their sexual feelings about each other, and thus prevent any airing of individual needs and preferences concerning both erotic play and intercourse itself. This is obviously self-defeating. Spouses spend incalculable hours freely discussing their money problems, their children's difficulties and matters crucial to homemaking. To be restrained by shyness, or by an irrational fear of wounding the other's feelings, from discussing freely and without reserve their needs, preferences, whims or possible dissatisfactions in one of the most important aspects of marriage is to threaten its chances of success.

There is a medical vocabulary available for such frank discussions, and there is certainly nothing awry with using whatever colloquial expressions come to mind or, if need be, the four-letter words which have a noble heritage in the Anglo-Saxon language.

There is one enemy to watch for in the conjugal establishment, and that is monotony. Both partners, having succeeded in building an enduring relationship, will want to guard against that faceless presence which would blunt the edge of sensual pleasure.

9

---•◆•---

TOWARD IDEAL ORGASM

HAVING INVESTED A WEALTH OF TENDER ARTISTRY AND BOLD inventiveness in the erotic delights of foreplay, it would be a pity if conjugal partners were to squander their accumulated fund of sensual excitement in one instantaneous splurge. The youthful tend to spend their erotic fortunes this way, but then their funds are quickly replenished. Mature man seeks, if possible, a high and lingering return on his lovingly tended investment. He wants as prolonged an orgastic experience as physiology will permit.

For many centuries, scholarly erotologists have tried to devise means of delaying the fleeting orgastic moment, to double or triple the time spent on the uppermost peaks of pleasure. They prescribed weird compounds of herbs, juices and animal essences to be applied to the husband's penis, his navel, the soles of his feet. Various unguents and incantations were offered the wife to encourage her climax, and some women were said to have learned arcane powers that would delay the male ejaculate. Hindu women, seeking to stay their orgasm, demanded a minimum of twenty minutes of penile insertion, and the man who could not last that long they contemptuously called a village rooster.

Is there a modern scientific prescription for prolonging the act of coitus? There is, and it consists not of magical medicaments but of a specific procedure for couples to follow. Being neither nostrum nor overnight miracle, it requires practice and development, particularly outside the conjugal bed. It can raise the temperature of passion in husbands and wives who already enjoy each other immensely. And for those who occasionally experience a lack of poignancy in their intercourse, or near-failure in their mutual orgasm, it may be of distinct benefit. Before describing this procedure, there are, however, certain observations to be made.

In ordinary coitus, the erect penis enters the tumid vagina and thrusting begins. Whatever the posture, the husband tries to make certain that he has sufficient staying power, after the excitement of insertion, to contain his orgasm. His sexual tension, at this point, is determined by the degree to which he has been stimulated during foreplay, by the vigor and speed of his thrusting and, to a more mystifying extent, by his psychophysical state.

There is a wide disparity among males in their ability to contain climax. It ranges from as short a time as ten seconds after insertion to as high as thirty minutes. A husband can end tension at will; he can make up his mind to ejaculate after seconds or minutes of thrusting. His capacity to withhold orgasm is another matter, and much less controllable. He may flirt on the brink and win or lose, depending often on the slightest triggering influence.

The wife, on the other hand, is somewhat differently oriented. She does not have her husband's problem of containment as he tries to control ejaculation until the beginning of her climactic surge. Like her husband, however, her progress toward orgasm is subject to the intensity of her excitement when entrance is made, to the force and fre-

quency of friction upon the clitoris and the vaginal vestibule, and also to her general emotional tone.

Furthermore, a wife is more susceptible to distraction
than her mate, around whose deaf ears the walls may topple
before he can be deflected from his orgastic goal. A wife
may lose some of her neuromuscular build-up when a door
is slammed, a child cries or some anxious thought occurs.
Also she can lose stride, as she moves toward orgasm, if a
husband should unthinkingly change position and interrupt the friction of the base of his penis upon the crucial
clitoral area.

What the Hindu women were alluding to when they
described some men as copulating roosters was their quick
and sudden thrusting within a short period of insertion.
In the hot urgency of youth, quick coitus is often customary and often leaves the young wife unsatisfied. Over
the long vista of marriage this swift and perhaps solo flight
is not the ideal. Man the adventurer and improviser seeks
to elaborate, to modulate his pleasure. The simple, instinc-
tive and rather primitive pelvic thrust is not enough for
his ranging curiosity. Besides, his sensory needs change
over the decades; he will think of keener stimulations to
keep sexual interest vivid and refreshed.

The method of thrusting is of interest to both husband
and wife. Usually the husband thrusts forcefully and deep.
When he becomes experienced and less precipitous, he will
alternate long strokes with shorter ones, no more than an
inch of penis length. Or he will rest briefly, then resume
short and long thrusting. To prolong coitus, to delay
ejaculation and give his wife sufficient time for her own
orgasm, he can take certain measures, with more or less
success. He can tighten the sphincter muscles of his anus,
hold tense the perineal muscle that extends from the anus

to the scrotum, hold his breath occasionally and, if he can, divert his thoughts to nonerotic channels. He may whisper affectionate or erotic words, inquire about the imminence of his wife's climax or engage in deep kissing. This is virtually the extent of the husband's contribution to the pacing of coitus after entrance is made.

His wife, meanwhile, is responding with forward movements of her pelvis, meeting his forward thrust; certainly she is not inert, receiving without giving. Many women in their forward movements, however, simply lift up their buttocks, which is not the same as tilting the pelvis. When the pelvis is tilted its lateral axis is changed, and something more is accomplished than simply moving toward the penis. Very importantly, the clitoris is exposed to certain and forceful pressure. The wife who can tilt her pelvis gains a measure of control over the timing of her orgasm; to an extent she holds the trigger to it. Obviously, tilting the pelvis requires more muscular virtuosity than merely lifting the buttocks, and a way to achieve this will soon be described.

Because she can secure this extra control over her orgastic success, her husband need not thrust so deeply and rapidly as a husband ordinarily does to expedite his wife's climax. With her newly gained pelvic tilt, he can dawdle, if he wishes, and enjoy slow and shallow thrusting, occasionally punctuated by a deeper one. Thus he delays ejaculation and the time of coitus is prolonged. Instead of being suddenly released, excitement rises from plateau to plateau where each may linger for a bit.

In the pelvic tilt, the wife is contributing to her own pleasure as well as to her husband's. But she can add still another string to her erotic bow. She may learn to exert upon his penis what may be called a vaginal clasp. This will intensify her husband's pleasure without necessarily accelerating his orgasm. It will also bestow a rather exquisite erotic sensation. The vaginal clasp is effected by contracting and relaxing, in turn, the system of muscles surrounding the vagina. Their power to please was not discovered yesterday; seven centuries ago, an author wrote in Sanskrit:

> The wife will remember that without an especial exertion of will on her part, the husband's pleasure will not be perfect. To this end she must ever strive to close and constrict the Yoni (vagina) until it holds the Linga (penis) as with a finger, opening and shutting at her pleasure, and finally acting as the hand of the girl who milks the cow. Her husband will then value her for the most beautiful queen in three worlds. So lovely and pleasant is she who constricts.

The pelvic tilt can be easily learned by any healthy wife; no unusual muscular development is required, and it can be mastered by faithfully performing certain simple exercises like those which some orthopedists recommend for the relief of lower back pain. Tilting the pelvis is, in fact, what theatrical dancers perform when they do the "bump."

The exercises are done in two positions: lying on the back with the knees drawn up, or standing with the back against a wall, the feet a few inches forward. In both positions, the action consists of tensing and turning in the buttocks, tightening the lower abdomen and, with a distinct thrust, snapping forward the pelvis. Visually, only the pelvis moves; no other area of the body is involved. After a little practice, such muscular control will be achieved that the pelvic tilt will be done rhythmically, effortlessly and with a certain sinuous beauty. The muscular coordination for the movement can even be rehearsed, undetected by others, while waiting for a bus or elevator. The erotic use of the pelvic tilt is effective in all coital postures with the exception of entrance from the rear; it is especially rewarding in the position of the wife astride.

The vaginal clasp is developed by a somewhat more subtle exercise. The area to be strengthened is the muscle system surrounding the vagina, consisting of the levator and constrictor muscles of the pelvic floor. The exercise consists of no more than contracting and relaxing, repeatedly, these muscles that cause the vaginal canal to open and close. When they are strengthened they will develop a clasping action not unlike that of a handshake. The problem is to become conscious of their location so that they can be voluntarily activated. One way is to simulate the contraction of those muscles that would be necessary if urination had to be prevented at all cost. The exercises described above for developing the pelvic tilt and the vaginal clasp need to be done daily, at least twenty times each, for about a month, to strengthen the muscles and develop the smooth coordination that will add so much to coitus.

A sensual refinement of the pelvic tilt is the pelvic roll. Professional dancers are often adept at this undulation of the loins and buttocks. To adapt this to coitus, considerable suppleness of the pelvic musculature is required. It is done by moving the pelvis circularly, to left and right, in the pattern of the figure eight. The stimulatory effect of the pelvic roll has been ecstatically described by some of the great Athenians, whose hetaerae apparently possessed remarkable pelvic virtuosity. In some preliterate societies, girls were sent to school for a forty-day course in learning to roll the pelvis in a manner described as "grinding flour."

Couples, by experimenting, will find their own ways of orchestrating their coital movements so that the husband's thrust is met with his wife's muscular response. How long orgasm can be postponed and pleasure prolonged is a matter of circumstance and the emotional state of the partners. At first the wife's muscular activity may precipitate her spouse's ejaculation rather than help him to contain it, until both achieve reciprocal skill. With practice the effect will be to intensify the erotic experience.

By enriching the act of intercourse with these muscular skills, not only will the wife raise its sensual level, she will also improve her own record of orgastic success. And she will give proof positive that she is an active participant, not merely a receiving vessel. There are husbands who can be quietly dismayed by a wife's lack of erotic adventuresomeness, however willing she may appear to be to begin coitus. Whether she employs the vaginal clasp, the pelvic tilt or roll, in sequence or in combination, she is in any case sending her husband a message of love, an erotic message that also has emotional meaning to him. Husbands, however tender and passionate, sometimes feel hollow and alone with a passive and unresponsive partner; they may even feel guilty over their own sexual zeal. Neither feeling tends to keep sexual interest alive.

Prolongation of coitus after entrance for the purpose of orgastic pleasure is not to be confused with a sexual practice known as *coitus reservatus*. This difficult and perhaps self-defeating mode of intercourse, sometimes called Karezza, was introduced during the last century in this country among a colony of eugenically mated couples having a quasi-religious motive. After entrance, the partners proceeded to make movements, but with great effort of will they avoided orgasm. According to the exponents, sexual excitement gradually subsided until normal circulation, and apparently peace of mind, was restored. The experiment, known as male continence, has since been medically discredited and has ended in oblivion.

The question of how often to have intercourse has bemused men's minds since Hercules gathered around him fifty virgins and impregnated each one of them within twelve hours; apparently only a god can summon such a supply of sexual vigor, let alone of willing partners. An eminent modern theologian has given the succinct answer to this occasionally puzzling question:

> There is as wide a variation in appetites and capacites in the realm of sex as in that of nutrition, and it is questionable whether one can go to excesses in one area any more than the other. The physiological limitations are rigid in both. As the intestines can hold only so much food, even those of a compulsive eater, the body can produce only so many orgasms, even that of a sexual athlete. There is a kind of "wisdom of the body" which simply paralyzes sexual desire when the limit has ben reached. The notion that man has more libido than he can handle seems to be a vestigial remnant of the prejudice against sex for pleasure.

It is well known how wide the variation is among individuals in their sexual needs. There are some couples who desire and have coitus twice daily for many years, others who are content with intercourse once or twice a week, or month. For some spouses, one conclusive orgasm at each coitus is enough for completion. There are a few young husbands who are capable of reaching a second orgasm a few minutes after the first, without loss of erection and no interval of rest. There is a small minority of

wives who can have three or more successive climaxes within minutes.

Sometimes there is a disparity of desire between husband
and wife. In good relationships, a disparity can always be
adjudicated by the simple process of accommodation. To
adjust to each other's needs, in sexual or material matters,
is a first principle in healthy marital union. For the wife
who may lag behind her husband's more frequent desire,
there is the deep satisfaction of knowing that she can give
pleasure to the man she loves.

The threat to many marriages comes not from differences in sexual desire but from monotony. Sexual boredom
may have several causes, but primary among them is the
repeated enactment of intercourse in one rigidly repeated
pattern of behavior. Only man, of all the living species,
can suffer boredom. And only man knows how to cure
himself of it.

One of the ways is to develop a repertory of love-postures
that provide variety, refresh the senses and are adapted to
the individual taste and unique physical structure of the
partners.

10

———◆·◆———

ANTIDOTES TO MONOTONY (1)

MARRIAGES DETERIORATE OR DISSOLVE FOR A COMPLEX OF causes. But the most common single cause to start a marriage on a downhill course is continuing dissatisfaction or disenchantment with the sexual act. Therapists and counselors agree that where a healthy hedonism continues to characterize the sexual relationship, the danger of discord, chronic quarreling and even infidelity is considerably lessened if not entirely removed. Some modern physicians, faced with certain typical psychosomatic disorders among their patients, specifically recommend more hedonistic practices in marital coitus.

One of the most dependable ways to attain a hedonistic attitude—that is, a joyfully sensual approach to coitus—is by the acquisition of a varied repertory of coital postures. The mere experimentation with such postures tends to banish nervous inhibition, reticence and awkward shyness which still cling to many supposedly modern marriages, sometimes for decades. Words in a book can accomplish something toward overcoming inhibition. Frank and loving talk between partners can achieve still more. The calm counsel of a sympathetic physician is also helpful. But only a course of continuing practice with a variety of coital postures can bring genuine liberation from inhibited coital behavior, and the comfort of mind that is essential to free, joyful sexual adventure within marriage.

Lovemaking postures can be active and vigorous, or they can be gentle, soothing, relaxed. In either form, there need be no fixed monotonous pattern.

Quiet lovemaking can also be adventurous. "The body in sacrificing to Venus," wrote Aloysia Sigea five centuries ago in Spain, "can take as many postures as there are ways in which it can bend and curve. It is as impossible to enumerate all these, as it is to say which is best fitted to give pleasure. Each acts in this respect according to his own caprice, according to place, time, and so on, choosing the one he prefers."

And she adds, "Love is not identical for each and all."

Many modern spouses, like many generations of spouses before them, tend to think of the frontal position with the wife supine and the husband above as the natural posture, and of all others as variations. Yet, oddly, it is not the natural posture in other lands, nor was it always in the West in other times. Among the ancient Egyptians, posterior entrance was considered natural, and the Greeks apparently preferred the woman-astride posture. Dr. Kinsey pointed out that South Sea islanders, spying on the good folk who came to bring them European civilization and religion in the nineteenth century, dubbed the standard Western position the "missionary position."

Scholars of cultural history have speculated that this so-called natural position became so during the centuries in northern Europe when the marital act was performed only under heavy bedcoverings, never in the open and never in the nude. Another speculation is that it developed out of wartime conquest and rape.

Whatever its origin, its survival bears witness that it is

highly satisfactory. It is comfortable, it yields pleasurable and loving body contact, and if it is monotonous that is not a defect of the posture but a lack of repertoire in the partners, one that can easily be remedied. Its single disadvantage—that it pins and virtually immobilizes the wife—can be partially overcome by variations which will be described in this chapter. But when the wife's role as equal and highly versatile partner is given full rein in other postures, an occasional return to the near-passivity of the standard position will come as a pleasant variation rather than a rigid rule.

For partners who have already discovered them, the novelty in the postures that follow may be in one or another variation which is new to them. For other partners, many postures in this category will be new. To experiment with them, and add to their repertoire those that are pleasurable, will be to add the essential ingredient of variety to the sexual relationship.

In every couple's life there are times when lovemaking of a gentle kind is desirable or perhaps merely more inviting than the more active postures. The postures that will be described here are not especially strenuous; the more active and adventurous ones will be detailed in the next chapter. Yet, within the following group will be found postures that lend themselves to variation, and hence to novelty. Some will be found suitable for special conditions, such as pregnancy, or when one or both partners are corpulent, or when one is tense, fatigued or for other reasons inclined to take a more passive role.

In the standard frontal posture the wife is, of course, lying on her back, and the husband places himself over her, breast to breast. Ordinarily she spreads her legs wide to receive him. A firm pillow under her hips will enhance the depth of penetration. She may also lift her legs with bent knees, place her soles on the bed and push, thus gaining mobility for upward thrusting to meet her husband's downward movements. Or she may lift her legs free, either one or both, for a variation in the angle of thrust.

She can lift either one or both legs and embrace her husband's waist with them. Bringing both her legs together around his waist will bring her buttocks somewhat together and increase the closeness of the genital clasp. Or she can lift her legs high enough so that her husband, pressing toward her breast, presses also against the undersides of her thighs, thus bringing a new area into pleasurable contact for both.

She can also lower her legs completely and slip them under her husband's on the bed, bringing them together. This intensifies the genital clasp, often with the effect of reviving a waning erection, and it also brings her clitoral area into closer contact with her husband's body, intensifying her own arousal to orgasm.

The husband can increase his wife's ability to participate in movement if he supports some of his weight on his forearms and knees.

An exact reverse to this position is the frontal posture with the wife above. This is a restful position for the husband; it also gives a more active role to the wife. The husband lies outstretched on his back with legs extended. The wife lies forward on his breast, spreading her thighs so that they flank his. She can support herself on her forearms, placed beside his shoulders, and on her knees, until he effects entrance. From these points of support, she then has considerable power for rhythmic pelvic movement. Her husband has somewhat less mobility, depending upon how much of her weight she allows to rest on him. He may lift his knees between her thighs, resting his soles on the bed, for additional leverage. His arms are free to embrace his wife's body or clasp her buttocks to him.

For a variation, if the wife is somewhat smaller and lighter than her husband, she can place her legs over his, only slightly flanking them, and he can then lift and spread his legs wide, at the same time spreading hers. This adds agreeable contact of the thighs, and brings the buttocks in apposition for more complete penetration.

Another face-to-face position, reclining on the side, is a restful one for both partners, for a change or when the wife is pregnant. The partners lie on their sides, facing each other. To effect entrance, the wife flexes the leg on which she is lying and lifts the other leg, resting it on her husband's thigh or around his waist if that is comfortable for her. The husband may also move so that his torso is at an angle to his wife's. When union is acomplished, they may lie half on their sides and half on their backs. The comfort of this position compensates for somewhat limited movement. As a variant, the partners may draw together for a closer embrace, with the husband's arm underneath him bearing some of his weight so that the wife's leg does not tire. She can also extend her legs together for a closer genital clasp.

There is a more active version of the side posture. In this, the husband faces toward his wife but places himself diagonally to her. She, also on her side facing toward him, spreads and raises both legs with knees flexed so that they slip under his armpits. Entrance is thus effected, and the husband can place his hands on the upper surface of his wife's flexed thighs, or on her buttocks, to draw her toward him in thrusting.

The position recommended during the wife's pregnancy,

for both comfort and safety, is the posterior position, re-clining on the side. Both partners lie on their sides, the husband behind his wife and somewhat at a diagonal angle to her torso. She flexes her legs and draws them forward as far as is comfortable for her, and arches her buttocks slightly backward so that her husband can make entrance. The position is rather restricted as to movement, and penetration cannot be deep. But for the husband it is entirely adequate, and by stimulating the clitoris manually after entrance he can also bring his wife to orgasm.

The classic wife-astride position has been extolled in all the ancient cultures, and it has been rediscovered by modern spouses. Possibly it contributes more to total hedonism than any other customary posture. It has advantages for both partners: for the husband, a stimulating view of his wife's body; for the wife, an unequaled opportunity to contribute actively to her husband's and her own erotic pleasure.

The husband lies outstretched on his back, and the wife straddles his hips, either squatting or kneeling according to her preference. When entrance is desired, she lowers herself slowly on his erect penis, with either partner guiding entrance. She can then rest her buttocks on his thighs, stretching her legs out forward and supporting herself with her hands on the bed for better freedom of motion. Or she can continue kneeling, deriving motive power from her thigh muscles. If she supports her weight somewhat on either her hands or her knees, her husband has some range of movement, especially if he lifts his knees and presses his soles on the bed. Thus he affords his wife a backrest.

Some wives are more comfortable kneeling than squatting in the astride position. In kneeling the back can be arched without strain. It also allows a greater range of movement for the husband and added maneuverability for the wife.

The husband lies on his back with legs outstretched and together. The wife kneels astride him at the hips, lowers herself to effect union, and then places her hands behind her on the bed so that she leans back at about a 45-degree angle. Variations depend upon her suppleness and energy. She can remain on both knees, arched backward on her hands, to exert thrust and meet her husband's thrust. She can rest on one knee and extend the other leg with knee bent, with the sole of that foot on the bed. Her husband can lift one knee or both, deriving leverage from his sole on the bed and at the same time supporting his wife's back. She can extend both legs backward and lie forward on her husband's breast, continuing to support some of her weight on her knees and her hands, which are now extended forward. This will bring her to the position previously described. In this position, her husband can lift his legs to embrace her thighs and thus help to press her toward him. A wife who is light in weight with respect to her husband will do well with these variations.

The posterior position, kneeling, is probably the most ancient in sexual history. The wife is on her belly, with head, arms and bosom resting on the bed, half-kneeling so that her back is arched and her buttocks elevated. Her husband kneels behind her, his thighs between hers. His hands are free for foreplay at her breasts and clitoris, and to embrace her at the waist and draw her close for entrance, while continuing to maintain pressure at the clitoris and vaginal vestibule. Although the wife can contribute little in the way of active foreplay, the husband has a pleasurable view, both have tactile sensations in the apposition of the wife's back, buttocks and thighs to the husband's breast, belly and thighs, and both have leverage for full penetration. In this, as in most rear-entrance coitus, the husband should remember that stimulation of the clitoris and vestibule are important to his wife's arousal.

Posterior coitus is also traditionally accomplished with both spouses standing; historically it was employed for quick or stolen coition. Within the conjugal bedroom, it is, of course, not stolen and it need not be quick, but can be as leisurely and pleasurable as any other posture. The wife bends well forward over some article of furniture, perhaps the footboard of the bed if there is one. She spreads her legs; if she is shorter than her husband she may stand on a stool or a high firm cushion. Her husband stands behind her and effects entrance. With their firm stance, both have leverage for full penetration and for vigorous thrusting by the husband.

The posterior position can be effected with the wife astride. In this, the husband lies on his back with his legs outstretched, or he can raise his knees with his soles on the bed for his wife's added support. His wife faces toward his feet and straddles his hips, by kneeling, leaning forward and arching her back so that her husband can effect entrance. She can then continue in a squatting or kneeling position, supporting her own weight enough to give her husband some range of thrust. She can extend her legs backward, flanking his sides, supporting herself forward on her hands or holding his knees if they are raised. A very supple, slender wife can arch backward to rest her head on her husband's breast, while he raises his knees between her legs to maintain the union.

In a variation of this the husband lies on his back with a pillow under his hips, his legs spread and drawn up high out of his wife's way. She kneels on the bed with her back to him, her knees also wide apart so that her calves rest against the outsides of his upper thighs or his hips. She lowers her upper torso to the bed and lifts her buttocks high enough to effect union. She can then raise her torso as far as is comfortable, while he lowers his legs until his soles rest on the bed. She can embrace his knees for support and thrust, while her husband with his hands free can lean forward to embrace her around the waist and draw her to him.

Still another posterior position is one with the wife reclining. More comfort, but somewhat less mobility, for the wife is achieved in this than in other posterior positions. She lies on her belly with a high, firm pillow under her pelvis to elevate her buttocks. A good support for her in this position is a wedge-shaped pillow such as those used for backrests when reading in bed: laid flat on the bed, with the thick end of the wedge pointing toward her genitals, it provides an inclined plane rising from her breast to her buttocks. The husband kneels behind her, his breast on her back. His legs may spread and straddle her thighs, or they may come between her thighs, whichever is more functional. In this position he can engage in foreplay and also effect entrance, and he has full mobility for thrusting.

For couples who possess a high antique bed, or after placing enough firm pillows on a modern bed to raise the wife to an adequate height, a classic position from antiquity can be re-enacted. The wife lies on her back at the foot of the bed (if it has no footboard) or else at its side, with her buttocks close to the edge and her legs spread and raised. Her husband stands before her and effects entrance. If he is muscular and she is slight, and if despite pillows she is still too low for him, he can clasp her buttocks and draw her upward toward him while she guides him in making entrance. She can embrace his hips with her legs for added support. He has a firm stance on the floor for power in thrusting.

A similar position with the husband standing can be arranged for posterior coition, according to an early Arabic writer.

Standing coitus is of very ancient origin and is immortalized in Hindu sculpture. Both partners stand erect and face to face. The partners needs to be about equal in height, or the shorter one can stand on a sturdy stool or box or step. The husband may wish to have the wall or some reliable support at his back or side, to maintain his balance. The wife lifts and turns one leg outward to permit entrance. She may then stand on both feet, effecting a close genital clasp, and with this firm stance she can cooperate with her husband in pelvic motion, which is likely to be strong and unrestricted in this position.

The same posture can be taken for posterior entrance, but in this case the wife will spread her legs widely and arch her back, and the husband may have to crouch somewhat to effect entrance.

Coitus seated in a chair, face to face, is companionable and highly erotic. With the use of a sturdy chair without arms, it offers another opportunity for an excursion away from the bed; the traditional low slipper chair found in many bedrooms is convenient for this. The husband seats himself and takes his wife astride and facing him on his lap. Her feet, resting on the side rungs of the chair or on the floor if the chair is low, give her some control in lowering her buttocks slowly to effect union, and in continuing pelvic motion. The husband has not much mobility, but both partners may have pleasure in the novelty and the close embrace of the posture.

For posterior coitus in the same setting, the wife straddles her husband's lap backward, bending at the hips and elevating her buttocks until successful union is accomplished. If no sturdy armless chair is available, seated coitus may be accomplished at the corner of a bed or couch, although not so comfortably.

There are several positions for a corpulent wife and a lean husband, and vice versa. A stout wife lies on her side facing her husband, who is also on his side, his hip supported by a pillow. He raises her upper thigh as high as possible so that it rests on his waist. The pillow under his hips keeps much of his weight from resting on her other thigh, sparing her possible discomfort.

An obese husband with protuberant stomach places his slender wife on her back, lifts up her thighs and kneels between them. The wife bends her knees and draws them close to her chest. He grasps her buttocks and draws her toward him, and makes entrance. A slender wife with a corpulent husband will find the wife-astride position convenient in any of its variations.

When both spouses are corpulent, the most satisfactory are the posterior postures.

A muscular husband and a petite wife may enjoy standing coition in the "clinging vine" position famed in Oriental art and literature. It may be accomplished without the aid of a stool and without beginning in a sitting posture if the couple will stand in a doorway or hallway. The husband lifts his wife so that her legs embrace his waist. She leans away from him, resting her back and shoulders against the wall behind her. She braces one foot against the opposite wall, while her other leg is slung over her husband's arm. With his free arm he supports her back. After entrance the husband may walk to a bed or hassock and sit down; his wife embraces him with both arms around his neck and both legs curled around his waist.

11

---·•·---

ANTIDOTES TO MONOTONY (2)

TRADITIONAL MARRIAGE GUIDES USUALLY MAKE THE IMPLI-cation that a coital posture, once assumed, is a set thing, fixed, static, like a pose in sculpture.

But coitus is not necessarily like that. It need not always be static; it can be, for variety's sake, dynamic and active. The very words "posture" and "position" in this sense are misnomers, unless they are understood as simply starting points for movement, in the same way that the five basic ballet positions are only starting points for a sequence of steps.

Adventurous lovers, particularly those who are some-what athletic, occasionally discover a part of this truth for themselves. Through happenstance or imagination, they find new ways to approach each other's bodies, new sur-faces to place in apposition, areas that were previously un-awakened to erotic sensation. But the whole adventure of postural variations, the *kinesthesia* of erotic pleasure, would be almost unknown to modern lovers were it not for a Bombay physician who painstakingly assembled a definitive collection of unusual postures from world sex-ual history.

This *kinesthetic* pleasure, or pleasure in the sensation of movement from one position to another within the coital embrace, is something that lovers are not likely to come upon without instruction. And yet it is not new. Like many of the arts of man, it has been explored and developed in past cultures more leisurely than our own, and has been forgotten. The classic erotic literature refers to postures in numerical terms—36, 48, multiples of 9, or any combination of magic numbers—so that the modern reader tends to dismiss the whole idea of large numbers of possible variations as poetic license, ancestral boasting or perhaps no more than the sheer exuberance of successful lovers.

Yet the many varieties of coital postures are real, and their numbers do actually run into the hundreds. One reliable figure is 206, all normal, all affording coital junction of the male and female genital organs with penetration leading to orgasm.

Many are, of course, near-duplicates. Some require the agility of trapeze artists to accomplish. But among them are a goodly number of comfortable, practical and highly rewarding new-old ways for married lovers to enjoy each other. With even a small part of the repertoire given in these pages, there need never be any danger of monotony in the conjugal bedroom.

It is worth emphasizing that the occasional experimentation with such novel modes of intercourse as will be described here offers not the slightest danger of compromising either conscience or scruple. The more relaxed one can be in the absolute privacy of sexual life, the more receptive to pleasure and hence the greater the possibility of an enduring and healthy marital relationship. Psychologists and physicians favor marital hedonism because it presents at least one means of overcoming the tensive effects of inhibition which may contribute to many kinds of emotional and physical symptoms. Any pleasure that can be both sexually rewarding and therapeutic at one and the same time would certainly seem to deserve consideration.

Not all the postures will work perfectly the first time; some margin must be allowed for error. And it may be found that some are best attempted when the husband is in absolute control of his ejaculation, perhaps the second time around. Some may be so swiftly arousing that they need several practice attempts for timing. And some are so relaxed in performance that they lead naturally and pleasantly to sleep.

Some of these postures require more space than the ordinary twin bed. For partners who do not have a double or oversized (Hollywood) bed, an area of floor will do, with rug or carpeting and, for added softness, perhaps a comforter spread with a sheet.

The first and simplest kinesthetic variation is that of the standard frontal posture. On a wide bed, the traditional face-to-face position with the husband above is assumed. The husband makes entrance. In tight embrace, breast to breast, both straighten the leg on the same side. The wife pushes with the sole of the opposite foot against the floor or bed. The husband also pushes with one hand, holding his wife firmly clasped to him with the other arm. Together they roll over so that they are in reversed position, he underneath and she on top.

Partners of approximately equal weight may wish to roll gently during coitus on a wide bed or carpeted floor. Union can be effected as the partners please, provided they are eventually breast to breast, arms and thighs tightly entwined about each other. Now with a slight push of hand, elbow, knee or foot against the surface on which they are lying, they roll over—side, back, side, back—as far as space permits, and if they have enjoyed the gentle jogging motion they can reverse direction and roll back again.

A husband may sometimes choose to approach his drowsing wife. This variation is for partners who share a double or oversize bed. The wife is lying on her side, facing her husband, her under leg drawn up. Lifting her upper leg, the husband slides down until he is lying on his side, at right angles to her, and he thus effects entrance. She can hook her free leg around to embrace his body; he can place his free hand on her shoulder to gain leverage in thrusting. Or he can lie quiescent, draw her to him so that they are breast to breast, and embrace her buttocks, both still on their sides. For a further kinesthetic variation, he helps her to raise her torso over him, and elevates his knees with his soles on the bed, so that she is astride him with his thighs as a backrest. In this regular astride position, the wife can begin whatever pelvic movements please them both.

A wife can also be approached when she is lying on her side with her back to the edge of her bed. Her husband sits on the bed, lifts her upper leg and slips under it with his torso across her other thigh, supporting his weight on his elbow. In effect they are in diagonal frontal position, and he thus accomplishes entrance. For a kinesthetic variation, she now draws up her lower leg and pushes up from the bed, while he turns on his back, until she is up and astride with her knees straddling his hips. His feet remain on the floor, giving him added leverage in helping his wife to the new position, and in thrusting.

Probably the following posture was devised in a bygone Arabic era when carpets and cushions were spread on the floor for lovemaking. On a wide bed, or the floor, the wife lies comfortably on her side, her body flexed at the hips in a right angle, her legs outstretched. Her husband places himself in the identical position behind her, but in reverse, his head behind her feet, his feet behind her head. He slips his torso between her legs, rests on one elbow and makes entrance. For leverage in thrusting, he may arch backward, still reclining on his side, at the same time pulling her toward him with his hand (or both hands if she will not mind the weight of his torso on her thigh).

Partners capable of prolonging coitus may wish to try this variation in an oversize bathtub, chaise or bed with high pillows. In the center of the bed, chaise or tub, entrance is made with the wife astride and her feet forward. At this stage, the partners are breast to breast, clasping each other, their legs spread and outstretched. They may wish to proceed to orgasm at this point. Or they may wish to prolong the embrace. In the latter case, both can lean back against whatever backrests have been provided, and maintain genital union. In the tub, foam rubber pillows can be used, and their feet can be raised against the ends of the tub for additional comfort. In a bed, high pillows at each end will support their backs; this is also a posture suitable for a mechanically adjustable bed, with its ends raised. In a chaise longue indoors, pillows are needed only at one end; on a terrace or garden chaise whose ends are elevated, pillows are probably not needed. If they are in bed, the partners may wish to go to sleep without relinquishing the position, thus practicing a kind of *coitus reservatus* but to orgasm. Outdoors, all that is needed is grass or sand and backrests for two.

If vigor is somewhat diminished after a first coitus, a second embrace, more restful and novel, may be desired. The partners are stretched head to feet and feet to head, lengthwise on their sides and facing each other, so that their genitals are in apposition. Each may rest on the other's thigh and engage in such erotic play as pleases them both, including oral or manual caressing. When entrance is desired, it can be effected if the husband maneuvers to a somewhat diagonal angle while the wife still reclines on her side.

Ovid advised wives who boast of fine backs and buttocks to favor the posterior position. In this variation the husband lies on his back, a firm pillow under his buttocks. The wife faces toward his feet and straddles him on her knees; both adjust their positions until entrance is made. She may then lie forward between his legs, her own legs extended. He may rise to a partly sitting position, grasp her hips and pull her toward him rhythmically. Or, for better thrust, they can clasp hands and pull toward each other, first one and then the other. It can be done on any ordinary-sized bed.

This posterior posture requires some dexterity. The wife is lying on her side in the center of a wide bed or on the floor, her body flexed at the hips so that her torso and legs are at right angles. The husband places himself behind her, on his side and outstretched, at such an angle to her body that he can effect entrance. To avoid breaking the union, her husband holds her hips close to him while she performs this kinesthetic maneuver: she raises her legs and swings them over, at the same time turning on her back and then on the other side, sliding her head and torso in the opposite direction, so that she achieves a head to foot position. If this swiveling movement has gone well, she can now reverse the motion and return to the original posture.

Another posterior posture requires that partners have both dexterity and firm thigh muscles. The wife lies outstretched on her side in the center of an ordinary bed, and raises her upper leg. The husband places himself diagonally behind her, his torso between her thighs and his hip resting on her lower leg. He can thus effect entrance, and she can clasp his body below the hips with one or both her legs. He holds her about the waist and upper body with his arms and draws her rhythmically to him.

The following posture brings together areas of the body which have probably never met in this way before, with consequent novel stimulation although without the warmth of a total embrace. The wife lies on her right side, with her knees drawn up to her chest. Her husband also lies on his right side with his knees similarly drawn up, but his head is toward the opposite direction. The bodies meet flat against each other's posteriors; they press buttocks to buttocks as though sitting. In this position entrance is made. With their soles pressing each other's backs and the help of their hands on the bed, or clasping each other's hips, they can press rhythmically together. For variation, they can raise and entwine their upper legs, and with dexterity they can turn and lie end to end on their backs without losing the union. It is best achieved on an oversized bed or floor.

For this transverse posture with kinesthetic variations the wife should be supple enough to arch her back without discomfort; the bed should be double or oversized. The wife lies on her back with her head toward the head of the bed. Her thighs are spread and raised up out of her husband's way. The husband places himself crosswise on the bed, outstretched and on his side, in such a position that by pressing against her buttocks he can effect entrance. She will help him by bringing her feet down on the far side of his body and arching her back. Once union is accomplished, she can press her calves against his back, drawing him to her, and he can clasp her hips or possibly her shoulders with one or both hands, and thus gain leverage for thrusting.

For a kinesthetic variation: she extends one of her legs to the side and swivels her torso in the opposite direction, at the same time as her husband slowly turns on his back, and with some help from him she can swing around and lift so that she ends in an astride position. If the movements are slow and coordinated, this can be accomplished without breaking the union.

The following posture is designed for a muscular husband and a lightweight wife. The wife lies on her back with thighs outspread. The husband kneels between her thighs, stoops and pulls her toward him, lifting her buttocks. He makes entrance with her help. Now she has several options: she can allow her legs to remain relaxed, embrace his hips with them, rest them on his shoulders or help in thrusting by pressing her soles on the bed. Both partners should be in good muscular condition.

Here is a kinesthetic version of the wife-astride position requiring both partners to be supple. It is best done on a double bed or other wide surface. The husband is half sitting, half lying, with his back against an inclined backrest or a slope of pillows. His legs are spread and drawn up nearly to his chest. His wife kneels before him, straddling his drawn-up thighs, and effects union. She can now lean backward on her hands, while he leans forward. He can extend his legs to embrace her with his calves at her back, and she can lift her arms to embrace him. Thus interlocked, they can sink to one side or the other, with their mutual clasp of each other's bodies giving leverage for rhythmic movement.

The following posture is suitable only for a muscular husband and a lightweight wife. The bed can be of any size, twin or wider; the only accessory needed is a firm pillow. The husband lies fully outstretched on his back, with the pillow under his hips. The wife straddles his hips in a squatting position, and when entrance is made, she lowers her weight on his body and frees her legs. Now slowly, lifting and moving each leg in turn, she swivels in successive quarter turns to face to the side, toward his feet, to the other side, and again to the starting point face to face. She will have support from her hands on the bed, and her husband's hands are free to help her in lifting and moving her legs over his torso. If both are in exuberant mood and health, a form of sexual athleticism can be enjoyed by trying to make a number of full rotations before climax occurs.

This face-to-face posture requires strength and suppleness in both partners. The wife takes a position in the center of the bed on her knees, and then arches backward to rest on her hands or forearms. Her husband kneels in front of her, between her spread thighs, and effects entrance. He can then bend forward over her, resting on his hands, if she is strong enough to meet his thrust in this position. Or he can remain upright, clasping her hips and drawing her rhythmically to him. It can also be accomplished at the end of the bed with the husband standing on the floor.

This transverse posterior posture requires a wide bed or the floor, and possibly a firm pillow. The wife kneels in the center of the bed and bends forward, leaning on her hands so that her torso is horizontal. The husband places himself across the bed, at right angles to her body; his knees will be arched over one of her calves, and his torso, supported by an elbow, will lie across her other calf. The pillow under his hips helps him to elevate himself, while she in turn lowers her hips, pressing down to accomplish union. The husband has some upward leverage from his feet and elbows on the bed, and the wife has complete mobility from her knees and thigh muscles.

This is a classical Greco-Roman position, requiring a high bed or a number of pillows to raise the height, since the husband stands on the floor. The wife lies across the bed, her hips close to the edge and her legs extended and spread. Her husband stands before her, bends and pulls her buttocks toward him to effect entrance, with her guidance. She embraces his waist with her legs, or lifts one or both of them to his shoulders. He has ample thrust from his feet on the floor and she also has leverage with her arms and upper torso on the bed. It can be accomplished on any article of furniture high enough to bring the genitals of both to near or exact apposition.

A sitting posture, face to face with legs encircling each other, has been described earlier. Here it is offered with a variation. On a firm bed or on the floor, the partners sit facing each other, breast to breast. Each spreads the thighs to encircle the other's waist, the wife's thighs outside of and over the husband's. In this position, union is made in a close embrace of each other's bodies with both arms and legs. After entrance is made, each leans backward, resting on one or both hands, and then slides forward at the hips for complete penetration, with thrust from the angle of the torsos.

This kneeling posture by both partners requires a soft surface for kneeling on, but nothing else. The partners face each other, upright on their knees. The wife spreads her thighs. The husband, sinking somewhat on his heels, either draws her toward him or slides forward so that his knees are between her thighs, and access is possible. The embrace can be continued in this position. Or the partners can clasp each other and lower themselves to either side, forward, or backward, without relinquishing the union, and thus continue into other changes of position for further kinesthetic variety.

This posterior kneeling position was favored in Arabic cultures. Both partners kneel on a soft surface, the husband behind his wife, pressing his knees between her spread knees so that her calves flank his. He lowers his hips and draws her buttocks toward him so that she is actually kneeling straddled across his thighs. She may also lean forward and support herself with her hands on her thighs, to make union easier. When this has been accomplished, his hands are free to embrace and caress her, while she can reach backward with her hands to clasp his thighs or buttocks and thus deepen the union.

The "clinging vine" position may be accomplished sitting and standing, even walking but the husband had better be of sturdy build, and the wife petite, for this position which appears often in classic erotic literature. The husband sits on an armless chair, hassock or the side of the bed, his feet firmly planted on the floor. He takes his wife on his lap, straddling and facing him, and entrance is made. She wraps her arms and legs tightly around him. He rises to a standing position, supporting her with his hands under her buttocks. Both partners have excellent leverage for thrusting. The husband can rock and dandle his wife's body with pleasurable result. He may even walk with her, sit down again and complete coition on a chair or the side of a bed.

Coitus on a swing, the wife astride, is described in an

ancient Chinese amatory work as a means of coitus which involves perhaps the highest possible degree of kinesthesia. In the quotation below, the swinging hammock is probably none other than our familiar swing suspended by rope from the limb of a tree and wide enough for two:

> The man and the woman sit in a swinging hammock on New Year's Day (springtime), the woman placing herself on the man's lap, over his yard, which is standing. They then take hold of one another, she placing her two legs against his two sides, and set the swinging hammock in motion. And thus when the hammock goes on one side the yard comes out of her, and when it goes to the other side it goes into her, and so they go on swiving (copulating) without inconvenience or tire, but with endearment and tender braying, till depletion comes to both of them. This is called Congress of the New Year's Hammock.

12

THE DO'S AND DON'TS OF
SEXUAL RELATIONS

MARRIAGE IS NO MORE PERFECT THAN ANY OTHER OF MAN'S handiworks. A sexual relationship can be no better than the marriage of which it is a part. These two principles underline the basic truth that sex, marriage and the events in the lives of the partners are all interrelated.

A joyous and adventurous sex life sheds its glow over a marriage and lifts the spirits of its partners. By the same token, a flaw in the sex life drives a wedge between husband and wife and may weaken other relationships. It may impair a husband's productivity in his work. It may interfere with a wife's performance as a mother. It may diminish the psychic or physical health of either.

The sexual relationship has another, less obvious characteristic. It tends to absorb and magnify not only its own flaws but also the dissatisfactions and disturbances in other areas of the partners' lives. It takes into its sexual realm not only the troubles that husband and wife feel in their relationship with each other, but the troubles that afflict them in other aspects of their lives.

Job or money worries, anxieties about the children, irritations with the house, the neighbors or community, anx-

ious strivings for social status—any of these can be translated into sexual ineffectiveness or discontent. Almost any
aspect of the environment, internal or external, can be
drawn into the stream of this most powerful and intimate
relationship.

This close interchange between our sexual life and our
total environment is a fact of civilized existence. From this
hard reality, we must expect that occasional impairments
of potency and desire will arise. In the following re-
minder of basic sexual principles, ways to cope with such
problems will be explored and methods suggested to pro-
tect sexual happiness throughout the various stages of
marriage.

*Communication is the lifeline of continuing sexual
pleasure.* In the sexual relationship, small dissatisfactions
tend to become big ones, and temporary difficulties may
leave permanent scars. When a disturbance is transient, it
is good to know that it will pass. It can then be taken in
stride, and not be allowed to build misunderstanding and
resentment between partners. If the trouble is chronic or
likely to endure for any length of time, there is clearly all
the more reason to air and explore it, correct it if possible
and detour it if necessary.

Communication between husband and wife is thus of
the greatest importance. And yet, perversely, communication is often the first casualty when anything goes wrong.
At the time when it is most needed, the ability to talk
things over is most likely to become paralyzed.

A wife may be suffering a local disorder which makes
intercourse painful, or perhaps only unesthetic, and she is
restrained by embarrassment from telling her husband why
she declines his sexual advances. She does not realize that
their sexual harmony is far more deeply disturbed by her

unresponsiveness than it could possibly be by the simple medical facts. A graver disability, such as a cardiac condition, may impose genuine restrictions on the partners; yet if it is openly and lovingly discussed, their sexual life can be redesigned to meet the physical limitations of one of them. Or one of the partners may be so profoundly absorbed in a project or a professional crisis that sexual desire is for a time entirely absent. If for some reason the all-absorbing situation is not shared, the partner is almost bound to feel baffled, rejected, resentful or hurt.

In the closest of all human relationships, it seems obvious that husbands and wives should be able to talk to each other freely. In actual fact, many loving partners bring with them into marriage some habitual reserves. One man keeps his serious business worries to himself under the illusion that he is sparing his wife, when the truth is that she is far more troubled by his unexplained lack of desire than she would be by sharing his anxieties. Another man is irritated by his wife's prolonged cosmetic devotions at night but he refrains from protest out of a mistaken masculine resignation toward women's ways. If she knew, she would feel flattered by his impatience and would cheerfully forego her bedtime ritual.

Feminine reticence is more frequent and potentially more troubling to sexual enjoyment. A wife is often peculiarly unable to tell her husband about some discontent with his mode or manner of lovemaking. This is not necessarily feminine inhibition. A loving wife intuitively protects her husband's image of himself as a virile male and a competent lover, and she may fear to hurt his self-confidence by criticizing him.

This is an error of judgment on her part. The male is proud of his virility and perhaps sometimes mistakenly proud of his skill, but he is also interested in his wife's pleasure. Her sexual satisfaction is a large factor in his total enjoyment of sex, and her unexpressed discontent can become a subtle block to their mutual sexual freedom. The longer she nurtures the discontent, the more difficult it becomes to express it. She needs to exert herself, not in concealing it, but in finding words to communicate it that will not be a criticism but a positive contribution to their pleasure in each other.

Health is a mutual concern and is directly related to sexual desire. More often than is realized, sexual desire and effectiveness run at a low key because of the low energy levels of one or the other partner. Acute illness is immediate and urgent and we give it prompt attention. But a low state of physical health very often goes unrecognized and results in a slow but devastating attrition of the sexual life.

Sex is a combined physical and psychic function that involves the whole individual. Its finest enjoyment, its success in attaining adventure, depend upon both physical and psychic health. Such physical conditions as anemia, subnormal metabolism, thyroid dysfunction, chronic digestive distress, can subtly undermine the sex life. So can chronic psychological states of tension, anxiety or depression. Husbands and wives owe an obligation to themselves and their partners to maintain their health of mind and body, and to seek medical help when something seems amiss.

In an ideal environment there would presumably be no need to advise readers of such a book as this one on maintaining their physical health. Partners who accept the high human privilege of enjoying life together would rationally care for their health as a matter of course. A wife would give thought to the planning and preparation of food as a contribution to happiness no less than to health; out of the abundant American diet it is no problem to choose well balanced, wholesome meals that also please the palate and make eating together part of the pleasure of living together. Healthy lovers would automatically respect the normal needs for restful sleep, recreation and pleasurable physical activity. They would be aware that a high metabolic level, one of the signs of good health, is a precondition for sturdy potency and lively sexual desire.

All that would be true in an ideal environment. But every setting in which human life is lived has its stresses, and the modern urban-suburban way of life presents a number of concealed health hazards. Most men and many women travel considerable distances to their work, so that despite the shorter working day, the occupational hours are actually long. Two of the three daily meals are likely to be hurried and probably ill planned. Travel, work and many recreational activities are sedentary and indoors. The sum of these environmental conditions is to impose on us habits that are exactly opposite to our best health interests.

Thus instead of taking our good health for granted, we are obliged to give some thought to maintaining it. Natural appetite is no longer a guide to wholesome eating; we have to guard against the random hungers of tension, boredom and mental or nervous fatigue, none of which use up a fraction of the food and drink they induce us to absorb. We find we must count calories against overeating for an underactive body. The simple question of fitting enough physical exercise into our lives to keep joints flexible and muscles in tone becomes a matter for conscious planning.

Overweight and underexercise are unquestionably the prime health hazards of our time. The relationship of high-fat foods and cholesterol to cardiovascular ills is still debated, but the connection of these ills with overweight is not in doubt. Most cardiologists now agree that exercise is a safeguard against heart disease. And heart disease is a direct threat to the enjoyment of sexual adventure.

Apart from this, the enforced sedentary way of life has nearly infinite potential effects on the body systems, all of which are physiologically attuned to active use of the musculature. Sitting for long periods, a hazard by and of itself, is a most unphysiological posture which strains the skeletal and circulatory systems and contributes to lower back pain, poor gastric and intestinal function, a slow return of the blood from the feet and a consequent burden on the heart. We would be better off to do our talking, thinking, traveling and television viewing lying down. The Roman banqueters had a sound idea in their dining couches; if big business management were even keener than it is in protecting the health of its expensive executives, we might see sofas replacing the chairs around the corporation board table.

We need not frighten ourselves with specters of grave illness in order to give thought to protecting our health against these built-in stresses in our way of life. American women have on the whole made great advances in weight control, thanks largely to the urging of fashion and esthetics. Loving wives also do their best to keep their husbands from developing expanding waistlines and flabby muscles. But they cannot wet-nurse a man into doing what is good for him. A man who ignores his wife's gentle reminders may reduce her to nagging, an unloving and unlovely form of care. If for nothing else, a man should care for his health in order to continue and increase his enjoyment of sex.

Ordinarily we would not think of sensible health rules as related to our sexual lives. But in literal fact, everything we do that guards and increases our physical well-being is a direct contribution to sexual potency and desire. All the powers of a healthy body enter into the enjoyment of sex. Everything that debilitates the body impoverishes sex, and everything that builds health enriches sex.

About this there are specific findings. Nutritionists have pointed out that with all our vaunted abundance there is much concealed malnutrition in the United States, not among the disadvantaged but among the prosperous and well-fed, indeed the overfed. Despite popular education in nutrition, many American families still ignore the simple rules of a balanced diet and the simple methods of preparing food to conserve nutritional values. Malnutrition, as we know, lowers the energies in general and specifically it leads to a lowered sexual drive in both appetite and performance. As for exercise, one of its salutary effects is to improve metabolism, and good metabolism is a basic condition for vigorous sexual responses.

Overweight and underexercise do not in themselves curtail sexual drive, but they surely limit sexual adventure. We have spent many pages in this book guiding the reader toward an adventurous enjoyment of sex; the adventurous spirit is a first requisite, but it goes without saying that sexual adventurers have need of reasonably active, capable bodies. Many of the postural variations might daunt partners who have settled for middle-aged muscles at the age of thirty-five. Yet they are performed without strain by couples in their fifties who have enjoyed their bodies enough to keep them trim, resilient and youthful.

Conjugal lovers who are enjoying their healthy bodies at any age surely agree in wanting to continue enjoying them. Minding calories and tending muscles can be a burdensome bore when one must do it alone, but as part of a campaign of healthy sexual pleasure for two it becomes no burden but a game. A noted psychologist declares that it is a sign of maturity to like what is good for us. Once we have regained the feeling of a sensibly fed and wholesomely active body, there is no room for doubt that it is good for us and we like it.

A flaw in the sexual relationship may cause psychosomatic illness. We have long known that psychological disturbances, such as irritability, excessive anxiety, emotional instability, excessive dependence on stimulants and sedatives and similar neurotic behavior patterns, are often related to a sexual dissatisfaction. Medical men today also observe that many apparently unrelated physical symptoms may arise from the same origin. Chronic headache, insomnia, fatigue, overweight, functional digestive and intestinal disorders, even allergies have been known to disappear when a sexual discontent has been uncovered and remedied.

Although the conscientious physician may do his best to trace such a symptom to its hidden origin, his efforts are likely to be fruitless without cooperation and honest self-searching by the patient and in fact by both partners. Here the illness of one is most clearly the concern of both, not only in its effects but in the search for its possible source.

Since functional ailments are bound to diminish or temporarily impair sexual potency and desire, the emotional support of a loving partner is of utmost value. It is of value in all illness, whether physical or psychic, acute or chronic, but in the functional illnesses that have no discoverable organic cause the partner's role can be crucial. The interplay between psyche and soma, mind and body, is subtle and often escapes exact definition, but its power is beyond doubt. All illness, whatever its origin, has an impact on the mind and emotions, and correspondingly an improved emotional climate has a beneficial effect on the source of the illness.

The primary emotional hazard of illness is that it throws the sufferer into a helpless state like that of childhood and calls forth the dependent attitudes of childhood. Illness creates around the patient a wall of self-centered anxiety, isolating him or her from the active, outgoing interests and enjoyments of adult relationships, including the sexual.

To break through this wall, the sufferer needs strong motivation. This comes most effectively from a partner who shows a steady interest in the sufferer's strengths rather than weaknesses. A positive, deeply loving concern takes account of weakness and pain but seeks ways to keep alive the joys of good health and the hope of recapturing them.

One of the most effective sources of healthy motivation is the enjoyment of sex. Sex is usually the first casualty of illness, and often unnecessarily. More often than not, the sexual relationship can be maintained despite disability through illness or accident, within the restrictions imposed by the physician. An orthopedist tells of a wife who asked him how she could keep her husband sexually happy through long months of immobility following an accident. The physician, welcoming this as an ideal way to maintain his patient's morale, approved her suggestion for manual and oral lovemaking, and found the resulting improvement in the injured man's rate of recovery worth noting.

The effect was not only psychic but physical, in terms of the improved functioning of all the body's systems.

To ask one's physician specific questions and elicit specific medical approval is the task of the healthy partner. Usually, the physician will not take the initiative in such matters. Hence the notes on postural variations detailed in this book can serve an additional purpose in helping to frame questions for such a consultation.

Menstruation, pregnancy and menopause are not illnesses but may obstruct sexual happiness. These biological phenomena are normal, healthy and common to human females of all cultures since the beginning of man's life on earth, and there is no reason why they should cause more than a transient ripple in the sexual life of the partners. Yet for the very reason that they are ancient, and surrounded with the profound mystery of life and birth, through the millennia they have been shrouded in rigid ritual and taboo. Shreds of these age-old prohibitions still cling in our attitudes today in the midst of twentieth-century scientific knowledge.

The physiological facts can be briefly reviewed. At birth the girl child has all her organic equipment for child-bearing in immature form: the uterus or womb, the twin ovaries containing the cells that will later develop into ova to be fertilized by sperm for new life, the breasts that will one day provide milk for her babies, and the glands that will regulate all these activities. At puberty this mechanism comes into operation. Thereafter roughly once each month a ripe ovum is released from one of the ovaries, and for the next several days the uterus wall becomes enriched with cells and extra blood supply in preparation for a possible pregnancy.

If the ovum is fertilized, the pregnancy results and men

struation is suspended until after the baby is delivered and the organs return to their nonpregnant normal state. If no pregnancy takes place, the waiting ovum disintegrates, and at a hormonal signal the uterus discharges its supplementary cells and blood supply. At menopause, the regulating glands gradually cease to produce their hormones, menstruation ends, and the child-bearing phase of life is over.

Each woman experiences these phenomena in her individual way. For all but a few there is no physiological reason for distress and little discomfort. Most women are not aware of ovulation, the midmonth ripening and release of the ovum; a few women are aware of a faint twinge or other signal that it is taking place. As menstruation approaches, some swelling and tenderness of the breasts is fairly general; a woman with a tendency toward constipation or bloating may find that these discomforts are accentuated. Some girls and young women suffer dysmenorrhea, or menstrual cramps, sometimes with backache or headache. Usually these symptoms disappear as the reproductive mechanism matures or with the birth of the first child; exercise and improved posture often help.

Similarly, pregnancy is mostly comfortable for women in good health; morning sickness is not inevitable, and with modern dietary supplements, active exercise and weight control, we hear little of tooth decay, sciatic and lower back pain, and difficulty in getting around during the heavy last weeks. Modern obstetrics aids delivery and repairs minor tissue damage on the spot, preventing the lifelong "women's troubles" that once invalided many women after childbirth. Breast feeding is being rediscovered as a safe, convenient, inexpensive and healthy way of launching a baby, and incidentally as nature's way of accelerating the return of the mother's body to its normal shape.

Finally, menopause no longer has the physical and psychic impact it once exerted. As with some women in pregnancy, the glandular changes may bring some symptoms, for which medicine now has a variety of ameliorative measures. The end of child-bearing in itself is of no practical significance, since most women have ended their childbearing long before and are already engaged in a new phase of activities and interests.

Since the normal female body in good health has little trouble with these biological functions, they do not physically interfere with the sexual life. Menopause is for many women a time of second sexual blooming when they are released from all concerns with pregnancy and can bring their full capacity for pleasure and adventure to their sexual life. Pregnancy brings an interruption of a few weeks before and after delivery under medical orders; otherwise it need have no effect except for a variation in postures for comfort's sake. Menstruation (note below) is no longer considered an inevitable interruption of the sexual life.

What problems these biological episodes in a woman's life may present to sexual happiness are now looked upon as mainly psychic. Some wives, and occasionally some husbands, are still haunted by undefined residues of old wives' tales—for example, that sudden whims and appetites during pregnancy must be indulged, or that some emanation from a menstruating woman is lethal to plants and flowers, or that during pregnancy a woman should not have intercourse at the normal time of her menstrual period. Such beliefs have no scientific basis. They stem from the ancient times when men had no scientific method and relied on magical interpretations to explain nature's mysteries.

When a woman clings to such fragments of superstition against scientific disproof, and allows them to interfere with her readiness for sexual enjoyment with her husband at such times, psychiatrists look to a deeper level for the explanation. They see in this an unconscious technique of avoidance of the sexual relationship, perhaps stemming from an immature inability to accept the role of an adult woman with its full biological and emotional richness of experience.

This need not be a grave problem requiring psychiatric help. When it exists, it is most often only a shadow on sexual happiness, and it can be dispelled. A joyful, adventurous approach to sex can be a key to the resolution of a wife's sexual immaturity in this respect, since it joins the hedonism of youth to sexual sophistication.

Menstruation today presents no obstacle to pleasurable intercourse. With the last of the old wives' tales brushed aside, it is possible now to take into account the fact that many women experience heightened sexual desire during the menstrual period, and can take steps to satisfy it with pleasure to their husbands and themselves. Today, with all our hygienic facilities, any problems that arise are purely esthetic, and with a little ingenuity these can be forestalled by douching in advance of intercourse and the use of a diaphragm.

During the time of heavy flow the genital area may be too congested for comfortable intercourse. Normally the menstrual flow subsides after the first day or two, and is further slowed during active sexual response. Gynecologists point out that the area of the vagina above the position of the diaphragm is adequate to contain some twelve hours of normal flow, so that the temporary stoppage can cause no discomfort and, of course, do no harm.

Why heightened sexual desire occurs during the menstrual period cannot be physiologically explained, but whatever the reason, women are today liberated to respond to a husband's desire and their own whatever the time of month.

When contraception is desired, the right choice is most important to the sexual life. An unreliable method of contraception does not eliminate the fear of an unwanted pregnancy, which can be inhibiting to sexual pleasure, especially for the wife. An awkward or unesthetic method obviously interferes with free enjoyment. Even an efficient, inconspicuous method can be used with poor timing so that it becomes intrusive and disturbing.

Devices or methods that are harmful to health are, of course, excluded. Other considerations are the religious and moral principles of the partners, and their individual needs or preferences. For all these reasons, husband and wife should have full information on the available methods and should explore each other's feelings about them no less than their own.

The birth control movement in modern times arose first out of concern for the health of women and the welfare of children among the poor. Among the privileged, some form of contraception has been quietly practiced for centuries, out of custom and convenience. In recent decades the pursuit of family happiness and the most advantageous conditions for child rearing stimulated the spread of education in planned parenthood. Today the rapid increase of the earth's population has made control an international problem.

All these urgencies intensified the medical and pharmaceutical search for safe, simple and reliable contraception. The outstanding result has, of course, been the contraceptive pill. Other methods, however, are still widely in use.

One of these, the diaphragm, continues to be preferred by knowledgeable women for habitual use. Another, the condom, continues useful under particular circumstances. Some other methods are disapproved by the medical profession as either ineffectual or harmful. Following is a digest of facts and judgments on contraceptive methods in current use.

The contraceptive pill has been tested and found efficacious. It definitely and with certainty prevents conception by preventing ovulation. About two million women in this and other countries are using this biological form of birth control.

The drug has been cleared for use by the United States Food and Drug Administration. It should be noted, however, that the clearance is valid for only two consecutive years. Thus far it is not known what effects may result if the pill is taken for a longer period. Physicians do not know for certain whether fertility might be affected after ten or more years of use.

The oral contraceptive is a hormone drug; its basic ingredient is derived from Mexican yams. It is similar to the natural hormone progesterone, which halts ovulation when a woman becomes pregnant. Some users experience a pregnancy type of discomfort, such as nausea, swelling of the breasts, dizziness, but these usually disappear after a few months of use.

One pill is taken daily for twenty consecutive days of each menstrual cycle, on a schedule prescribed by a physician; regular menstruation continues. To be effective, administration must begin on the fifth day of the cycle.

The oral contraceptive is biological, and thus differs from mechanical and chemical forms of intervention of the past. Its safety for a period of two years is not disputed. Its convenience, compared to other means, must remain a personal decision arrived at with the help of a physician.

It is also recommended by physicians for particular situations, such as the honeymoon. Married couples embarking on a vacation might also wish to avail themselves of its convenience and its value in facilitating spontaneous sex during a carefree holiday. To insure its effectiveness, it is advisable to begin taking it two months in advance.

The vaginal diaphragm is still for many women the contraceptive of choice. This is, of course, a mechanical form of prevention; the thin rubber disk with its flexible rim is inserted in the vagina in such a position that it covers the cervix and prevents entrance of sperm into the uterus. With a spermicidal jelly spread on both surfaces and the rim, it provides a very high degree of protection. Since a proper fit is essential, the diaphragm is fitted by a physician, who also instructs in its insertion and removal and prescribes a spermicidal jelly. A refitting is necessary after each childbirth until the next pregnancy is sought.

Most women experience no difficulty in using a diaphragm, and its presence is not usually troubling to either partner in intercourse. Since the sperms are active for several hours, the diaphragm is conveniently removed in the morning, after intercourse the previous night, usually with a douche of warm water with two to four tablespoons of ordinary household vinegar.

Taking time for insertion of the diaphragm can be

awkward if the wife waits for foreplay to reach an advanced stage of excitement. With experience she can easily prepare for lovemaking in the same way as she may put on a favorite nightdress or dab of perfume. Many women make ready even without advance hints, preferring to take their contraceptive precautions automatically and then put them out of mind. Wives who cherish the privilege of adventurous and spontaneous lovemaking think it no sacrifice to insert a diaphragm as routinely as they brush their teeth; they are thus able to respond uninhibitedly to husbandly advances at any time.

The condom, or male sheath, still has its advocates. This is the only mechanical device for the husband's use and is probably the oldest device still employed. Formerly made of thin animal membrane (whence its traditional but inaccurate name, "fish skin") it now comes more often in rubber or latex. The membrane type must be moistened in water before use. All kinds should be examined in advance for imperfections or leaks. Another source of unreliability is that a condom may break or slip off during intercourse.

Some physicians still consider the condom the most reliable contraceptive. Although its use somewhat blunts the husband's pleasure, some husbands use it in combination or alternately with the wife's use of the diaphragm. The interruption of foreplay for its application may be unwelcome except for experienced lovers who are habituated to its use. The use of the condom may also be helpful to husbands who are prone to premature ejaculation.

The rhythm or "safe period" method is reliable for a percentage of women. This requires neither mechanical nor chemical aid; it is based on the assumption that fertility in the female exists only for a limited period during the menstrual cycle and that intercourse at other times cannot result in conception.

The major difficulty is in determining this period of fertility with exactness. The menstrual cycle varies greatly among women and undergoes changes even for the same woman. Some women are regularly irregular, so to speak, and women who ordinarily have a steady cycle may find that it is subject to change following childbirth, during times of emotional stress and in a variety of other circumstances. Clinical records indicate that in individual instances, women have become pregnant at just about every part of the menstrual cycle.

Correct calculation of the fertile period, made in collaboration with a physician, is important both to partners who want a pregnancy and to those who do not want one. While the rhythm of fertility-infertility is easy to arrive at in theory, for practical purposes it needs to be precise, particularly when it is depended upon as the sole or principal method of avoiding pregnancy. To date there are two ways of calculating, both requiring the keeping of careful records.

One way is for the woman to keep a calendar record of her menstrual periods for a number of months. A calculation is then made of a safe period that will cover the widest variations in her cycle.

The second way is to keep a record of her temperature on awakening every morning throughout the cycle for a number of months. The basal body temperature of women rises at the time of ovulation. From this temperature record a physician will advise on a "safe period."

Because it is a "natural" method, depending not upon mechanical or chemical intervention but upon the physiological cycle of fertility, the rhythm method is acceptable, under prescribed conditions, to the Roman Catholic Church among other faiths.

Disapproved by many physicians as unreliable although harmless are these methods: Douching, even immediately after intercourse, may not be soon enough to intercept all the active spermatozoa. A further objection is that douching with any but the mildest antiseptic is irritating to sensitive tissues. Psychologically, hurrying to arise in order to douche for contraceptive purposes is disturbing to both partners and makes impossible the close, restful embrace so valuable to the loving relationship.

Vaginal sponges with foaming tablets, spermicidal suppositories, spermicidal creams and jellies introduced by applicators, are all contraceptive methods that supposedly provide both mechanical and chemical protection. In fact they are not reliable because they may fail to foam or spread or may fail to cover the cervix adequately.

Disapproved as possibly harmful to health are these: The cervical cap of metal or plastic, to be removed at menstruation, is potentially irritating to the tissues. The rubber cap, fitted to cling to the cervix by occlusion and to be inserted before intercourse, may not be irritating but it requires more skill than a diaphragm for proper insertion, and it may become disloged during intercourse.

The button or stem pessary and the cervical ring, usually of silver or gold and designed to be left more or less permanently in place, are rejected by physicians as possibly causing irritation, infection and subsequent complications.

Coitus interruptus, or withdrawal immediately before ejaculation, the most ancient of contraceptive methods, is disapproved as injecting strain and psychological tension into the husband's enjoyment of sex, and in many instances depriving the wife of full sexual completion.

Knowledge of the male and female erogenous zones is important to both partners. Many husbands approach their wives with great love and tenderness but only a rather vague notion of the kind of caresses that are most generally stimulating to women. Even more frequently, wives are willing but uncertain in offering genital caresses to a husband. Every individual has his or her preferences, and with experience and mutual guidance the partners learn the preferred modes of stimulation, their own as well as each other's. The following is a general description of the erogenous zones of each sex.

The head, or glans, of the clitoris protrudes from the anterior (bellyside) wall of the vaginal vestibule, and is the specific part that is responsive to gentle but firm stroking movements, at precisely the pressure desired. Stimulation is applied with one or several fingers, or with the tongue, and the stroking movement should impinge also upon the labia minora, or small lips. As distinguished from the labia majora, or large outerlips, which are not very sensitive to touch, the small inner lips are richly endowed with nerves.

The vaginal vestibule directly at the entrance to the vagina (known as the orifice or introitus) is actually a continuation of the inner lips. In intercourse, after insertion, this highly sensitive area outside of the vagina receives its stimulation from the base of the penis and the pressure of the husband's pubic bone. When such pressure is lacking, as in posterior positions, the husband should encircle his wife with his arm and manually stimulate the clitoris and nearby areas.

If there is to be extravaginal intercourse, as in a time of illness or impotence, or because of lack of contraceptive preparation, a husband may bring his wife to complete orgasm by those tactile measures which are most pleasing to her. He might begin, if desired, with gentle oral stimulation of the clitoris and adjacent areas of the vaginal vestibule and inner lips. He might follow with firmer and continuous stroking by the fingers, avoiding a rubbing movement, which may sometimes cause anesthesia of the area instead of tumescence and orgasm.

Although the vaginal cavity itself is not erotically sensitive, there is considerable sensitivity in the anterior wall just inside the entrance. The levator muscles surrounding the vagina produce erotic sensation under pressure of coitus. The perineum, essentially the same in both male and female, and situated between the genitalia and the anus, is a source of considerable arousal. It is well supplied with sensory nerves, and touch or pressure is pleasurable to the female and brings the male quickly to erection. In deep penetration of the vagina, the female derives additional erotic sensation because of the pressure upon perineal nerves.

Tactile stimulation of the anal area is for about 50 per cent of males and females a source of erotic excitement; for those who are susceptible it may be added to the repertory of love-play. The male's scrotum, the skin that encompasses the testes, is not a very potent source of arousal. Some males are aroused by tactile stimulation of the scrotum alone, but usually an active pressure upon the testes is needed to evoke erotic response.

The head, or glans, of the penis is the area most sensitive to tactile stimulation, particularly the undersurface below the cleft. Forward pressure of the shaft toward the head and a squeezing together of the upper and lower areas of the shaft, thus stimulating some of the deep-seated nerves, cause intense sexual response. In foreplay, titillation of the skin of the penis without pressure produces slighter but more prolonged stimulation. In oral intercourse, the shaft is manually stimulated while the head is held between the lips as far as the cleft and titillated.

The lips and their interior surfaces, the tongue and the whole interior of the mouth are for most individuals sources of high erotic sensitivity. It may be said that the two areas of the body of both males and females that are most sensitive erotically are the mouth and the genitalia. In the sexual practices of many cultures, these two areas are often brought into direction apposition. The constraints that prohibit such contact derive from social proprieties, from moral codes and from notions about cleanliness. The play of the lips and tongue upon the lobes and orifices of the partner's ear is another source of keen, if not particularly long-lasting, excitement.

Other areas of the body capable of producing erotic pleasure when touched, caressed or otherwise manually or orally stimulated are the nape of the neck, the throat, the soles of the feet, the palms of the hand, the armpits, the tips of the fingers, the sides of the fingers, the toes, the navel area, the small of the back at the center, the entire abdominal and pubic area, the female breasts, the buttocks and the insides of the thighs. Teeth and hair may even be sensitive, since nerves exist at their bases. Alone, some of these areas are insufficient sources of arousal, but they contribute to the chain of tactile events that lead to total tumescence, with accruing pleasure on the way. It may in fact be said that the entire surface of the body is potentially one erogenous zone, any part of which can be eroticized in the course of sexual practice.

13

---•◆•---

PROBLEMS OF POTENCY
AND DESIRE

IN THE PREVIOUS CHAPTERS WE HAVE DEALT WITH SEXUAL
problems arising in common experience. In this chapter
ways of managing specific sexual inadequacies will be considered, particularly female frigidity and male impotence,
in the presence of which sexual adventure cannot be satisfactorily attained.

*A wife's fear that she may be frigid, or her assumption
that she is frigid, is one of the most nagging obstacles to
sexual happiness for both partners.* Because of its insidious
effect, the whole concept of frigidity in women needs to be
thoroughly aired.

There is a simple fact of nature, that while orgasm for
the male is essential for the continuation of the race,
orgasm for the female has no such biological inevitability.
The male must rise to climax and ejaculation in order to
deposit his sperm, but the female can conceive and bear
children without ever experiencing orgasm. As one author-
ity put it, male organism is a necessity, female orgasm a
luxury.

That is the biological view. But biologically it is also
true that both sexes are completely equipped for sexual

satisfaction. To the wife who wishes to enjoy full partnership with her husband, and to the husband whose sexual
enjoyment is complete only when his wife shares it, the
wife's ability to achieve orgasm can scarcely seem like a
luxury.

Although the husband is generally the initiator and
leader in sex, he cannot go far without a willing partner.
Doubt about her joyful participation is deeply inhibiting
to his sense of adventure and indeed to his pleasure in sex
altogether. A loving husband is as profoundly troubled by
his wife's failure to achieve orgasm as she is herself. Both
husband and wife expect that she will share with him the
whole range of pleasure, not isolated parts of it—and as
often as possible.

This expectation is, of course, a recent development, and
it may be unprecedented in history. The question of a
woman's sexual enjoyment scarcely arose before the sexual
revolution that gave women equal partnership with men.
The intimidating phrase, female frigidity, was coined in
this century.

Possibly because it is such a new idea, the range of
women's sexual response is a subject of considerable dis-
agreement among professional authorities and of considerable confusion among women themselves. A few psychiatrists take the extreme view that anything less than the
most intense orgastic climax, on most if not all occasions
of intercourse, should be ranked as frigidity. A more general opinion is that frigidity is a term to be applied to
women who experience neither desire nor response in any
degree, and they are extremely rare. Except for these, there
are no frigid women. There are only women who have
been blocked or retarded in developing their full sexuality.

It is now established that while women are characteristic·

ally slower in arousal, especially by psychological stimuli, they are capable of as full and intense sexual satisfaction as men. It is further established that, contrary to popular belief, intellectual development does not chill feminine sexuality. Rather it seems to encourage liberation from prudery and rigid patterns of sexual behavior. The statistical pattern reveals that college women on the average make better sexual partners that women of lesser educational background.

It is also now generally agreed that although capability for sexual pleasure is inborn in both sexes, orgasm is on the whole a learned experience for the female, compared with the almost automatic biological response of climax and ejaculation in the male.

A wife who is troubled by her sexual response does well to remember this difference between the sexes. Her husband was capable of physiological climax almost from the day he reached puberty, while she may still be in the process of learning. Her responses may still be diffused, still incompletely focused on the genital sensations that lead to orgasm.

The record of female learning is clear in the experience of a vast majority of women. Those with a history of extensive premarital petting arrive at orgasm in marital sex sooner than those who come to marriage with little previous petting experience. Those who have had sexual experience before marriage do even better. Most significant is the fact that whatever a woman's capability at the beginning of her sexual experience, she improves steadily in her achievement of orgasm throughout the first ten years of her marriage.

This statistical promise of improvement may not, of course, reassure entirely a wife who is discontented with her sexual response. If after several years of a good marriage she becomes anxious, then it is time to recognize and investigate her difficulty.

Trivial psychological discomforts can be at fault. Until she reaches an assured skill in rising to climax, a woman can be easily disturbed by minor distractions of which her husband, with the sexual singlemindedness characteristic of the male, is not even aware. The physical setting for lovemaking is likely to be important to her. Her rising pleasure can be short-circuited by the fear of intrusion; a secure privacy may be crucial to her. She can be set back by a flapping window shade or a light shining in her eyes. The interruption for a contraceptive measure may depress the level of her arousal to the point of no return. (For suggestions on the management of contraception see the preceding chapter.)

Disturbances of this sort are superficial and need only to be recognized in order to be remedied. Others may go somewhat deeper and take more effort to discover and overcome.

It should be understood at the outset that for both sexes, although the mechanisms of sexual climax are physiological, physiological climax is only part of sexual satisfaction. This is true for men as well as women. A man may release his physical tension by the physiological mechanism, as he may satisfy physical hunger by eating a meal. A man may be conditioned to taking his sex commercially, without any pretense at personal relationship, but this is sexual convenience, not sexual fulfillment. The total sexual experience involves love and continuing companionship, for a husband as well as for a wife.

When things are going well, it is hard to say whether the psychic content of sex is larger for the wife than for her husband. When things go wrong, however, the psychic factor tends to loom large. Whether or not there is some other cause, physical or psychic, for a woman's lack of orgastic success, anxiety itself is a powerful added obstacle to her satisfaction.

Anxiety may be the main trouble. Many a woman enters her first sexual relationship with unrealistic expectations of immediate and dramatic orgastic experience. For some women this does occur, but it is not general. Yet if this was her expectation, and she suffered disappointment, she may have set up a pattern of tenseness and anxiety from the outset. Coupled with this there are likely to be some remnants of virginal inhibitions and fears of which she herself may be unaware. Traces of modesty and embarrassment, and the somewhat deeper fear of abandoning oneself to the powerful stream of sexual excitement, are part of the sexual immaturity with which most girls come to womanhood in our culture. These generate their own anxieties and tensions in the early days of sexual experience. When anxiety about the lack of orgastic success is added, the pattern is self-feeding and self-perpetuating.

Often a woman needs only to recognize this kind of tension in herself in order to become free of it. Within the comfort of a good marital relationship, she may find it relatively easy to shake off whatever maidenly fears and restraints still cling to her. At the same time she can put all suspicion of frigidity out of her mind. She can accept her womanly sexuality as a fact, and relax in the certainty that she will achieve reliable orgastic success.

Her first step toward liberation is to help her husband find the effective ways to give her pleasure. It used to be fashionable to hold the husband to blame for his wife's poor sexual response; either he was not attentive enough or he was unskilled in his techniques. Today it is more justly assumed that even a most loving and attentive husband, who has cultivated the art of arousal, may benefit by some guidance from his wife in the kind of lovemaking she prefers. Her readiness to give her husband this kind of guidance acts as an immediate key to her own sexual liberation. Also, with the single act of articulating her desires in specific terms, she has drawn closer to her husband in intimacy and put herself on the path to achieving more frequent orgasm. As she gains sophistication, she may alter her specifications for pleasure, thus proving to her husband that she is genuinely interested in sexual adventure and in the way he pursues it. The very act of experimentation loosens constraints that may be thwarting a wife's orgasm and is a first step toward hedonism in the marital relationship.

A wife's ignorance of her own body and its capabilities is often an obstacle to her orgasmic success. At least one psychiatrist begins therapy with discontented wives by describing to them what the female orgasm is like. Many girls come to marriage inexperienced and inadequately genitalized, and even after years of marriage they may still be uncertain of the sequence of sensations that result in orgasm. The right caress at the right time may make the difference between disappointment and orgastic success. If a wife actually does not know or has not yet discovered what can best bring her to full arousal and satisfaction, this is surely the best possible cue for throwing off inhibition and joining her husband on a frank voyage of sexual adventure and discovery. In this conjugal quest for sensuality she has nothing to lose and may gain the key to total pleasure.

For many, perhaps most women, a deliberate rejection of anxiety about their sexual capacity is enough to free them for orgasm. If a woman couples with this a healthy willingness to follow her own and her husband's impulses toward a variety of caresses and lovemaking modes, she may soon find herself experiencing the full tide of arousal and climax.

Some psychic obstacles are more deeply rooted. Special fears may haunt a wife, and unconsciously these may inhibit her in fully participating in the sexual act. A fear of pregnancy is often expressed by women to their physicians; some psychiatrists interpret this as a fear not of pregnancy as such but of the full maturity of womanhood, including fully developed sexuality. By her inability to achieve orgasm a woman may be unknowingly clinging to childhood and rejecting her adult womanly role. In some few instances a woman may be inhibited in her sexual responses by the reverse fear, that of infertility, as though she were afraid of being proved less than a complete woman.

Fairly commonly revealed in therapy are a childhood fear of sex itself, a buried guilt over masturbation dating from parental expressions of disapproval, or a guilt over pleasure of any kind and a fear of punishment to follow. Sometimes there is a fear of strong feeling and particularly of sexual feeling, an inability to let go, to expose oneself and give rein to one's impulses.

Some of these fears may be recognized by patient self-examination. Some, too deeply buried, may need the help of a professional counselor or therapist to uncover. It is not usually essential to trace such difficulties to their origin in childhood. Bringing them to light, so that one can recognize their childish unreality, is often enough to dissipate them. As these psychic obstacles are gradually cleared away, orgasm may be expected to occur more often, more strongly and more pleasurably.

Physical causes of sexual inadequacy are the simplest to remedy. An inborn lack of nerve endings in the genital area, and particularly in the clitoris, is so extremely rare that it can be dismissed. Two minor anatomical hindrances are capable of immediate remedy by the physician in his examining room. The more usual of these is the resistant hymen. This membrane, which is usually perforated at first intercourse, has been known to persist through several years of marriage and the beginning of a pregnancy. The other is a prepuce, or foreskin, covering the head of the clitoris and preventing its stimulation in intercourse. Anatomically the clitoris is the female equivalent of the penis in the male, and occasionally, although infrequently, it develops with a similar protective foreskin.

Other physical causes are also readily apparent. Poor general health, a local disorder that causes pain or itching, chronic indigestion with heartburn or gassiness are all obvious deterrents to sexual adventure as they are indeed to general happiness.

Glandular disturbances are sometimes a cause of sexual ineffectiveness. There are some glandular conditions, such as defective thyroid function, that affect other physical systems and naturally the sexual function as well. A glandular disorder would be likely to reveal itself in other symptoms besides the sexual.

Some claims have been made for sex hormones in the treatment of female frigidity and male impotence. Results have been unreliable and success, if any, seldom lasts; any temporary improvement is usually attributed to the psychological effect of the mere idea of treatment. This is a common phenomenon in medical practice.

Individual differences in sexuality do exist. Constitutional differences also need to be taken into consideration.

Some people are more excitable, others more placid by temperament; some respond more and some less quickly and intensely to stimuli of all kinds.

Like height, weight, sharpness of vision and hearing and most other characteristics, the degree of sexual drive is not identical among human beings but follows a statistical curve within the normal range. At one end of the curve is the woman described by some psychiatrists as the "all-mother": she is placid, even-tempered, devoted to her home and children, content to give her husband the sexual gratification he desires, but she has little sexual drive of her own and is not troubled by her failure to achieve orgasm. At the other extreme is the highly sexed woman who is frequently conscious of desire, quickly aroused to sexual excitement and usually achieves orgasm as a matter of course.

Most individuals cluster around the center or median point of the curve, which represents the average. Most women experience a rise and fall in desire within a limited range of variation. For some, the sexual appetite rises markedly just before or just after menstruation. Desire is commonly stimulated on a trip or vacation, after a festive evening or sometimes as a reaction from grief or loss. Desire may be dampened by fatigue or worries.

Orgasm need not be invariable. In a good marriage, both appetite and pleasure tend to increase with experience. The experience of bearing a child may also release a new intensity of sexual enjoyment. Most women usually become aware of their own desire in response to their husband's expression of desire. In a good relationship, a wife willingly receives her husband even when she herself is not especially desirous. If she does not rise to a peak of gratification, she enjoys the close communion and basks happily in her husband's love and the pleasure he takes in her.

Thus, with most women, while orgasm is frequent it is not invariable, nor does it on every occasion reach the highest degree of intensity. Most wives do not consider an invariable orgasm of the highest intensity to be essential to their sexual happiness. Wives who do not invariably reach orgasm nevertheless consider themselves full partners in sexual pleasure with their husbands. They are equally ready for novelty and adventure in the sexual partnership, aware that more frequent and more intense orgasm is likely to be the outcome.

Cultivating a state of mind for lovemaking is an essential womanly skill. The erotically receptive state of mind is one that most wives acquire with experience. A wife responds to her husband's desire with desire of her own, and shows it freely without constraint. She prepares herself for love-making by putting aside distractions and shedding anxieties; there is nothing more anti-erotic than a fussing, fretting, tense and anxious wife. The more unhurried and unworried she is, the more welcoming she is to the rise of her own desire and that of her husband, and the sooner she is likely to achieve her full sexual capabilities.

Quarrels and disagreements are, of course, inevitable in marriage, but they have no place between lovers. Angers and resentments cannot be taken to bed. Some partners enjoy sex together even in bitterness; for them sex may be more an expression of hostility than of love. For most, however, the sexual experience is at its best when both partners feel close and loving and give themselves up freely to total mutual hedonism.

Male impotence, from whatever cause, is a rare condition. The fear of impotence, however, is widespread, deeply rooted and extremely ancient. It appears to have existed in men of virtually every culture and for all we know it may have troubled prehistoric man in his cave. Certainly the search for aphrodisiacs and magical potency restorers is as old as the oldest medical records. Apparently it has been characteristic of the human male through the ages to measure his value as a man by his sexual potency.

In cultures that prized a large family of predominantly male children, whether for survival of the clan or expansion of power and property, a man's capacity to impregnate numerous wives and concubines was critically important. Potency and fertility were identified in the male; if a wife failed to conceive it was her fertility that was in question, not her husband's. So long as a man could achieve an erection he was assumed to be capable of fathering offspring, and the more impressive his erections the more likely he was to have sons rather than daughters.

This linkage of potency with fertility still clings in popular belief, although it has no scientific validity whatever. Male fertility depends upon the number of sperms produced in the testicles and conveyed through the lengthy journey to the penis in vital condition. Male potency is the ability to achieve erection and ejaculation. The only connection between potency and fertility—and a significant one for fatherhood—is that erection and ejaculation are the natural means by which sperm can be deposited in the female vagina and make conception possible. Fertility is dependent upon potency to that extent, but potency is in no way dependent upon fertility. Yet the myth persists, and a man who discovers that he is infertile tends to feel that he may be lacking in potency in some way.

In a healthy male, sexual potency is a powerful function and not easily disturbed. So strong and persistent is male potency that even castration, if performed after the reproductive system has become mature, may not destroy the male capacity for desire and erection. Many are the tales of harem eunuchs who were caught *in flagrante delicto* with their master's female property. That such tales have been based in fact is evidenced by modern cases of patients who have undergone castration because of disease, or had their prostate glands surgically removed, and yet retained a degree of potency.

When a man's physical health is not in question, the psychic factor appears to be crucial in sustaining his potency. Lesser animals than man have confirmed this experimentally. In one animal laboratory an old, battered tomcat was the undisputed lord of the feline population and treated like a prizewinning thoroughbred by his caretakers. This animal, although castrated, continued to function sexually with no sign of impairment, simply on the basis of psychophysical habit patterns established by long experience and maintained with undamaged self-confidence.

Apart from impotence as a result of illness, debility or physical damage to the organ or the nerve centers that control it, two principal forms of potency disturbances are recognized, both of them having psychological or emotional origins. One is transitory, the other is stubbornly embedded in the psyche.

Transitory impotence can be embarrassing but is not significant. It can occur to any man under special circumstances. "Honeymoon impotence" was a traditional fear of bridegrooms, induced by the sudden release from restraint, anxiety at approaching a virginal bride and too much to drink at the wedding feast. Erotic poets throughout history made rueful verse out of a situation in which, after long pursuit of a much desired mistress, the victorious lover found himself physically unable to enjoy his prize. A normal, loving husband may suffer temporary impotence under particular conditions of tension or stress. The only possible response for both partners is to shrug off the occurrence as having no importance, and wait until next time.

Also transitory and unimportant except for the moment is the subsidence of a husband's erection through a mishap in the course of lovemaking. Sometimes, after extensive foreplay or postural experimentation, or an irritating interruption, the ability to continue the erection may not be equal to the demand made upon it in a particular instance. Such minor misadventures have no bearing on potency or love and are only a temporary check on enjoyment.

Persistent potency disturbance may arise from deep psychological sources. Emotional problems of long duration can reveal themselves in loss of potency. Therapy has brought to light such causes as a man's unresolved childhood attachment to his mother, with whom he unconsciously identifies his wife; fear of a punishing father image; buried guilt about stolen childhood experiences of masturbation or sexual experiment; fear of castration by the female; latent homosexual tendencies. The disturbance may show itself in total or partial inability to achieve erection, in persistent premature ejaculation or sometimes in an inability to feel pleasure although the physiological forms of potency are undisturbed. Usually in such conditions the potency disturbance is only one of many other symptoms. Medical advice is needed, and some form of psychotherapy is likely to be recommended.

Some males during foreplay ejaculate before entrance or immediately upon entrance so that their wives cannot achieve orgasm. Psychiatrists list this as a form of potency disturbance. Premature ejaculation, however, is a relative description. Some males are unable to thrust after entrance for more than ten or twenty seconds without ejaculating. If female orgasm has been reached because of a high pitch of arousal, male ejaculation cannot be described as premature, no matter how quickly it has occurred. Inexperienced husbands, particularly youthful ones, occasionally ejaculate prematurely; with experience a husband develops control and adapts his pace to his wife's speed of response. Premature ejaculation happens, if rarely, to experienced husbands when under some emotional stress or after long abstinence.

Many men worry needlessly about aging and potency. As middle age approaches, they become concerned about paunches, thinning hair and most of all about their dwindling physical powers. They tend to be panicked by the passing years, are especially disturbed by the meaningless symbolism of a fiftieth or sixtieth birthday, as if sexual potency were determined chronologically, not psychophysically. Like the wife who fears she is frigid, these men, by their anxiety, may bring about the very condition they fear.

Today we know that sexual pleasure can be happily prolonged into later years. In recent decades there has been a remarkable increase in the number of married couples who continue to enjoy pleasurable sexual intercourse well into their fifties, sixties, seventies and even into their eighties. Our improved standard of health is, of course, the prime reason for this phenomenon. Good sexual function in later years requires an adequate hormonal balance, an unimpaired emotional life and a disease-free body. With these budgets in reasonable balance, sexual life goes on almost literally from the cradle to the grave.

Studies have shown that sexual vigor begins to decline at about age eighteen in the male and in the middle to late twenties in the female. From these ages onward there is a descending curve of sexual activity so gradual that it is measurable from year to year in mere percentage points.

Between the tenth year of marriage and the twenty-fifth, for example, the decrease of coital frequency is so slight that only couples who have kept faithful bookkeeping accounts would be aware of the difference. A wife's orgastic experience will ordinarily dwindle from once a week at age fifty to slightly less than three times a month at age sixty. Where sexual interest between man and wife has been kept alive throughout marriage, interrupted only by transitory illness and occasional separations, happy coitus may be enjoyed almost indefinitely; in some instances men and women have been sexually active in their nineties.

The facts about aging today are so reassuring that the traditional anxiety has less and less power to trouble either a man's mind or his potency. Statistically, only 27 per cent of American men lose their sexual powers by the age of seventy. The other 73 per cent continue to enjoy a degree of sexual adequacy long past the Biblical life span, and some even become fathers at this late age. The twin keys to long-lived enjoyment of potency are good health and a good history of sexual happiness.

When there is a disparity of desire in later years, certain accommodations can be made. In the early years of marriage, a husband's desire for coitus exceeds that of his wife. As they pass through and beyond middle age, desire will become more nearly equalized, and sometimes a wife's desire for coitus will outstrip her spouse's. Where there is no disparity, there is no problem, but there may occasion-

ally develop differences in potency that are troublesome
to the relationship.

Changes in the body's metabolism, persistent tension, the
overuse of certain drugs, may cause the husband to be only
partially potent. Despite his desire, erection will be less
than rigid or tend to subside too quickly. This may recur
with increasing frequency in later years, and at a period
when a wife's zest for intercourse is barely diminished. An
increasing number of women are in fine sexual fettle
throughout their fifties and sixties, according to Kinseyan
studies. Hence the problem may arise whether a wife will
continue to be sexually content when a husband's erections
have become less than reliable.

Authorities agree that it is not necessary to discontinue
sexual relations because of a husband's partial or subsiding
erection. An increase of mutual genital stimulation, sufficient to bring each partner to the brink of orgasm, often
makes it possible for the husband to make entrance and
after a few thrusts to proceed directly to climax before
there is time for the erection to subside. A husband's lack
of a complete erection also need not spell the end of sexual
activity for partners who have had a good sexual history
together. Manual and oral stimulation to mutual orgasm is
greatly preferable to the alternative of no sex at all. The
abandonment of sex may only serve to accentuate the husband's sense of failure and thus delay his return to potency.
Oral-genital stimulation to orgasm is feasible in a head to
foot posture, either with both partners on their sides or
the wife beneath and the husband above, so that mouth
and genitals are in apposition.

*Sex hormones to revive waning potency in later years
have had varying success and are occasionally unsafe.* Many
physicians are wary about prescribing the male sex hor-

mone, testosterone, for middle-aged men whose potency is failing. Arriving at the optimum dosage for each individual need presents the most difficulty; too little is useless and a slight excess may adversely affect the pituitary and other glands, and actually precipitate total sexual impotence, leaving the patient worse off than before hormone treatment began.

When testosterone has been given experimentally to normal males and females who have no potency problem, the effect has been to intensify sexual desire and increase orgastic potency. Administered to females who have diminished desire, testosterone may temporarily increase sexual response. But when given to males who suffer total or partial loss of potency, the results have been inconclusive.

An increased level of sex hormones in the adult body, whether by synthetic or natural means, does not necessarily increase sexual capacity. Nor are all sex hormones produced in the testes and ovaries, as was believed not so long ago; they are additionally secreted elsewhere in the body. This is one reason why castration or prostatectomy in the adult male or ovariectomy in the adult female does not inevitably spell the end of sexual potency.

Medical opinion suggests that when sexual potency has become seriously deficient, other causes besides a lowered hormone level should be sought, especially psychological and emotional factors.

Of tradition's long list of aphrodisiacs, all are hoaxes and at least two are dangerous to health. The shores of sexual history are so littered with recipes for sharpening the sexual appetite that the accumulated debris of quackery, superstition, mysticism and quasi-medicine may one day be huge enough to fill in a subcontinent, and thus serve at least one useful purpose. Each culture in the past has put faith in its favorite love philtres, whether the genitals of bulls, crocodiles and hedgehogs, or apples soaked in the hollow of the beloved's armpit.

The novelist Norman Douglas summed up the centuries' accretion of remedies and rejuvenants for lagging sexual impulses:

> Put not your trust in Arabian skink, in Roman goose-fat or Roman goose tongues, in the arplan of China that "maketh a man renew his youth and astonish his household," in spicy culinary dishes, erongoe root, or the brains of lovemaking sparrows . . . in pine nuts, the blood of bats mingled with asses' milk, root of valerian, dried salamander, cyclamen, menstrual fluid of man or beast, tulip bulbs, fat of camel's hump, parsnips, hyssop, gall of children, salted crocodile, the aquamarine stone, pollen of date palm, the pounded tooth of a corpse, wings of bees, jasmine, turtles' eggs, applications of henna, brayed crickets or spiders or ants, garlic, the genitals of hedgehogs, Siberian iris, rhinoceros horn . . . , the blood of slaughtered animals, artichokes, honey compounded with camel's milk, oil of champak, liquid gold, swallows' hearts, vineyard snails, fennel-juice, certain bones of the toad, sulphurous waters and other *aquae amatrices,* skirret-tubers or stag's horn crushed to powder: aphrodisiacs all, and all impostures.

Yet certain alleged aphrodisiacs keep recurring in history, even in our own enlightened century.

Two of these are harmful. Spanish fly is the popular name for one, the drug cantharides which, when taken internally, causes inflammation of the genito-urinary system. The other is yohimbine, an alkaloid derived from the bark of a West African tree used therapeutically to relieve cardiac symptoms, and unfortunately recommended in a popular marriage manual. Both are dangerous drugs, and neither is worth the risk to health in order to gain a mechanically stimulated form of excitation.

Raw eggs in quantity, caviar and seafood, especially oysters, are other recurrent themes in the lexicon of modern love doctors. These suggest at least a dietetic approach to the maintenance of sexual potency that is more rational than applying ginger and cinnamon to the testicles or ambergris to the vagina.

More effective for wooing Venus than anything in history's fraudulent pharmocopeia of love is modern medicine's recommendation: a balanced diet that includes a proper daily intake of proteins found in milk, cheese, eggs, fish, meat and dried legumes; moderate exercise in the open air; physiological sleep without drugs; and freedom from emotional conflict.

A third-century medico-literary text thus defines *The True Aphrodisiac:*

> A woman, the mention of whose name alone is delightful to the heart, the sight of whose beauty gives each time unprecedented pleasure, who is like a noose for the entrapping of all the senses and who is vowed to follow the inclinations of her husband; one whose real ornaments are her esthetic accomplishments, graceful charms, beauty of limbs and youth, who is pure, who is bashful in public but unabashed in the boudoir, who is sweet-tongued, whose desire is commensurate with that of her husband; such a woman is the best aphrodisiac for a man.

An
Appendix
of Historical Interest

A BRIEF ANTHOLOGY OF POETRY, HUMOR
FOLKLORE AND INSTRUCTION

———◆———

The sexual instinct is more poignant and over-mastering, more ancient than any as a source of beauty. Color and song and strength and skill—such are the impressions that male and female have graved on each other's hearts in their moments of most intense emotional exaltation. Their reflections have been thrown on the whole world. When the youth awakes to find a woman is beautiful, he finds, to his amazement, that the world also is beautiful. Who can say in what lowly organism was stored the first of those impressions of beauty, the reflections of sexual emotion, to which all creators of beauty—whether in the form of the Venus of Milo, the Madonna di San Sisto, Chopin's music, Shelley's lyrics—can always appeal, certain of response? One might name finally as the highest, most complex summit of art reached in our own time—a summit on which art is revealed in its supreme religious form —Wagner's "Parsifal." These things sprang from love, as surely as the world would have been wellnigh barren of beauty had the sexual method of reproduction never replaced all others. Beauty is the child of love; the world, at least all in it worth living for, was the creation of love.

—FROM "THE NEW SPIRIT" BY HAVELOCK ELLIS

AUTHOR'S NOTE

The history of Western sexuality is a many-colored fabric. Cultural threads of varied hues and textures have been woven into it and produced a diversity both astonishing and illuminating. Greek classicism, Old Testament Hebraism, Teutonic tribal customs, medieval Courts of Love, Arabic eroticism, Christian theology, Elizabethan ribaldry, are but a few of the strands that have lent depth and richness to modern man's lovemaking and the sexual codes he subscribes to.

Over the centuries man has reflected the culture of his times through his art and literature; a segment of this is properly concerned with the modes and manners of his sexual activities and how he feels about them. Consequently there has grown a vast treasury of works of an amatory and sexual nature by men of letters, poets, painters and sculptors who have treated the sexual impulse honestly and without subterfuge, as a part of the stuff of life. Among the writers are Chaucer, Rabelais, Boccaccio, Shakespeare, Robert Burns, Mark Twain, Horace, Juvenal, Martial, Ovid, Petronius, Sir Richard Burton, the scholarly translator of Arabic and Hindu erotological classics, and many English poets.

A sampling of written classics follows in this appendix, affording a historical panorama of human sexuality and also contributing, in the broad adult sense, to sexual education. The selections, ranging from the Bible to Ben Jonson, are in widely varying veins, for as the poet Louis Untermeyer has written, "The language of love can be beautiful or bawdy, naively simple or boldly salacious, elegantly baroque or coarse and common as the vernacular, or, in certain moments, a wild mixture of all of these."

CONTENTS

The Song of Songs from the *Bible*
Poems from Greece and Rome
A Breton Folk Tale
Poems of 17th-Century England

SELECTIONS FROM

Venus and Adonis by William Shakespeare
The Perfumed Garden by Cheikh Nefzaoui
The Decameron by Giovanni Boccaccio
The Memoirs of Jacques Casanova
The Loves of Ovid

INSTRUCTIONS FROM

The Kama Sutra of Vatsyayana
The Ananga-Ranga or *The Hindu Art of Love*
Manual of Classical Erotology
by Friedrich Karl Forberg

FOLKLORE FROM THE ARABIC
Book of Exposition

SHORT STORIES BY
Honoré de Balzac
Guy de Maupassant

WRITINGS BY
Havelock Ellis

The Song of Songs

[from the *Bible*]

———•———

1

LET HIM kiss me with the kisses of his mouth:
For thy love is better than wine.
Because of the savor of thy good ointments
Thy name is as ointment poured forth;
Therefore do the virgins love thee.

Draw me. We will run after thee.

The king hath brought me into his chambers.
We will be glad and rejoice in thee,
We will remember thy love more than wine:
The upright love thee.

I am black, but comely,
O ye daughters of Jerusalem,
As the tents of Kedar,
As the curtains of Solomon.

Look not upon me, because I am black,
Because the sun hath looked upon me:
My Mother's children were angry with me;
They made me the keeper of the vineyards;
But mine own vineyard have I not kept.

Tell me, O thou whom my soul loveth,
Where thou feedest,
Where thou makest thy flock to rest at noon:
For why should I be as one that turneth aside
By the flocks of thy companions?
"If thou know not, O thou fairest among women,
Go thy way forth by the footsteps of the flock,
And feed thy kids beside the shepherds' tents."

I have compared thee, O my love,
To a company of horses in Pharaoh's chariots.
Thy cheeks are comely with rows of jewels,
Thy neck with chains of gold.
We will make thee borders of gold
With studs of silver.

While the king sitteth at his table
My spikenard sendeth forth the smell thereof.

A bundle of myrrh is my wellbeloved unto me;
He shall lie all night betwixt my breasts.
My beloved is unto me as a cluster of camphire
In the vineyards of En-gedi.

"Behold thou art fair, my love;
Behold, thou art fair;
Thou hast doves' eyes.
Behold, thou art fair, my beloved, yea pleasant;
Also our bed is green.
The beams of our house are cedar,
And our rafters are fir."

2

I am the rose of Sharon,
And the lily of the valleys.
As the lily among thorns,
So is my love among the daughters.
As the apple tree among the trees of the wood,
So is my beloved among the sons.

I sat down under his shadow with great delight,
And his fruit was sweet to my taste.
He brought me to the banqueting house,
And his banner over me was love.

Stay me with flagons, comfort me with apples
For I am sick of love.
His left hand is under my head,
And his right hand doth embrace me.

I charge you, O ye daughters of Jerusalem,
By the roes, and by the hinds of the field,
That ye stir not up, nor awake my love,
Till he please.

The voice of my beloved!
Behold, he cometh leaping upon the mountains,
Skipping upon the hills.
My beloved is like a roe or a young hart.
Behold, he standeth behind our wall,
He looketh forth at the windows,
Showing himself through the lattice.
My beloved spake, and said unto me,

"Rise up, my love, my fair one, and come away.
For lo, the winter is past.
The rain is over and gone;
The flowers appear on the earth;
The time of the singing of birds is come,
And the voice of the turtle is heard in our land;
The fig tree putteth forth her green figs,
And the vines with the tender grape give a good smell.
Arise, my love, my fair one, and come away.

"O my dove, that art in the clefts of the rock,
In the secret places of the stairs,
Let me see thy countenance,
Let me hear thy voice;
For sweet is thy voice,
And thy countenance is comely."

Take us the foxes,
The little foxes, that spoil the vines:
For our vines have tender grapes.
My beloved is mine, and I am his:
He feedeth among the lilies.
Until the day break, and the shadows flee away,
Turn, my beloved, and be thou like a roe
Or a young hart upon the mountains of Bether.

3

By night on my bed I sought him whom my soul loveth:
I sought him, but I found him not.

I will rise now,
And go about the city in the streets,

And in the broad ways I will seek him whom my soul loveth:
I sought him, but I found him not.
The watchmen that go about the city found me:
To whom I said, "Saw ye him whom my soul loveth?"

It was but a little that I passed from them,
But I found him whom my soul loveth:
I held him, and would not let him go,
Until I had brought him into my mother's house,
And into the chamber of her that conceived me.

I charge you, O ye daughters of Jerusalem,
By the roes, and by the hinds of the field,
That ye stir not up, nor awake my love,
Till he please.

Who is this that cometh out of the wilderness
Like pillars of smoke, perfumed with myrrh and frank-
      incense,
With all powders of the merchant?
Behold his bed, which is Solomon's;
Threescore valiant men are about it, of the valiant of Israel.
They all hold swords, being expert in war:
Every man hath his sword upon his thigh
Because of fear in the night.

King Solomon made himself a chariot
Of the wood of Lebanon.
He made the pillars thereof of silver,
The bottom thereof of gold,
The covering of it of purple,
The midst thereof being paved with love,
For the daughters of Jerusalem.

Go forth, O ye daughters of Zion,
And behold king Solomon
With the crown wherewith his mother crowned him in the
    day of his espousals,
And in the day of the gladness of his heart.

4

Behold, thou art fair, my love;
Behold, thou art fair;
Thou hast doves' eyes within thy locks:
Thy hair is as a flock of goats that appear from mount
    Gilead.
Thy teeth are like a flock of sheep that are even shorn,
Which came up from the washing;
Whereof every one bears twins,
And none is barren among them.
Thy lips are like a thread of scarlet,
And thy speech is comely;
Thy temples are like a piece of pomegranate
Within thy locks;
Thy neck is like the tower of David
Builded for an armory,
Whereon there hang a thousand bucklers,
All shields of mighty men.
Thy two breasts are like two young roes that are twins,
Which feed among the lilies.

Until the day break, and the shadows flee away,
I will get me to the mountain of myrrh,
And to the hill of frankincense.

Thou art all fair, my love;
There is no spot in thee.
Come with me from Lebanon, my spouse,
With me from Lebanon:
Look from the top of Amana,
From the top of Shenir and Hermon,
From the lions' dens,
From the mountains of the leopards.

Thou hast ravished my heart, my sister, my spouse;
Thou hast ravished my heart with one of thine eyes,
With one chain of thy neck.
How fair is thy love, my sister, my spouse!
How much better is thy love than wine!
And the smell of thine ointments than all spices!
Thy lips, O my spouse, drop as the honeycomb:
Honey and milk are under thy tongue;
And the smell of thy garments is like the smell of Lebanon

A garden inclosed is my sister, my spouse;
A spring shut up, a fountain sealed.
Thy plants are an orchard of pomegranates,
With pleasant fruits; camphire, with spikenard,
Spikenard and saffron;
Calamus and cinnamon,
With all trees of frankincense;
Myrrh and aloes,
With all the chief spices:
A fountain of gardens,
A well of living waters,
And streams from Lebanon.

Awake, O north wind; and come, thou south;
Blow upon my garden,
That the spices thereof may flow out.
Let my beloved come into his garden,
And eat his pleasant fruits.

5

"I am come into my garden, my sister, my spouse:
I have gathered my myrrh with my spouse;
I have eaten my honeycomb with my honey;
I have drunk my wine with my milk:
Eat, O friends;
Drink, yea, drink abundantly, O beloved."

I sleep, but my heart waketh:
It is the voice of my beloved that knocketh, saying,
"Open to me, my sister, my love, my dove, my undefiled:
For my head is filled with dew,
And my locks with the drops of the night."

I have put off my coat; how shall I put it on?
I have washed my feet; how shall I defile them?
My beloved put in his hand by the hole of the door,
And my bowels were moved for him.
I rose up to open to my beloved;
And my hands dropped with myrrh,
And my fingers with sweet-smelling myrrh,
Upon the handles of the lock.

I opened to my beloved;
But my beloved had withdrawn himself, and was gone;

My soul failed when he spake:
I sought him but could not find him;
I called him, but he gave me no answer.

The watchmen that went about the city found me,
They smote me, they wounded me;
The keepers of the walls took away my veil from me.
I charge you, O daughters of Jerusalem,
If ye find my beloved, that ye tell him,
That I am sick of love.

"What is thy beloved more than another beloved,
O thou fairest among women?
What is thy beloved more than another beloved,
That thou dost so charge us?"

My beloved is white and ruddy,
The chiefest among ten thousand.
His head is as the most fine gold;
His locks are bushy, and black as a raven;
His eyes are as the eyes of doves by the rivers of waters,
Washed with milk, and fitly set;
His cheeks are as a bed of spices,
As sweet flowers;
His lips like lilies, dropping sweet-smelling myrrh;
His hands are as gold rings set with the beryl;
His belly is as bright ivory overlaid with sapphires;
His legs are as pillars of marble,
Set upon sockets of fine gold;
His countenance is as Lebanon,
Excellent as the cedars;
His mouth is most sweet:

Yea, he is altogether lovely.
This is my beloved,
And this is my friend,
O daughters of Jersualem.

6

"Whither is thy beloved gone,
O thou fairest among women?
Whither is thy beloved turned aside?
That we may seek him with thee."

My beloved is gone down into his garden,
To the bed of spices,
To feed in the gardens, and to gather lilies.
I am my beloved's, and my beloved is mine:
He feedeth among the lilies.

Thou art beautiful, O my love, as Tirzah,
Comely as Jerusalem,
Terrible as an army with banners.
Turn away thine eyes from me,
For they have overcome me:
Thy hair is as a flock of goats
That appear from Gilead.
Thy teeth are as a flock of sheep
Which go up from the washing,
Whereof every one beareth twins,
And there is not one barren among them.
As a piece of a pomegranate are thy temples
Within thy locks.

"There are threescore queens, and fourscore concubines,
And virgins without number,
My dove, my undefiled is but one;
She is the only one of her mother,
She is the choice one of her that bare her.
The daughters saw her and blessed her;
Yea, the queens and the concubines, and they praised her."

"Who is she that looketh forth as the morning,
Fair as the moon, clear as the sun,
And terrible as an army with banners?"

I went down into the garden of nuts
To see the fruits of the valley,
And to see whether the vine flourished,
And the pomegranates budded.
Or ever I was aware,
My soul made me
Like the chariots of Ammi-nadib.

"Return, return, O Shulamite;
Return, return, that we may look upon thee."

What will ye see in the Shulamite?

"As it were the company of two armies."

7

How beautiful are thy feet with shoes,
O prince's daughter!
The joints of thy thighs are like jewels,

The work of the hands of a cunning workman.
Thy navel is like a round goblet,
Which wanteth not liquor;
Thy belly is like an heap of wheat
Set about with lilies;
Thy two breasts are like two young roes that are twins;
Thy neck is as a tower of ivory;
Thine eyes like the fishpools of Heshbon,
By the gate of Bath-rabbim;
Thy nose is as the tower of Lebanon
Which looketh toward Damascus;
Thine head upon thee is like Carmel,
And the hair of thine head like purple—
The king is held in the galleries.
How far and how pleasant art thou,
O love, for delights!

This thy stature is like to a palm tree,
And thy breasts to clusters of grapes.
I said, "I will go up to the palm tree,
I will take hold of the boughs thereof."
Now also thy breasts shall be as clusters of the vine;
And the smell of thy nose like apples;
And the roof of thy mouth like the best wine for my beloved,
That goeth down sweetly,
Causing the lips of those that are asleep to speak.

I am my beloved's,
And his desire is toward me.

Come, my beloved,
Let us go forth into the field;
Let us lodge in the villages;

Let us get up early to the vineyards;
Let us see if the vine flourish,
Whether the tender grapes appear,
And the pomegranates bud forth.
There will I give thee my loves.

The mandrakes give a smell,
And at our gates are all manner of pleasant fruits,
New and old, which I have laid up for thee,
O my beloved.

8

O that thou wert my brother,
That sucked the breasts of my mother!
When I should find thee without, I would kiss thee;
Yea, I should not be despised.

I would lead thee, and bring thee into my mother's house,
Who would instruct me:
I would cause thee to drink of spiced wine,
Of the juice of my pomegranate.

His left hand should be under my head,
And his right hand should embrace me.

I charge you, O daughters of Jersualem,
That ye stir not up, nor awake my love,
Until he please.

"Who is this that cometh up from the wilderness,
Leaning upon her beloved?"

I raised thee up under the apple tree:
There thy mother brought thee forth;
There she brought thee forth that bare thee.

Set me as a seal upon thine heart,
As a seal upon thine arm:
For love is strong as death;
Jealousy is cruel as the grave:
The coals thereof are coals of fire,
Which hath a most vehement flame.

Many waters cannot quench love,
Neither can the floods drown it:
If a man would give all the substance of his house for love,
It would utterly be contemned.

"We have a little sister,
And she hath no breasts:
What shall we do for our sister
In the day when she shall be spoken for?

"If she be a wall,
We will build upon her a palace of silver:
And if she be a door,
We will inclose her with boards of cedar."

I am a wall,
And my breasts like towers:
Then was I in his eyes as one that found favor.

Solomon had a vineyard at Baal-hamon;
He let out the vineyard unto keepers;
Every one for the fruit thereof
Was to bring a thousand pieces of silver.

My vineyard, which is mine, is before me:
Thou, O Solomon, must have a thousand,
And those that keep the fruit thereof two hundred.

Thou that dwellest in the gardens,
The companions hearken to thy voice:
Cause me to hear it.

Make haste, my beloved,
And be thou like to a roe or to a young hart
Upon the mountain of spices.

Poems from Greece and Rome

[The first five poems are from Louis Untermeyer's *An Uninhibited Treasury of Erotic Poetry*, copyright 1963, published by Dial Press; the first two are his adaptations of Petronius, the last three are his adaptations from *The Greek Anthology*.]

A Plea for Haste

WHY THIS delay? Why waste the time in kissing?
   What is the very meaning of a kiss?
Think of the best, the ultimate joy we're missing!
   Hasten the moment of our mutual bliss!

Think of the night the little lamplight faltered
   And you lay under me. What love and laughter
We shared that night till morning! Nothing's altered.
   So come to bed; there's time for dawdling after.

A Plea for Postponement

IT's ALL too swift; it's over all too soon—
The quickened pace, the gasps, the final swoon,
The sudden dying down of flame and fire,
The loosened limbs, the loss of all desire.
Let us control it; love is far more than
The itching heat of a stray dog—or man.
Let us put off the moment, let us wait
Before we lose all sense and consummate

What we might well conserve. Let lips and hands
Do all we want to answer our demands.
Let eager mouths and teasing tongues fulfill
Our deepest need until . . . until . . . until . . .

LOVESICK

I LONG to be the wanton breeze
    That, blowing wayward everywhere,
Plucks at your loosened robe, and frees
    Your bosom beautiful and bare.

I long to be the rose you wear
    Between your little breasts, too sweet
For rude exploring hands, and there
    I'd give your heart an added beat.

I long to be the virgin zone,
    That zealous guardian, trim and tight;
I'd clasp you till the day was done
    And lie beside you all the night.

AGELESS

Now CHARITO is sixty. But her hair
Is dark; her ample bosom's firm and fair;
Her skin is like a young girl's, warm and white;
Her legs and thighs are fashioned to delight.

Her years are in her favor, for she knows
Tricks that a novice never could disclose.
Yes, she is sixty; but, still full of fire,
She'll do, my friend, whatever you desire.

CONSUMMATION

NOW PUT aside the flute; sing no sweet air;
   This is no time for either songs or hymns.
Remove that hindering robe; take down your hair;
   Let naked limbs be locked with naked limbs.

Your thinnest tissued gown is like a wall
   Around some town that must be breached at will.
Now breast to breast, mouth to mouth, till all
   Is plunged into the depths, and we lie still.

THE NATURE OF LOVE

by Lucretius

FOR LOVE, and love alone of all our joys,
By full possession does but fan the fire;
The more we still enjoy, the more we still desire.
Nature for meat and drink provides a space,
And, when receiv'd, they fill their certain place;
Hence thirst and hunger may be satisfied,
But this repletion is to love denied:
Form, feature, color, whatsoe'er delight
Provokes the lover's endless appetite,
These fill no space, nor can we thence remove
With lips, or hands, or all our instruments of love:
In our deluded grasp we nothing find,
But thin aerial shapes, that fleet before the mind.
As he, who in a dream with drought is curst,
And finds no real drink to quench his thirst,
Runs to imagin'd lakes this heat to steep,
And vainly swills and labors in his sleep;

So love with phantoms cheats our longing eyes,
Which hourly seeing never satisfies:
Our hands pull nothing from the parts they strain,
But wander o'er the lovely limbs in vain.
Nor when the youthful pair more closely join,
When hands in hands they lock, and thighs in thighs they
    twine,
Just in the raging foam of full desire,
When both press on, both murmur, both expire,
They grip, they squeeze, their humid tongues they dart,
As each would force their way to t'other's heart:
In vain; they only cruise about the coast;
For bodies cannot pierce, nor be in bodies lost,
As sure they strive to be, when both engage
In that tumultuous momentary rage;
So 'tangled in the nets of love they lie,
Till man dissolves in that excess of joy.
Then, when the gather'd bag has burst its way,
And ebbing tides the slacken'd nerves betray,
A pause ensues; and nature nods a while,
Till with recruited rage new spirits boil;
And then the same vain violence returns,
With flames renew'd th'erected furnace burns;
Again they in each other would be lost,
But still by adamantine bars are cross'd.
All ways they try, successless all they prove,
To cure the secret sore of lingering love.

The Maiden Well Guarded

[A Breton folk tale from *The Way of a Virgin*]

———•———

There lived a maiden whose mother guarded her with infinite care lest some youth should do her ill; and she was brought up in all innocence. And when she begged to go to gatherings even as other maids of her age, her mother was wont to answer her, saying:

"Nay, my daughter, thou shalt not go, for there thou art like to lose thy maidenhead."

One day, nevertheless, Pierre, the maiden's lover, who was a good lad and quiet, came seeking to conduct her to an assembly, and both lad and maid besought the mother to let them go. In the end she consented, thinking in herself that Pierre was too honest to do her daughter ill, and she enjoined him guard her well.

Behold, then, these two on their way; and as they went, the maiden said:

"My mother hath strictly enjoined me guard my maidenhead. It seemeth that at assemblies one is in case to lose it. How best preserve it?"

"Hath not thy mother shown thee a method of so doing?"

"Yea," answered the maiden, "she hath enjoined me to press my thighs tightly together."

Quitting the road, they entered a wood wherein were several streamlets, which one crossed by means of planks.

Even as the maid walked upon one of these planks Pierre, who marched behind her, cast a stone into the water hard by the girl.

"Alas!" cried the maiden. "What will my mother say? Behold, my maidenhead hath fallen in the water and is lost!"

"Fear not," answered the lad. " 'Tis fortunate I am here. I will restore it thee. Come with me 'neath the trees, and say naught if the business hurteth thee, for 'tis all for thy good."

Then Pierre, in very sooth, "put back" the maidenhead for her, and shortly afterward they came to the second plank. Even as the girl stood upon it, two or three frogs, slumbering at the streamside, were affrighted and hopped into the water, which spirted up 'neath the maiden.

"Ah! Pierre!" cried she. " 'Tis lost again! It seemeth that it was not firm. 'Twas most wrong of thee not to have put it back more firmly."

"Say no more," answered Pierre. "I will again put it back."

And when the maidenhead had been put back for the second time, they went on, reaching the assembly, where they diverted themselves as did the others.

On their return journey, even as the young girl passed over a plank, Pierre cast in the water an apple which he had in his pocket.

"What will my mother say?" cried the girl. " 'Tis the third time I have lost it today!"

"Fear not," quoth Pierre. "I am about to sew it on again."

When the maidenhead had been resewed, the girl, who was acquiring a taste for this form of embroidery, said to Pierre:

" 'Tis not sewn sufficiently firm."

"Indeed it is."

" 'Tis not."

"But I have no more thread."

"Miserable deceiver!" cried the girl. "He saith he hath no more thread, yet all the while he possesseth two great balls of it!"

Poems of 17th-Century England

I WILL ENJOY THEE NOW

[From *A Rapture* by Thomas Carew]

I WILL enjoy thee now, my Celia, come,
And fly with me to Love's Elysium . . .

Come, then, and mounted on the wings of Love
We'll cut the flitting air and soar above
The monster's head, and in the noblest seats
Of those blest shades quench and renew our heats.
There shall the queens of love and innocence,
Beauty and Nature, banish all offense
From our close ivy-twines; there I'll behold
Thy baréd snow and thy unbraided gold;
There my enfranchised hand on every side
Shall o'er thy naked polish'd ivory slide.
No curtain there, though of transparent lawn,
Shall be before thy virgin-treasure drawn;
But the rich mine, to the enquiring eye
Exposed, shall ready for mintage lie,
And we will coin young Cupids. There a bed
Of roses and fresh myrtles shall be spread,
Under the cooler shades of cypress groves;
Our pillows of the down of Venus' doves,
Whereon our panting limbs we'll gently lay,
In the faint respites of our active play;

That so our slumbers may in dreams have leisure
To tell the nimble fancy our past pleasure,
And so our souls, that cannot be embraced,
Shall the embraces of our bodies taste.
Meanwhile the bubbling stream shall court the shore,
The'enamor'd chirping wood-choir shall adore
In varied tunes the deity of love;
The gentle blasts of western winds shall move
The trembling leaves, and through their close boughs
    breathe
Still music, whilst we rest ourselves beneath
Their dancing shade; till a soft murmur, sent
From souls entranced in amorous languishment,
Rouse us, and shoot into our veins fresh fire,
Till we in their sweet ecstacy expire.
Then, as the empty bee that lately bore
Into the common treasure all her store,
Flies 'bout the painted field with nimble wing,
Deflow'ring the fresh virgins of the spring,
So will I rifle all the sweets that dwell
In my delicious paradise, and swell
My bag with honey, drawn forth by the power
Of fervent kisses from each spicy flower.
I'll seize the rosebuds in their perfumed bed,
The violet knots, like curious mazes spread
O'er all the garden, taste the ripen'd cherry,
The warm firm apple, tipp'd with coral berry;
Then will I visit with a wand'ring kiss
The vales of lilies and the bower of bliss;
And where the beauteous region doth divide
Into two milky ways, my lips shall slide
Down those smooth alleys, wearing as they go,
A track for lovers on the printed snow;

Thence climbing o'er the swelling Apennine,
Retire into thy grove of eglantine,
Where I will all those ravish'd sweets distill
Through Love's alembic, and with chemic skill
From the mix'd mass of one sovereign balm derive,
Then bring that great elixir to thy hive.

Now in more subtle wreaths I will entwine
My sinewy thighs, my legs and arms with thine;
Thou like a sea of milk shalt lie display'd
Whilst I the smooth calm ocean invade
With such a tempest, as when Jove of old
Fell down on Danaë in a storm of gold;
Yet my tall pine shall in the Cyprian strait
Ride safe at anchor and unlade her freight:
My rudder with thy bold hand, like a tried
And skilful pilot, thou shalt steer, and guide
My bark into love's channel, where it shall
Dance, as the bounding waves do rise or fall.
Then shall thy circling arms embrace and clip
My willing body, and thy balmy lip
Bathe me in juice of kisses, whose perfume
Like a religious incense shall consume,
And send up holy vapors to those powers
That bless our loves and crown our sportful hours,
That such halcyon calmness fix our souls
In steadfast peace, as no affright controls.
There no rude sounds shake us with sudden starts;
No jealous ears, when we unrip our hearts,
Such our discourse is; no observing spies
This blush, that glance traduce; no envious eyes
Watch our close meetings; nor are we betray'd
To rivals by the bribèd chambermaid.

No wedlock bonds unwreathe our twisted loves,
We seek no midnight arbor, no dark groves
To hide our kisses; there the hated name
Of husband, wife, lust, modest, chaste, or shame,
Are vain and empty words, whose very sound
Was never heard in the Elysian ground.
All things are lawful there, that may delight
Nature or unrestrainèd appetite.
Like and enjoy, to will and act is one:
We only sin when Love's rites are not done . . .

Daphne hath broke her bark, and that swift foot
Which th'angry gods had fastened with a root
To the fixed earth, doth now unfettered run
To meet th'embraces of the youthful Sun.
She hangs upon him like his Delphic lyre;
Her kisses blow the old and breathe new fire . . .

Come then, my Celia, we'll no more forbear
To taste our joys, struck with panic fear,
But will depose from his imperious sway
This proud usurper and walk free as they.

WHEN WE COURT AND KISS

by Thomas Campion

I CARE not for these ladies,
That must be wooed and prayed:
Give me kind Amarillis,
The wanton country maid.

Nature art disdaineth,
Her beauty is her own.
    Her when we court and kiss,
    She cries, "Forsooth, let go!"
    But when we come where comfort is,
    She never will say "No!"

If I love Amarillis,
She gives me fruit and flowers:
But if we love these ladies,
We must give golden showers.
Give them gold, that sell love,
Give me the nut-brown lass,
    Who, when we court and kiss,
    She cries, "Forsooth, let go!"
    But when we come where comfort is,
    She never will say "No!"

These ladies must have pillows,
And beds by strangers wrought;
Give me a bower of willows,
Of moss and leaves unbought,
And fresh Amarillis,
With milk and honey fed;
    Who, when we court and kiss,
    She cries, "Forsooth, let go!"
    But when we come where comfort is,
    She never will say "No!"

*   *   *

To Celia

by Ben Jonson

Come, my Celia, let us prove,
While we may, the sports of love;
Time will not be ours for ever;
He at length our good will sever;
Spend not then his gifts in vain.
Suns that set may rise again;
But if once we lose this light,
'Tis with us perpetual night.
Why should we defer our joys?
Fame and rumor are but toys.
Cannot we delude the eyes
Of a few poor household spies;
Or his easier ears beguile,
So removed by our wile?
'Tis no sin love's fruit to steal,
But the sweet theft to reveal:
To be taken, to be seen,
These have crimes accounted been.

The Vine

by Robert Herrick

I dreamed this mortal part of mine
Was metamorphosed to a vine,
Which, crawling one and every way,
Enthralled my dainty Lucia.
Methought, her long small legs and thighs

I with my tendrils did surprise;
Her belly, buttocks, and her waist
By my soft nervelets were embraced:
About her head I writhing hung,
And with rich clusters hid among
The leaves, her temples I behung:
So that my Lucia seemed to me
Young Bacchus ravished by his tree.
My curls about her neck did crawl,
And arms and hands they did enthrall,
So that she could not freely stir,
All parts there made one prisoner.
But when I crept with leaves to hide
Those parts which maids keep unespied,
Such fleeting pleasures there I took
That with the fancy I awoke;
And found, ah me! this flesh of mine
More like a stock than like a vine.

* * *

To His Mistress Going to Bed

by John Donne

COME, MADAM, come, all rest my powers defy,
Until I labor, I in labor lie.
The foe ofttimes having the foe in sight,
Is tired with standing though he never fight.
Off with that girdle, like heaven's zone glittering,
But a far fairer world encompassing.
Unpin that spangled breastplate which you wear
That th'eyes of busy fools may be stopped there.

Unlace yourself, for that harmonious chime
Tells me from you that now it is bedtime.
Off with that happy busk, which I envie,
That still can be, and still can stand so nigh.
Your gown going off such beauteous state reveals
As when from flowery meads th'hills shadow steals.
Off with that wiry coronet and show
The hairy diadem which on you doth grow;
Now off with those shoes, and then safely tread
In this love's hallowed temple, this soft bed.
In such white robes, heaven's angels used to be
Received by men. Thou, angel, brings't with thee
A heaven like Mahomet's paradise; and though
Ill spirits walk in white, we easily know,
By this these angels from an evil sprite:
Those set our hairs, but these our flesh upright.

License my roving hands, and let them go,
Before, behind, between, above, below.
O my America! my New-found-land,
My kingdom, safliest when with one man manned,
My mine of precious stones, my empery.
How blest am I in this discovering thee!
To enter in these bonds is to be free;
Then where my hand is set my seal shall be.

Full nakedness! All joys are due to thee,
As souls unbodied, bodies unclothed must be
To taste whole joys. Gems which you women use
Are like Atlanta's ball cast in men's views
That when a fool's eye lighteth on a gem
His earthly soul may covet that, not them.
Like pictures or like book's gay covering made
For laymen are all women thus arrayed;

Themselves are mystic books, which only we
(Whom their imputed grace will dignify)
Must see revealed. Then since that I may know,
As liberally as to a midwife show
Thyself: cast all, yea, this white linen hence;
There is no penance due to innocence.

To teach thee, I am naked first. Why, then,
What need'st thou have more covering than a man?

WHILE ALEXIS LAY PREST

by John Dryden

WHILE Alexis lay prest
In her arms he loved best
With his hands round her neck
And his head on her breast
He found the fierce pleasure too hasty to stay
And his soul in the tempest just flying away.

When Celia saw this,
With a sigh and a kiss,
She cried, "Oh, my dear, I am robbed of my bliss!
'Tis unkind to your love, and unfaithfully done,
To leave me behind you, and die all alone."

The youth, though in haste
And breathing his last
In pity died slowly, while she died more fast;
Till at length she cried, "Now, my dear, now let us go:
Now die, my Alexis, and I will die too!

Thus entranced they did lie,
Till Alexis did try
To recover new breath that again he might die,
Then often they died; but the more they did so,
The nymph died more quick, and the shepherd more slow.

I DREAMED MY LOVE

Anonymous

I DREAMED my love lay in her bed:
　　It was my chance to take her:
Her legs and arms abroad were spread;
　　She slept; I durst not wake her.
O pity it were, that one so fair
　　Should crown her love with willow;
The tresses of her golden hair
　　Did kiss her lovely pillow.

Methought her belly was a hill
　　Much like a mount of pleasure,
Under whose height there grows a well;
　　The depth no man can measure.
About the pleasant mountain's top
　　There grows a lovely thicket,
Wherein two beagles trampled,
　　And raised a lively pricket.

They hunted there with pleasant noise
　　About the pleasant mountain,
Till he by heat was forced to fly,
　　And skip into the fountain.

The beagles followed to the brink,
  And there at him they barked;
He plunged about, but would not shrink;
  His coming forth they waited.

Then forth he came, as one half lame,
  Were weary, faint, and tired;
And laid him down betwixt her legs,
  As help he had required.
The beagles being refresht again,
  My love from sleep bereavèd;
She dreamed she had me in her arms,
  And she was not deceivèd.

She Lay All Naked

Anonymous

She lay all naked in her bed,
  And I myself lay by;
No veil but curtains about her spread,
  No covering but I.
Her head upon her shoulders seeks
  To hang in careless wise,
And full of blushes were her cheeks,
  And of wishes were her eyes.

Her blood still fresh into her face,
  As on a message came,
To say that in another place
  It meant another game;

Her cherry lips moist, plump, and fair,
   Millions of kisses crown,
Which ripe and uncropt dangled there
   And weighed the branches down.

Her breasts, that well'd so plump and high,
   Bred pleasant pain in me,
For all the world I do defy
   The like felicity.
Her thighs and belly, soft and fair,
   To me were only shown:
To see such meat, and not to eat,
   Would anger any stone.

Her knees lay upward gently bent,
   And all lay hollow under,
As if on easy terms, they meant
   To fall unforc'd asunder;
Just so the Cyrian Queen did lie,
   Expecting in her bower;
When too long stay had kept the boy
   Beyond his promised hour.

"Dull clown," quoth she, "why dost delay
   Such proffered bliss to take?
Canst thou find out no other way
   Similitudes to make?"
Mad with delight I thundering
   Threw both my arms about her,
But pox upon't 'twas but a dream
   And so I lay without her.

As on Serena's Panting Breast

Anonymous

As ON Serena's panting breast
   The happy Strephon lay,
With love and beauty doubly blest
   He passed the hours away.

Fierce rapture of transporting love
   And pleasure struck him dumb;
He envied not the powers above
   Nor all the joys to come.

As zealous bees far off do rove
   To bring their treasure home,
So Strephon ranged the field of love
   To make his honey-comb.

Her ruby lips he sucked and pressed
   From whence all sweets derive;
Then, buzzing 'round her snowy breast,
   He crept into the hive.

The Squire

by the Earl of Harrington

LAST NIGHT, when to your bed I came,
You were a novice at the game,
I've taught you now a little skill
But I have more to teach you still,

Lie thus, dear Sir, I'll get above,
And teach you a new seat of love;
When I have got you once below me,
Kick as you will, you shall not throw me;
For tho! I ne'er a hunting rid,
I'll sit as fast as if I did,
Nor do I stirrup need,
To help me up upon my steed.

   This said, her legs she open'd wide,
And on her lover got astride
And being in her saddle plac'd
Most lovingly the squire embrac'd
Who viewed the wanton fair with wonder,
And smil'd, to see her keep him under,
While she, to shew she would not tire,
Spur'd like a fury on the squire,
And tho' she ne'er had rid in France,
She made him caper, curvet, dance,
Till both of them fell in a trance.

   'Twas long e'er either did recover
At last she kissed her panting lover,
And, sweetly smiling in his face,
Ask'd him, "How he liked the chase?"
He scarce could speak, his breath was short,
But sobbing, answer'd "Noble sport;
I'd give the best horse in my stable,
That either I or you were able
To ride another, for I own
There never was such pastime known;"

   This answer pleased the frolic maid,
She sucked his breast, and, laughing, said,
"If you, good Sir, resolve to try
Another gallop here am I,

Ready to answer your desire,
Nor will you find me apt to tire
In such a chase: I'll lay a crown,
Start you the game, I'll run it down."
     The squire o'erjoyed at what she said,
Hugg'd to his breast the sprightly maid;
For he was young and full of vigour,
And Cherry was a lovely figure,
Was ever cheerful, brisk and gay,
And had a most enticing way.
She kiss'd his eyes, she bit his breast,
Nor did her nimble fingers rest,
Till he had all his toil forgot,
And found his blood was boiling hot,
While Cherry (who was in her prime
Still knew, and always nick'd her time)
Bestrid the amorous squire once more,
And gallop'd faster than before,
Fearing the knight might interrupt her,
She toss'd and twirl'd upon her crupper;
Nor did she let her tongue lay idle,
But thrust it in by way of bridle,
And giving him a close embrace,
Did finish the delightful chase.

THE PENITENT NUN

Anonymous

DAME JANE A sprightly Nun, and gay,
   And formed of very yielding Clay,
Had long with resolution strove
   To guard against the Shafts of Love.

Fond Cupid smiling, spies the Fair,
   And soon he baffles all her Care,
In vain she tries her Pain to smother,
   The Nymph too frail, the Nymph too frail, becomes a
      Mother.
But now these little Follies o'er,
   She firmly vows she'll sin no more;
No more to Vice will fall a Prey,
   But spend in Prayer each fleeting Day.
Close in her Cell immur'd she lies,
   Nor from the Cross removes her Eyes;
Whilst Sisters crouding at the Crate,
   Spend all their Time, spend all their Time in Worldly
      Prate.
The Abbess, overjoy'd to find
   This happy Change in Jenny's Mind,
The rest, with Air compos'd, addressing,
   "Daughters, if you expect a Blessing,
"From pious Jane, Example take,
   "The World and all its Joys forsake."
"We will (they all replied as One)
   "But first let's do as Jane has done."

JOHN AND JOAN

Anonymous

THERE WAS a Maid the other Day,
Which in her Master's Chamber lay;
As Maidens they must not refuse,
In Yeomans Houses thus they use
In a Truckle-bed to lye,
Or another standing by:

Her Master and her Dame
Said she shou'd do the same.

This Maid cou'd neither rest nor Sleep,
  When that she heard the Bed to crack;
Her Master Captive busie was,
  Her Dame cry'd out, you hurt my Back:
Oh Husband you do me wrong,
You've lain so hard my Breast upon;
You are such another Man,
You'd have me do more than I can:
Tush Master, then says Joan,
Pray let my Dame alone;
What a devilish Squalling you keep,
That I can neither rest nor Sleep.

This was enough to make a Maiden sick
  And full of Pain;
She begins to Fling and Kick,
  And swore she'd rent her Smock in twain:
But you shall hear anon.
There was a Man his name was John,
To whom this Maid she went alone,
And in this manner made her moan;
I prithee John tell me no Lie,
What ails my Dame to Squeak and Cry?
I prithee John tell me the same,
What is't my Master gives my Dame?

It is a Steel, quoth John,
  My Master gives my Dame at Night:
Altho' some fault she find,
  I'm sure it is her Heart's Delight:

And you Joan for your part,
You love one withal your Heart.
Yes, marry then quoth Joan,
Therefore to you I make my moan;
If that I may be so bold,
Where are these things to be sold?
At London then said John,
Next Market day I'll bring thee one.

What will a good one cost,
    If I shou'd chance to stand in need?
Twenty Shillings, says John,
    And for Twenty Shillings you may speed:
Then Joan she ran unto her Chest,
And fetch'd him Twenty Shillings just;
John, said she, here is your Coin,
And I pray you have me in your mind:
And out of my Love therefore,
There is for you two Shillings more;
And I pray thee honest John Long,
Buy me one that's Stiff and Strong.

To Market then he went,
    When he had the Money in his Purse;
He domineer'd and vapour'd
    He was as stout as any Horse:
Some he spent in Ale and Beer,
And some he spent upon good Cheer;
The rest he brought home again,
To serve his turn another time:
Welcome home honest John,
God a mercy gentle Joan;

Prithee John let me feel,
Hast thou brought me home a Steel?

Yes, marry then quoth John,
And then he took her by the Hand;
He led her into a Room,
Where they cou'd see neither Sun or Moon:
Together John the Door did clap,
He laid the Steel into her Lap:
With that Joan began to feel,
Cuts Foot, quoth she, 'tis a dainty Steel:
I prithee tell me, and do not lye,
What are the two Things hang thereby?
They be the odd Shillings, quoth John,
That you put last into my Hand:
If I had known so much before,
I wou'd have giv'n thee two Shillings more.

Selections from Venus and Adonis

by William Shakespeare

———•◦•———

O, WHAT a war of looks was then between them!
Her eyes petitioners to his eyes suing;
His eyes saw her eyes as they had not seen them;
Her eyes woo'd still, his eyes disdain'd the wooing:
 And all this dumb play had his acts made plain
 With tears, which chorus-like her eyes did rain.

Full gently now she takes him by the hand,
A lily prison'd in a gaol of snow,
Or ivory in an alabaster band;
So white a friend engirts so white a foe:
 This beauteous combat, wilful and unwilling,
 Show'd like two silver doves that sit a-billing.

Once more the engine of her thoughts began:
'O fairest mover on this mortal round,
Would thou wert as I am, and I a man,
My heart all whole as thine, thy heart my wound;
 For one sweet look thy help I would assure thee,
 Though nothing but my body's bane would cure thee.'

'Give me my hand,' saith he; 'why does thou feel it?'
'Give me my heart,' saith she, 'and thou shalt have it;
O, give it me, lest thy hard heart do steel it,
And being steel'd, soft sighs can never grave it:
    Then love's deep groans I never shall regard,
    Because Adonis' heart hath made mine hard.'

* * *

'Who sees his true-love in her naked bed,
Teaching the sheets a whiter hue than white,
But, when his glutton eye so full hath fed,
His other agents aim at like delight?
    Who is so faint, that dares not be so bold
    To touch the fire, the weather being cold?'

* * *

'I know not love,' quoth he, 'nor will not know it,
Unless it be a boar, and then I chase it;
'Tis much to borrow, and I will not owe it;
My love to love is love but to disgrace it;
    For I have heard it is a life in death,
    That laughs, and weeps, and all but with a breath.'

* * *

'You hurt my hand with wringing; let us part,
And leave this idle theme, this bootless chat;
Remove your siege from my unyielding heart;
To love's alarms it will not ope the gate:
    Dismiss your vows, your feigned tears, your flattery;
    For where a heart is hard they make no battery.'

'What! canst thou talk?' quoth she, 'hast thou a tongue?
O, would thou hadst not, or I had no hearing!
Thy mermaid's voice hath done me double wrong;
I had my load before, now press'd with bearing:
    Melodious discord, heavenly tune harsh-sounding,
    Ear's deep-sweet music, and heart's deep-sore wounding.

'Had I no eyes but ears, my ears would love
That inward beauty and invisible;
Or were I deaf, thy outward parts would move
Each part in me that were but sensible:
    Though neither eyes nor ears, to hear nor see,
    Yet should I be in love by touching thee.

'Say, that the sense of feeling were bereft me,
And that I could not see, nor hear, nor touch,
And nothing but the very smell were left me,
Yet would my love to thee be still as much;
    For from the stillitory of thy face excelling
    Comes breath perfumed, that breedeth love by smelling.'

* * *

And at his look she flatly falleth down,
For looks kill love, and love by looks reviveth:
A smile recures the wounding of a frown;
But blessed bankrupt, that by love so thriveth!
    The silly boy, believing she is dead,
    Claps her pale cheek, till clapping makes it red;

And all amazed brake off his late intent,
For sharply did he think to reprehend her,
Which cunning love did wittily prevent:
Fair fall the wit that can so well defend her!

For on the grass she lies as she were slain,
Till his breath breatheth life in her again.

He wrings her nose, he strikes her on the cheeks,
He bends her fingers, holds her pulses hard,
He chafes her lips; a thousand ways he seeks
To mend the hurt that his unkindness marr'd:
   He kisses her, and she, by her good will,
   Will never rise, so he will kiss her still.

The night of sorrow now is turn'd to day:
Her two blue windows faintly she upheaveth,
Like the fair sun, when in his fresh array,
He cheers the morn, and all the earth relieveth:
   And as the bright sun glorifies the sky,
   So is her face illumined with her eye;

* * *

'O, where am I?' quoth she; 'in earth or heaven,
Or in the ocean drench'd, or in the fire?
What hour is this? or morn or weary even?
Do I delight to die, or life desire?
   But now I lived, and life was death's annoy;
   But now I died, and death was lively joy.

'O, thou didst kill me: kill me once again:
Thy eyes' shrewd tutor, that hard heart of thine,
Hath taught them scornful tricks, and such disdain,
That they have murder'd this poor heart of mine;
   And these mine eyes, true leaders to their queen,
   But for thy piteous lips no more had seen.

* * *

'A thousand kisses buys my heart from me;
And pay them at thy leisure, one by one.
What is ten hundred touches unto thee?
Are they not quickly told and quickly gone?
    Say, for non-payment that the debt should double,
    Is twenty hundred kisses such a trouble?'

'Fair queen,' quoth he, 'if any love you owe me,
Measure my strangeness with my unripe years:
Before I know myself, seek not to know me;
No fisher but the ungrown fry forbears:
    The mellow plum doth fall, the green sticks fast,
    Or being early pluck'd is sour to taste.

'Look, the world's comforter, with weary gait,
His day's hot task hath ended in the west;
The owl, night's herald, shrieks, 'tis very late;
The sheep are gone to fold, birds to their nest;
    And coal-black clouds that shadow heaven's light
    Do summon us to part, and bid good night.

'Now let me say "Good night," and so say you;
If you will say so, you shall have a kiss.'
'Good night,' quoth she; and ere he says 'Adieu,'
The honey fee of parting tender'd is:
    Her arms do lend his neck a sweet embrace;
    Incorporate then they seem; face grows to face.

Till breathless he disjoin'd, and backward drew
The heavenly moisture, that sweet coral mouth,
Whose precious taste her thirsty lips well knew,
Whereon they surfeit, yet complain on drouth:
    He with her plenty press'd, she faint with dearth,
    Their lips together glued, fall to the earth.

Now quick desire hath caught the yielding prey,
And glutton-like she feeds, yet never filleth;
Her lips are conquerors, his lips obey,
Paying what ransom the insulter willeth;
    Whose vulture thought doth pitch the price so high,
    That she will draw his lips' rich treasure dry.

And having felt the sweetness of the spoil,
With blindfold fury she begins to forage;
Her face doth reek and smoke, her blood doth boil,
And careless lust stirs up a desperate courage,
    Planting oblivion, beating reason back,
    Forgetting shame's pure blush and honour's wrack.

Hot, faint and weary, with her hard embracing,
Like a wild bird being tamed with too much handling,
Or as the fleet-foot roe that's tired with chasing,
Or like the froward infant still'd with dandling,
    He now obeys, and now no more resisteth,
    While she takes all she can, not all she listeth.

*   *   *

'Sweet boy," she says, 'this night I'll waste in sorrow,
For my sick heart commands mine eyes to watch.
Tell me, love's master, shall we meet tomorrow?
Say, shall we? shall we? wilt thou make the match?'
    He tells her, no; to-morrow he intends
    To hunt the boar with certain of his friends.

'The boar!' quoth she; whereat a sudden pale,
Like lawn being spread upon the blushing rose,
Usurps her cheeks; she trembles at his tale,
And on his neck her yoking arms she throws:

She sinketh down, still hanging by his neck,
He on her belly falls, she on her back.

Now is she in the very lists of love,
Her champion mounted for the hot encounter:
All is imaginary she doth prove,
He will not manage her, although he mount her;
   That worse than Tantalus' is her annoy,
   To clip Elysium, and to lack her joy.

Even so poor birds, deceived with painted grapes,
Do surfeit by the eye and pine the maw,
Even so she languisheth in her mishaps
As those poor birds that helpless berries saw.
   The warm effects which she in him finds missing
   She seeks to kindle with continual kissing.

But all in vain; good queen, it will not be:
She hath assay'd as much as may be proved,
Her pleading hath deserved a greater fee;
She's Love, she loves, and yet she is not loved.
   'Fie, fie,' he says, 'you crush me; let me go;
   You have no reason to withhold me so.'

'Thou hadst been gone,' quoth she, 'sweet boy, ere this,
But that thou told'st me thou wouldst hunt the boar.
O, be advised: thou know'st not what it is
With javelin's point a churlish swine to gore,
   Whose tushes never sheathed he whetteth still,
   Like to a mortal butcher, bent to kill.

*   *   *

'Lie quietly, and hear a little more;
Nay, do not struggle, for thou shalt not rise:
To make thee hate the hunting of the boar,
Unlike myself thou hear'st me moralize,
   Applying this to that, and so to so;
   For love can comment upon every woe.

'Where did I leave?' 'No matter where,' quoth he;
'Leave me, and then the story aptly ends:
The night is spent.' 'Why, what of that?' quoth she.
'I am,' quoth he, 'expected of my friends;
   And now 'tis dark, and going I shall fall.'
   'In night,' quoth she, 'desire sees best of all.'

Selections from
The Perfumed Garden

by Cheikh Nefzaoui

———•◆•———

[The frank and insistent emphasis upon the genital aspects of sex is a quality peculiar to all Arabic erotology. In the early Moslem world, the sexual act was joined to religious veneration with an earthiness and fervor unequaled in any other culture excepting the Hindu. The excerpts which follow, believed to have been written in the sixteenth century for the Bey of Tunis, reflect the polygamous structure of the society, its seriousness about the minutiae of copulation, as well as its playful attitudes. It believed in the highest possible erotic joy for all, taking the trouble even to design special coital postures for the corpulent and the physically disabled.]

CONCERNING PRAISEWORTHY MEN

I HAVE seen women trying to find in young men
The durable qualities which grace the man of full power,
The beauty, the enjoyment, the reserve, the strength,
The full-formed member providing a lengthened coition,
A heavy crupper, a slowly coming emission
A lightsome chest, as it were floating upon them;

236

The spermal ejaculation slow to arrive, so as
To furnish forth a long drawn-out enjoyment.
His member soon to be prone again for erection,
To ply the plane again and again and again on their vulvas,
And between his arms I am like a corpse without life.
Every part of my body receives in turn his love-bites,
And he covers me with kisses of fire;
When he sees me in heat he quickly comes to me,
Then he opens my thighs and kisses my belly,
And he puts his tool in my hand to make it knock at my
    door.
Soon he is in the cave, and I feel the pleasure approaching.
He shakes me and thrills me, and hotly we both are
    working,
And he says, 'Receive my seed!' and I answer, 'Oh give it,
    beloved one!
It shall be welcome to me, you light of my eyes!
Oh, you man of all men, who fillest me with pleasure.
Oh, you soul of my soul, go on with fresh vigour,
For you must not yet withdraw it from me; leave it there,
And this day will be then finished free of all sorrow.'
He has sworn to God to have me for seventy nights,
And what he wished for he did in the way of kisses and
    embraces during all those nights.

* * *

There is a story that once there lived a king named
Mamoum, who had a court fool of the name of Bahloul,
who amused the princes and Vizirs.

One day this buffoon appeared before the King, who was
amusing himself. The King bade him sit down, and then
asked him, turning away, "Why hast thou come, O son of
a bad woman?"

Bahloul answered, "I have come to see what has come to our Lord, whom may God make victorious."

"And what has come to thee?" replied the King, "and how art thou getting on with thy new and with thy old wife?" For Bahloul, not content with one wife, had married a second one.

"I am not happy," he answered, "neither with the old one, nor with the new one; and moreover poverty overpowers me."

The King said, "Can you recite any verses on this subject?"

The buffoon having answered in the affirmative, Mamoum commanded him to recite those he knew, and Bahloul began as follows:

"Poverty holds me in chains; misery torments me.
I am being scourged with all misfortunes;
Ill luck has cast me in trouble and peril,
And has drawn upon me the contempt of man.
God does not favour a poverty like mine;
That is opprobrious in every one's eyes.
Misfortune and misery for a long time
Have held me tightly; and no doubt of it
My dwelling house will soon not know me more."
Mamoum said to him, "Where are you going to?"
He replied, "To God and his prophet, O prince of the
    believers."

"That is well!" said the King; "those who take refuge in God and his Prophet, and then in us, will be made welcome. But can you now tell me some more verses about your two wives, and about what comes to pass with them?"

"Certainly," said Bahloul.

"Then let us hear what you have to say!"

Bahloul then began thus with poetical words:

"By reason of my ignorance I have married two wives—
And why do you complain, O husband of two wives?
I said to myself, I shall be like a lamb between them;
I shall take my pleasure upon the bosoms of my two sheep,
And I have become like a ram between two female jackals,
Days follow upon days, and nights upon nights,
And their yoke bears me down both during days and nights.
If I am kind to one, the other gets vexed.
And so I cannot escape from these two furies.
If you want to live well and with a free heart,
And with your hands unclenched, then do not marry.
If you must wed, then marry one wife only.
One alone is enough to satisfy two armies."

When Mamoum heard these words he began to laugh, till he nearly tumbled over. Then as a proof of his kindness, he gave to Bahloul his golden robe, a most beautiful vestment.

Bahloul went in high spirits towards the dwelling of the Grand Vizir. Just then Hamdonna looked from the height of her palace in that direction, and saw him. She said to her servant, "By the God of the temple of Mecca! There is Bahloul dressed in a fine gold-worked robe! How can I manage to get possession of the same?"

The servant said, "Oh, my mistress, you would not know how to get hold of that robe."

Hamdonna answered, "I have thought of a trick to do it, and I shall get the robe from him."

"Bahloul is a sly man," replied the servant. "People

think generally that they can make fun of him; but, for God, it is he who makes fun of them. Give the idea up, mistress mine, and take care that you do not fall into the snare which you intend setting for him."

But Hamdonna said again, "It must be done!" She then sent her servant to Bahloul, to tell him that he should come to her. He said, "By the blessing of God, to him who calls you, you shall make answer," and went to Hamdonna.

Hamdonna welcomed him and said: "Oh, Bahloul, I believe you come to hear me sing." He replied. "Most certainly, oh, my mistress! She has a marvelous gift for singing," he continued. "I also think that after having listened to my songs, you will be pleased to take some refreshments." "Yes," said he.

Then she began to sing admirably, so as to make people who listened die with love.

After Bahloul had heard her sing, refreshments were served; he ate and he drank. Then she said to him, "I do not know why but I fancy you would gladly take off your robe, to make me a present of it." And Bahloul answered: "Oh, my mistress! I have sworn to give it to her to whom I have done as a man does to a woman."

"What! you know what this is, Bahloul?" said she.

"Whether I know it?" replied he. "I, who am instructing God's creatures in that science? It is I who make them copulate in love, who initiate them in the delights a female can give, show them how you must caress a woman, and what will excite and satisfy her. Oh, my mistress, who should know the art of coition if it is not I?"

Hamdonna was the daughter of Mamoum, and the wife of the Grand Vizir. She was endowed with the most perfect beauty; of superb figure and harmonious form. No one in her time surpassed her in grace and perfection. Heroes on seeing her became humble and submissive and looked down to the ground for fear of temptation, so many charms and perfections had God lavished on her. Those who looked steadily at her were troubled in their mind, and oh! how many heroes imperilled themselves for her sake. For this very reason Bahloul had always avoided meeting her for fear of succumbing to the temptation, and, apprehensive of his peace of mind, he had never, until then, been in her presence.

Bahloul began to converse with her. Now he looked at her and anon bent his eyes to the ground, fearful of not being able to command his passion. Hamdonna burnt with desire to have the robe, and he would not give it up without being paid for it.

"What price do you demand," she asked. To which he replied, "Coition, O apple of my eye."

"You know what that is, O Bahloul?" said she.

"By God," he cried; "no man knows women better than I; they are the occupation of my life. No one has studied all their concerns more than I. I know what they are fond of; for learn, oh, lady mine, that men choose different occupations according to their genius and their bent. The one takes, the other gives; this one sells, the other buys. My only thought is of love and of the possession of beautiful women. I heal those that are lovesick, and carry a solace to their thirsting vaginas."

Hamdonna was surprised at his words and the sweetness of his language. "Could you recite me some verses on this subject?" she asked.

"Certainly," he answered.

"Very well, O Bahloul, let me hear what you have to say." Bahloul recited as follows:

"Men are divided according to their affairs and doings;
Some are always in spirits and joyful, others in tears.
There are those whose life is restless and full of misery,
While, on the contrary, others are steeped in good fortune,
Always in luck's happy way, and favoured in all things.
I alone am indifferent to all such matters.
What care I for Turkomans, Persians, and Arabs?
My whole ambition is in love and coition with women,
No doubt nor mistake about that!
If my member is without vulva, my state becomes frightful,
My heart then burns with a fire which cannot be quenched.
Look at my member erect! There it is—admire its beauty!
It calms the heat of love and quenches the hottest fires
By its movement in and out between your thighs.
Oh, my hope and my apple, oh, noble and generous lady,
If one time will not suffice to appease thy fire,
I shall do it again, so as to give satisfaction;
No one may reproach thee, for all the world does the same.
But if you choose to deny me, then send me away!
Chase me away from thy presence without fear or remorse!
Yet bethink thee, and speak and augment not my trouble,
But, in the name of God, forgive me and do not reproach me.
While I am here let thy words be kind and forgiving.
Let them not fall upon me like sword-blades, keen and
    cutting!
Let me come to you and do not repel me.
Let me come to you like one that brings drink to the
    thirsty;
Hasten and let my hungry eyes look at thy bosom.
Do not withhold from me love's joys, and do not be bashful,
Give yourself up to me—I shall never cause you a trouble,
Even were you to fill me with sickness from head to foot.
I shall always remain as I am, and you as you are,

Knowing, that we are the servants, and you are the mistress.
Then shall our love be veiled? It shall be hidden for all
    time,
For I keep it a secret and I shall be mute and muzzled.
It's by the will of God, that everything is to happen,
He has filled me with love, and to-day I am in ill-luck."

While Hamdonna was listening she nearly swooned, and
set herself to examine the member of Bahloul, which stood
erect like a column between his thighs. Now she said to
herself: "I shall give myself up to him," and now "No I
will not." During this uncertainty she felt a yearning for
pleasure between her thighs, and Eblis made flow from her
natural parts a moisture, the forerunner of pleasure. She
then no longer combated her desire to cohabit with him,
and reassured herself by the thought: "If this Bahloul, after
having had his pleasure with me, should divulge it no one
will believe his words."

She requested him to divest himself of his robe and to
come into her room, but Bahloul replied, "I shall not undress till I have sated my desire, O apple of my eye."

Then Hamdonna rose, trembling with excitement for
what was to follow; she undid her girdle and left the room,
Bahloul following her and thinking: "Am I really awake
or is this a dream?" He walked after her till she had
entered her boudoir. Then she threw herself on a couch
of silk, which was rounded on the top like a vault, lifted
her clothes up over her thighs, trembling all over, and all
the beauty which God had given her was in Bahloul's
arms.

Bahloul examined the belly of Hamdonna, round like an
elegant cupola, his eyes dwelt upon a navel which was like
a pearl in a golden cup; and descending lower down there

was a beautiful piece of nature's workmanship, and the whiteness and shape of her thighs surprised him.

Then he pressed Hamdonna in a passionate embrace, and soon saw the animation leave her face; she seemed to be almost unconscious. She had lost her head; and holding Bahloul's member in her hands excited and fired him more and more.

Bahloul said to her: "Why do I see you so troubled and beside yourself?" And she answered: "Leave me, O son of the debauched woman! By God, I am like a mare in heat, and you continue to excite me still more with your words, and what words! They would set any woman on fire, if she was the purest creature in the world. You will insist on making me succumb by your talk and your verses."

Bahloul answered: "Am I then not like your husband?"

"Yes," she said, "but a woman gets in heat on account of the man, as a mare on account of the horse, whether the man be the husband or not; with this difference, however, that the mare gets lusty only at certain periods of the year, and only then receives the stallion, while a woman can always be made rampant by words of love. Both these dispositions have met within me, and, as my husband is absent, make haste, for he will soon be back."

Bahloul replied: "Oh, my mistress, my loins hurt me and prevent me mounting upon you. You take the man's position, and then take my robe and let me depart."

Then he laid himself down in the position the woman takes in receiving a man; and his verge was standing up like a column.

Hamdonna threw herself upon Bahloul, took his member between her hands and began to look at it. She was astonished at its size, strength and firmness, and cried: "Here we have the ruin of all women and the cause of many troubles. O Bahloul! I never saw a more beautiful dart than yours!" Still she continued keeping hold of it, and rubbed its head against the lips of her vulva till the latter part seemed to say: "O member, come into me."

Then Bahloul inserted his member into the vagina of the Sultan's daughter, and she, settling down upon his engine, allowed it to penetrate entirely into her furnace till nothing more could be seen of it, not the slightest trace, and she said, "How lascivious has God made woman, and how indefatigable after her pleasures." She then gave herself up to an up-and-down dance, moving her bottom like a riddle; to the right and left, and forward and backward; never was there such a dance as this.

The Sultan's daughter continued her ride upon Bahloul's member till the moment of enjoyment arrived, and the attraction of the vulva seemed to pump the member as though by suction: just as an infant sucks the teats of the mother. The acme of the enjoyment came to both simultaneously, and each took the pleasure with avidity.

Then Hamdonna seized the member in order to withdraw it, and slowly, slowly she made it come out, saying: "This is the deed of a vigorous man." Then she dried it and her own private parts with a silken kerchief and arose.

Bahloul also got up and prepared to depart, but she said, "And the robe?"

He answered, "Why, O mistress! You have been riding me, and still want a present?"

"But," she said, "did you not tell me that you could not mount me on account of the pains in your loins?"

"It matters but little," said Bahloul. "The first time it was your turn, the second will be mine, and the price for it will be the robe, and then I will go."

Hamdonna thought to herself, "As he began he may now go on; afterwards he will go away."

So she laid herself down, but Bahloul said, "I shall not lie with you unless you undress entirely."

Then she undressed until she was quite naked, and Bahloul fell into an ecstasy in seeing the beauty and perfection of her form. He looked at her magnificent thighs and rebounding navel, at her belly vaulted like an arch, her plump breasts standing out like hyacinths. Her neck was like a gazelle's, the opening of her mouth like a ring, her lips fresh and red like a gory sabre. Her teeth might have been taken for pearls and her cheeks for roses. Her eyes were black and well slit, and her eyebrows of ebony resembled the rounded flourish of the noun traced by the hand of a skilful writer. Her forehead was like the full moon in the night.

Bahloul began to embrace her, to suck her lips and to kiss her bosom; he drew her fresh saliva and bit her thighs. So he went on till she was ready to swoon, and could scarcely stammer, and her eyes got veiled. Then he kissed her vulva, and she moved neither hand nor foot. He looked lovingly upon the secret parts of Hamdonna, beautiful enough to attract all eyes with their purple centre.

Bahloul cried, "Oh, the temptation of man!" and still he bit her and kissed her till the desire was roused to its full pitch. Her sighs came quicker, and grasping his member with her hand she made it disappear in her vagina.

Then it was he who moved hard, and she responded hotly; the overwhelming pleasure simultaneously calmed their fervour.

Then Bahloul got off her, dried his pestle and her mortar, and prepared to retire. But Hamdonna said, "Where is the robe? You mock me, O Bahloul." He answered, "O my mistress, I shall only part with it for a consideration. You have had your dues and I mine. The first time was for you, the second time for me, now the third time shall be for the robe."

This said, he took it off, folded it, and put it in Hamdonna's hands, who, having risen, laid down again on the couch and said, "Do what you like!"

Forthwith Bahloul threw himself upon her, and with one push completely buried his member in her vagina; then he began to work as with a pestle, and she to move her bottom, until both again did flow over at the same time. Then he rose from her side, left his robe, and went.

The servant said to Hamdonna, "O my mistress, is it not as I have told you? Bahloul is a bad man, and you could not get the better of him. They consider him as a subject for mockery, but, before God, he is making fun of them. Why would you not believe me?"

Hamdonna turned to her and said, "Do not tire me with your remarks. It came to pass what had to come to pass, and on the opening of each vulva is inscribed the name of the man who is to enter it, right or wrong, for love or for hatred. If Bahloul's name had not been inscribed on my vulva he would never have got into it, had he offered me the universe with all it contains."

As they were thus talking there came a knock at the door. The servant asked who was there, and in answer the voice of Bahloul said, "It is I." Hamdonna, in doubt as to what the buffoon wanted to do, got frightened. The servant asked Bahloul what he wanted, and received the reply, "Bring me a little water." She went out of the house with a cup full of water. Bahloul drank, and then let the cup slip out of his hands, and it was broken. The servant shut the door upon Bahloul, who sat himself down on the threshold.

The buffoon being thus close to the door, the Vizir, Hamdonna's husband, arrived, who said to him, "Why do I see you here, O Bahloul?" And he answered, "O my lord, I was passing through this street when I was overcome by a great thirst. A servant came and brought me a cup of water. The cup slipped from my hands and got broken. Then our Lady Hamdonna took my robe, which the Sultan our Master had given me as indemnification."

Then said the Vizir, "Let him have his robe." Hamdonna at this moment came out, and her husband asked her whether it was true that she had taken the robe in payment for the cup. Hamdonna then cried, beating her hands together, "What have you done, O Bahloul?" He answered, "I have talked to your husband the language of my folly; talk to him, you, the language of thy wisdom." And she, enraptured with the cunning he had displayed, gave him his robe back, and he departed.

Putting the Devil in Hell

[from *The Decameron* by Giovanni Boccaccio]

———•———

Perhaps you, most gracious ladies, have never heard how the devil is put back into hell, so I am going to tell you. The information may help you save your souls, and make you realize that, although Love more willingly frequents gay palaces and downy chambers than humble cots, he does not fail, for all that, to assert his power in the recesses of the forests, and the barren mountains, and solitary caves. Indeed, we might truly conclude that all things are subject to his rule.

Once upon a time, there lived a very rich man in the city of Caspa, Barbary, who had, among other children, a young, pretty, and very charming daughter whose name was Alibech. Of course, she was not a Christian, but when she heard the praises of that faith from the mouths of many of the gentile inhabitants of the town, and the delight of serving God, she asked one of them how He might best be served with the least trouble. "They best serve God," he answered, "who flee from the things of the world, like those good souls who take refuge in the trackless desert of Thebais."

The girl, who was only about fourteen years old and very ingenuous for her age, stole away all alone the next morning, in search of the desert of Thebais, without telling anyone where she was going. It was no true call of religion that led her on, but a childish whim, yet it was sufficient to keep her on her way until she reached those lonely places, after great hardship.

At last she spied a little hovel at a distance, and going toward it, found a holy man standing at the threshold. He was astonished to see a pretty young girl in that place, and asked her what on earth she was seeking. She was inspired by God, she answered, and yearned to be of service to Him. She was in search of someone to show her how best to serve Him. The pious man, looking again at all her youthful charms, was seized with fear that if he let her stay, the devil might work him mischief. Praising her good intention, he feasted her with roots, herbs, wild apples and dates and a drink of water. Then, "Daughter," said he, "there's a holy man not so far from here who is a much better teacher for what you require, than I could ever be. Go, my dear, and seek him out." At that, he showed her the way. When she came to the holy gentleman, he received her with the selfsame words, until finally, as she proceeded, she came to the cell of a young sprig of a hermit by the name of Rustico, a devout youth, and the soul of sanctity. Alibech made the same request of him, that she had made of the others.

Now he wished to put his firmness of will to a stringent test, and did not send her away like his brethren, but kept her with him in his cell. At nightfall, he prepared her a little bed of palm leaves and told her to lie on it, which she did.

Before long, the surge of temptation began its assault upon Rustico's powers of resistance. Alas! it had a tremendous advantage over him! It was hardly worthwhile to

keep up the struggle, so turning right about, Rustico
yielded himself up, vanquished. Soon he flung pious medi-
tations, prayers and mortifications to the winds and fell
mentally to dallying with visions of the girl's youth and
loveliness. Moreover, he set about devising ways and means
of approaching her, and obtaining what he wanted, without
rousing in her mind any suspicion of his lecherous purpose. Paving the way with different questions, he learned
that she had never enjoyed a man, and was indeed as innocent as she seemed. Accordingly, he realized that the only
way to get to her, was to make her believe she was acting
in the service of God. To begin with, he showed her very
eloquently what a terrible enemy of Almighty God was the
devil; later, he gave her to understand that the most pleasing service she could render the Lord, was to put back
the devil in the hell to which He had condemned him.

"And how do you do that?" asked the girl.

"You'll know it soon enough," Rustico replied, "but you
must do whatever you see me do."

At that, he flung off the few clothes he wore and remained stark naked. Alibech followed his example. Then
he fell on his knees, as though he were about to pray, and
had her do likewise, facing him. At this juncture, Rustico
flared with hotter desire on seeing her so beautiful, and
Alibech stared, full of wonderment at the sight.

"Rustico," she asked, "what is that?"

"Ah, my daughter," said the monk, "this is the devil I
told you about. Look at him! See? He's giving me so much
trouble that I can scarcely bear it!"

"Praise be to God," exclaimed the girl. "I see now how
much better off I am! I haven't any such devil!"

"You're right," said Rustico, "but you have something
else I haven't, in place of this devil."

"Ooh, really!" said Alibech. "And what can it be?"

"It's hell itself, you have," replied Rustico. "I'm sure God sent you here for the good of my soul, because when this devil gives me so much trouble, it would be a great comfort to me to put him back into hell. You'll be doing the Lord a pleasure and a service, if you really came to this desert for that purpose."

Very earnestly Alibech answered: "Why father, of course, since I've this hell, you may put him back anytime you please."

"God bless you, daughter," said Rustico. "Let's proceed to it immediately, then, and put him in, so that he'll give me some peace."

As he spoke, he led the girl to one of their little pallets, and showed her what position to take in order to lock up the accursed of God. Alibech had never yet put any kind of devil into hell, and for the first time felt a little pain, which made her say: "I'm sure, father, that devil of yours must be a terror and a real enemy to God. Why, even hell itself, not to mention the rest of us, resents it when he's put back in it!"

"Daughter," said Rustico, "it will not always be that way." Indeed, to prevent its happening, they put the devil back into hell on six occasions before they left the bed, until the poor wretch had his pride so thrashed out of his head, that for the time being he was quite willing to remain in peace. Many a time thereafter they returned to the task, and as the girl went on, yielding herself obediently, she acquired a fondness for the game.

"I am beginning to understand," she remarked, "what those good men of Caspa meant, when they said it was such a delightful thing to serve God. I can't for the life of me think of anything else I ever did, that gave me as much pleasure as putting the devil back in hell. Do you know, I really think all people are fools, who spend their time at anything but the service of God."

Very often, therefore, she could come to Rustico, saying: "Father, I came here to serve God, not to waste my time. Come, let's get busy putting the devil back in hell."

Sometimes, when they were engaged in it, she would remark: "Do you know, Rustico, I wonder why the devil ever escapes from hell! If he remained there as gladly as hell welcomes and holds him, he'd never get out of it."

Alibech's frequent invitations, urging Rustico to the service of God, finally made him shiver with cold when another would have sweated; and he would admonish her that the devil was not to be punished or put back into hell, except when he raised his head with pride. "We've taken him down such a peg, by the grace of God," he added, "that he does nothing but pray the Lord to be left in peace."

So for a while, he succeeded in silencing her importunities; but when she saw he did not invite her to put the devil back in hell, she said to him, one day: "Listen, Rustico, if that devil of yours has had all the pride knocked out of him, this hell of mine doesn't give me a moment's rest. I think it's up to you to help me quiet the fury of my hell, the way I helped you to lower the pride of your devil!"

Rustico's sole nourishment consisted of roots and water, and he could therefore respond but poorly to the demands made upon him. Quite a lot of devils, he told her, were needed to quench hell, but he would do his best to help her, anyhow. Now and then, therefore, he would gratify her, but so infrequently, that it was like throwing a bean into a lion's mouth. Alibech thought she was not doing her duty by the Lord as assiduously as she desired, and complained, oftener than not.

However, while this argument was in progress between Rustico's devil, that could not, and Alibech's hell that would, a fire broke out in Caspa that destroyed Alibech's father in his own house, together with all his children and the rest of his family, leaving her his sole heir. A young man, called Neherbale, who had consumed all his goods in riotous living, learned somehow that Alibech was alive, and set out to look for her. He found her, just in time to prevent the court from appropriating her father's wealth, according to the law regarding the property of men dying without successor, and to Rustico's great relief, though much against her will, he took her back to Caspa, married her himself, and became joint heir to her father's rich estate.

There, when the women asked her, before the wedding, what she did in the desert to serve God, she replied she did His service by putting the devil back into hell, adding that Neherbale had been guilty of a grave sin by taking her away from so holy an occupation.

"Why, how do you put the devil back into hell?" the women asked her. Alibech showed them how it was done, by words and gestures. They laughed loud and long about it, and it's a common joke among them to this day.

"Don't take on about it, dear child," they consoled her. "We manage that service pretty well even here. Neherbale himself will serve the good Lord well enough, with your help."

They repeated the story to one another all over the city, until it became a popular saw, to the effect that the most pleasant service one could do the Lord, was to put the devil back in hell. The saying has even reached us across the sea, and is current to this day.

As for you, dear young ladies, if you are in need of God's grace, learn to put the devil back in hell, since it's highly agreeable to the Lord, and a joy to both parties—besides, much good might come of it.

A Selection from the
Memoirs of Jacques Casanova

Casanova and the two beautiful cousins Hedvige and Helene are strolling in a garden in Geneva. They are discussing the anatomy of the male, specifically the phenomenon of erection. Casanova continues:

"Yea, for this phenomenon springeth from desire, for 'tis very true that it would not have worked in me, sweet Hedvige, had I not found thee charming and had not what I had seen of thee given me the most seductive idea of the beauties I see not. Tell me frankly if, after feeling this rigidity of mine, thou dost not experience an agreeable sensation?"

"I confess it; 'tis precisely where thou pressest. Dost not feel as I, my dear Helene, an itching and a longing on listening to the very true discourse, given to us by this gentleman?"

"Yea, I feel it, but I feel it very often, without any discourse exciting it."

"And then," quoth I, "Nature forceth thee to appease it thus?"

"Not at all."

"Oh, that it were so, Hedvige! Even in sleep one's hand

strayeth there by instinct; and, lacking this easement, I have read that we should suffer terrible maladies."

And whilst we continued this philosophical converse, which the youthful theologian sustained with an authoritative tone, and which brought a look of voluptuousness to the lovely complexion of her cousin, we came to the edge of a fine pool where one descended by a marble staircase to bathe. Although it was chilly, our heads were warm, and it came to me to propose to the maidens that they put their feet in the water, assuring them that it would do them good and, if they permitted me, that I would count it an honour to remove their shoes and stockings.

"Come," said Hedvige, "I like the project well."

"I, too," said Helene.

"Seat yourselves, ladies, on the first stair."

Behold them, then, seated, and thy servant, on the fourth stair, busy unshoeing them, what time he extolled the beauty of their legs and made pretence to be incurious at the moment to see higher than the knee. Then, having gone down to the water, they had perforce to lift their garments, and in this business I encouraged them.

"Ah, well," remarked Hedvige, "men also have thighs."

Helene, who would have felt shame to show less courage than her cousin, did not hang back.

"Come, my charming naiads," quoth I, " 'tis enough. Ye will catch cold if ye remain for long in the water."

They reascended the staircase backwards, ever holding up their robes lest they might wet them; and it fell to me to dry their limbs with all the handkerchiefs that I possessed. This pleasant task permitted me to see and touch everything at my leisure, and the reader will scarce need my word to affirm that I made the best of my opportunity. The pretty niece (Hedvige) declared that I was too curious, but Helene let me have my way with an air so tender and so languid that I was hard pressed not to push the matter further. In the end, having again put on their shoes and stockings, I told them that I was enchanted to have viewed the secret charms of the two most lovely ladies in Geneva.

"What effect hath it on thee?" asked Hedvige of me.

"I dare not tell ye to look, but feel, both of ye."

"Bathe thou thyself also."

"Impossible. The business is too long for a man."

"But we have yet two full hours to remain here without fear of interruption from anyone."

This response caused me to see the happiness that awaited me; but I did not think fit to expose myself to an illness by entering the water in the state in which I was. Seeing a summer-house not far off and assured that M. Torchin would have left it open, I took my two beauties by the arms and led them hither, not letting them guess, however, my intentions.

The summer-house was full of vases of pot pourri, pretty engravings, and so forth; but what I valued most was a large and lovely divan, fit for repose and for pleasure. There, seated 'twixt these two beauties and lavishing caresses upon them, I said that I desired to show them that which they had never seen, at the same time exposing to their gaze the principle agent of humanity. They raised themselves to admire it, and then, taking the hand of each one of them, I procured for them a considerable pleasure; but, in the course of this labour, an abundant emission on my part caused them great amazement.

" 'Tis its speech," said I. "The speech of the great creator of men."

" 'Tis delicious!" cried Helene, laughing at the term 'speech.'

"I, too, have the power of speech," said Hedvige, "and I will show it thee, if thou wilt wait a moment."

"Put thyself in my hands, sweet Hedvige, I will spare thee the trouble of making it come thyself, and I will do it better than thee."

"I well believe it. But I have never done that with a man."

"Nor I," said Helene.

When they had placed themselves directly before me, their arms enlaced, I made them swoon away afresh. Then, having seated ourselves, what time my hand strayed all over their charms, I let them divert themselves at their leisure, till in the end I moistened their palms with a second emission of the natural moisture, which they examined curiously on their fingers.

Having once again put ourselves in a state of decency, we passed yet another half hour in exchanging kisses, after which I told them that they had rendered me partially happy, but, to make the work perfect, that I hoped they would devise a means of granting me their first favours. Then I showed them those preservative sachets which the English have invented in order to rid the fair sex of all fear. These little "purses," the use of which I explained to them, excited their admiration, and Hedvige said to her cousin that she would give thought to the matter. Become intimate friends and in good case to become even better, we took our way toward the house, where we found Helene's mother and the minister walking by the edge of the lake.

After dinner I went apart with Helene, who told me that her cousin and the pastor would sup with her mother on the following day.

"Hedvige," she added, "will stay and sleep with me, as

is ever her custom when she cometh with her uncle to sup. It remaineth to be seen if thou art willing to hide in a spot I will show thee to-morrow at eleven of the clock, in order to pass the night with us. Call on my mother at that hour to-morrow, and I will find means of showing thee the spot."

In the morning I paid the mother a visit, and as Helene was escorting me out, she showed me a closed door 'twixt the two stairs.

"At seven hours of the clock," said she, "thou will find it open, and when thou art within, put on the bolt. Take care lest any see thee as thou enter the house."

Casanova, in due course, takes up his position in the hiding place, and during his long wait for the two charmers, gives himself up to reflection on his past. The text continues:

In my long and profligate career, during which I have turned the heads of several hundreds of ladies, I have grown familiar with all methods of seduction; but it hath ever been my guiding principle never to press my attack against novices or those in whom prejudices were likely to prove an obstacle, save in the presence of another woman. Timidity, I soon discovered, maketh a girl averse from seduction; in company with another girl she is easily conquered; the weakness of one bringeth on the fall of the other.

Fathers and mothers are of contrary opinion, but they err. They will not trust their daughter to take a walk or go to a ball with a young man, but no difficulty is made if she hath another girl with her. I repeat—they err; if the young man hath the requisite skill, their daughter is lost.

A sense of false shame hindereth them from making a determined resistance to seduction, but, the first step taken, the fall cometh inevitably and rapidly. One girl, granting some small favour, straightway maketh her friend grant a much greater, thereby to hide her own blushes; and if the seducer be clever at his trade, the youthful innocent will soon have travelled too far to be able to draw back. In addition, the more innocent the girl, the greater her ignorance of seduction's methods. Ere she hath time to think, pleasure doth attract her, curiosity draweth her yet a little further, and opportunity doth the rest.

For example, 'twere possible I had been able to seduce Hedvige without Helene, but I am assured I had never succeeded with Helene had she not seen her cousin grant me certain licenses what time she took liberties with me —practices which she thought, doubtless, contrary to the modesty and decorum of a respectable young woman. I desire what I say to be a warning to fathers and mothers, and to secure me a place in their esteem, at any rate.

Shortly after the pastor had gone I heard three light knocks on my prison door. I opened it, and a hand soft as satin grasped mine. My whole being quivered. 'Twas Helene's hand, and that happy moment had already repaid me for my long waiting.

"Follow me softly," she said, in a low voice; but scarce had she closed the door ere I, in my impatience, clasped her tenderly in my arms, and caused her to feel the effect which her mere presence had produced on me, what time I assured myself of her docility.

"Be prudent, my friend," said she to me, "and come softly upstairs."

I followed her as best I might in the darkness, she leading me along a gallery into a room without light, the door of which she closed behind us, and thence into a lighted chamber, wherein was Hedvige, well nigh in a state of nudity. She came to me with open arms on the instant she saw me, and, embracing me ardently, signified her appreciation of my patience in my weary prison.

"Divine Hedvige," quoth I, "had I not loved thee madly, I had not stayed one fourth of an hour in that dismal cell; but for thy sake I would readily pass hours there daily till I quit this spot. But let us lose no time. To bed!"

"Do ye twain get to bed," quoth Helene. "I will couch on the divan."

"Oh!" cried Hedvige. "Think not so. Our fate must be exactly equal."

"Yea, beloved Helene," said I, embracing her. "I love you both with equal ardour, and these ceremonies but waste the time wherein I should be convincing ye of my passion. Follow my example. I am about to disrobe and place myself in the midst of the bed. Come lie beside me, and ye will see if I love ye as ye are worthy to be loved. If all be safe, I will remain till ye send me away, but whate'er ye do, of your mercy extinguish not the light."

In the twinkling of an eye, all the while discussing the theory of shame with Hedvige the theologian, I presented myself to their gaze in the costume of Adam. Hedvige, blushing but fearing, perchance, to depreciate herself in my opinion by any further reserve, parted with the last shred of modesty, citing the opinion of St. Clement Alexandrinus, who held that in the shirt lay the seat of shame.

I praised unstintingly her charms and the perfection of her form, thereby hoping to encourage Helene, who was disrobing but slowly; but a charge of mock modesty from her cousin had more effect than all my praises. At length this Venus was in a state of nature, covering her most secret parts with one hand, concealing one breast with the other, and seeming most sadly shamed of all she could not conceal. Her modest confusion, this strife twixt expiring modesty and growing passion, enchanted me.

Hedvige was taller than Helene, her skin was whiter, and her breast twice the size of her cousin's; but in Helene was more animation, her form was more sweetly moulded, and her bust was on the model of the Venus de Medici.

By degrees she became bolder, put at ease by her cousin, and we passed several moments in admiring each other; then to bed we went. Nature called loudly, and all we desired was to satisfy its demands. With a coolness that I did not fear would fail me, I made a woman of Hedvige, and when all was o'er she kissed me, saying that the pain was naught compared to the pleasure.

Next came the turn of Helene, who was six years younger than Hedvige; but the finest "fleece" that e'er I saw presented something of an obstacle. This she parted with her two hands, being jealous of her cousin's success; and although she was not initiated into the mysteries of love without woeful pain, her sighs were truly sighs of happiness as she responded to my ardent efforts. Her charms and vivacious movements caused me to shorten the sacrifice, and when I quitted the sanctuary my two beauties perceived I was in need of repose.

The altar was purified of the blood of the victims, and we all bathed, enchanted to serve one another.

Life returned to me 'neath their curious fingers, and the sight filled them with joy . . . For several hours I overwhelmed them with happiness, passing five or six times from one to the other before exhausting myself and arriving at the ecstatic spasm. In the intervals, perceiving them docile and desirous, I made them execute Aretin's most complicated postures, a business that amused them beyond measure. We were lavish with our kisses on whatever part took our fancy, and just as Hedvige applied her lips to the mouth of the pistol, it went off and the discharge inundated her face and her bosom. She was delighted, and studied the eruption to an end with all the curiosity of a physician.

The night seemed short, though we had not lost a moment's space, and at daybreak we had to part. I left them in bed, being fortunate to get away observed of none.

In the evening, after supper, Casanova contrives another meeting with his charmers.

. . . Going out with my heroines, I worked wonders. Hedvige philosophised over the pleasure, and told me that she would ne'er have tasted it had I not chanced to encounter her uncle. Helene did not speak; more voluptuous than her cousin, she swelled out like a dove, and came to life only to expire a moment after. I wondered at her amazing fecundity, although such is not uncommon; while I was engaged in one operation, she passed fourteen times from life to death. True, 'twas the sixth course I had run, so I made my pace somewhat slower to enjoy the pleasure she took in the business . . .

After passing another night with the cousins, Casanova again sets out on his travels; and here, for the time being, we will leave him.

The Impotent Lover

[from *The Loves of* Ovid]

———•—•———

EITHER SHE was foul, or her attire was bad,
Or she was not the wench I wished to have had.
Idly I lay with her, as if I loved not,
And like a burden grieved the bed that moved not.
Though both of us performed our true intent,
Yet could I not cast anchor where I meant.
She on my neck her ivory arms did throw,
Her arms far whiter than the Scythian snow.
And eagerly she kissed me with her tongue,
And under mine her wanton thigh she flung,
Yes, and she soothed me up, and called me "Sir,"
And used all speech that might provoke and stir.
Yet like as if cold hemlock I had drunk,
It mocked me, hung down the head and sunk.
Like a dull cipher, or rude block I lay,
Or shade, or body was I, who can say?
What will my age do, age I cannot shun,
Seeing in my prime my force is spent and done?
I blush, that being youthful, hot, and lusty,
I prove neither youth nor man, but old and rusty.
Pure rose she, like a nun to sacrifice,
Or one that with her tender brother lies.
Yet boarded I the golden Chie twice,

And Libas, and the white-cheeked Pitho thrice.
Corinna craved it in a summer's night,
And nine sweet bouts had we before daylight.
What, waste my limbs through some Thessalian charms?
May spells and drugs do silly souls such harms?
With virgin wax hath some abased my joints?
And pierced my liver with sharp needle-points?
Charms change corn to grass and make it die:
By charms are running springs and fountains dry.
By charms mast drops from oaks, from vines grapes fall,
And fruit from trees when there's no wind at all.
Why might not then my sinews be enchanted?
And I grow faint as with some spirit haunted?
To this, add shame: shame to perform it quailed me,
And was the second cause why vigor failed me.
My idle thoughts delighted her no more,
Than did the robe or garment which she wore.
Yet might her touch make youthful Pylius fire
And Tithon livelier than his years require.
Even her I had, and she had me in vain,
What did I crave more, if I ask again?
I think the great gods grieved they had bestowed,
This benefit: which lewdly I foreslowed.
I wished to be received in, in I get me.
Why was I blest: why made king to refuse it?
So in a spring thrives he that told so much,
And looks upon the fruits he cannot touch.
Hath any rose so from a fresh young maid,
As she might straight have gone to church and prayed?
Well, I believe, she kissed not as she should,
Nor used the sleight and cunning which she could.
Huge oaks, hard adamants might she have moved,
And with sweet words caused deaf rocks to have loved.

Worthy she was to move both gods and men,
But neither was I man nor lived then.
Can deaf ears take delight when Phaemius sings?
Or Thamyris in curious painted things?
What sweet thought is there but I had the same?
And one gave place still as another came.
Yet, notwithstanding, like one dead it lay,
Drooping more than a rose pulled yesterday.
Now, when he should not yet, he bolts upright,
And craves his task, and seeks to be at fight.
Lie down with shame, and see thou stir no more,
Seeing thou would'st deceive me as before.
Then cozenest me: by thee surprised am I,
And bide sore loss with endless infamy.
Nay more, the wench did not disdain a whit
To take it in her hand and play with it.
But when she saw it would by no means stand,
But still drooped down, regarding not her hand,
"Why mock'st thou me," she cried, "or being ill,
Why bade thee lie down here against thy will?
Either thou art witched with blood of frogs new dead,
Or jaded cam'st thou from some other's bed."
With that, her loose gown on, from me she cast her,
In skipping out her naked feet much graced her.
And lest her maid should know of this disgrace,
To cover it, spilt water on the place.

A Selection from The Kama Sutra

[by Vatsyayana]

———•———

[However poorly this famous Indian work has been
translated from the Sanskrit and bungled in reprinting, its
original meaning remains clear. The author, who is believed to have lived between the first and sixth centuries
A.D., wrote this at the close of his work:

"This work is not to be used merely as an instrument
for satisfying our desires. A person acquainted with the true
principles of this science (of love), who preserves his Dharma
(virtue or religious merit), his Artha (worldly wealth)
and his Kama (pleasure or sensual gratification), and who
has regard to the customs of the people, is sure to obtain
the mastery over his senses. In short, an intelligent and
knowing person, attending to Dharma and Artha and also
to Kama, without becoming the slave of his passions, will
obtain success in everything that he may do."

The *Kama Sutra* was reprinted in 1883 and dedicated
"to that small portion of the British public which takes
enlightened interest in studying the manners and customs
of the olden east." A selection from another Indian work
of a similar genre, *The Ananga-Ranga,* by Kalyana Mall,
follows this excerpt.]

ABOUT WOMEN ACTING THE PART OF A MAN; AND OF THE WORK OF THE MAN

When a woman sees that her lover is fatigued by constant congress, without having his desire satisfied, she should, with his permission, lay him down upon his back, and give him assistance by acting his part. She may also do this to satisfy the curiosity of her lover, or her own desire of novelty.

There are two ways of doing this, the first is when during congress she turns around, and gets on top of her lover, in such a manner as to continue the congress without obstructing the pleasure of it; and the other is when she acts the man's part from the beginning. At such a time, with flowers in her hair hanging loose, and her smiles broken by hard breathings, she should press upon her lover's bosom with her own breasts, and lowering her head frequently, should do in return the same actions which he used to do before, returning his blows and chaffing him, should say, "I was laid down by you, and fatigued by hard congress, I shall now therefore lay you down in return." She should then again manifest her own bashfulness, her fatigue, and her desire of stopping the congress. In this she should do the work of a man, which we shall presently relate.

Whatever is done by a man for giving pleasure to a woman is called the work of a man, and is as follows:—

While the woman is lying on his bed, and is as it were abstracted by his conversation, he should loosen the knot of her undergarments, and when she begins to dispute with him, he should overwhelm her with kisses. Then when his lingam is erect he should touch her with his hands in various places, and gently manipulate various parts of the body. If the woman is bashful, and it is the first time that they have come together, the man should place his hands between her thighs, which she would probably keep close together, and if she is a very young girl, he should first get his hands upon her breasts, which she would probably cover with her own hands, and under her armpits and on her neck. If however she is a seasoned woman, he should do whatever is agreeable either to him or to her, and whatever is fitting for the occasion. After this he should take hold of her hair, and hold her chin in his fingers for the purpose of kissing her. On this, if she is a young girl, she will become bashful and close her eyes. Anyhow he should gather from the action of the woman what things would be pleasing to her during congress.

Here a sage says that while a man is doing to the woman what he likes best during congress, he should always make a point of pressing those parts of her body on which she turns her eyes.

The signs of the enjoyment and satisfaction of the woman are as follows: her body relaxes, she closes her eyes, she put aside all bashfulness, and shows increased willingness to unite the two organs as closely together as possible. On the other hand, the signs of her want of enjoyment and of failing to be satisfied are as follows: she shakes her head, she does not let the man get up, feels dejected, bites the man, kicks him, and continues to go on moving after the man has finished. In such cases the man should rub the yoni of the woman with his hand and fingers (as the elephant rubs anything with his trunk) before engaging in congress, until it is softened, and after that is done he should proceed to put his lingam into her.

The acts to be done by the man are:

Moving forward
Friction or churning
Piercing
Rubbing
Pressing
Giving a blow
The blow of a boar
The blow of a bull
The sporting of a sparrow.

(1) When the organs are brought together properly and directly it is called "moving the organ forward."

(2) When the lingam is held with one hand, and turned all round in the yoni, it is called "churning."

(3) When the yoni is lowered, and the upper part of it is struck with the lingam, it is called "piercing."

(4) When the same thing is done on the lower part of the yoni, it is called "rubbing."

(5) When the yoni is pressed by the lingam for a long time, it is called "pressing."

(6) When the lingam is removed some distance from the yoni, and then forcibly strikes it, it is called "giving a blow."

(7) When only one part of the yoni is rubbed with the lingam, is it called the "blow of a boar."

(8) When both sides of the yoni are rubbed in this way, it is called the "blow of a bull."

(9) When the lingam is in the yoni, and moved up and down frequently, and without being taken out, it is called the "sporting of a sparrow." This takes place at the end of the congress.

When the woman acts the part of a man, she has the

following things to do in addition to the nine given above, viz.

The pair of tongs
The top
The swing.

(1) When the woman holds the lingam in her yoni, draws it in, presses it, and keeps it thus in her for a long time, it is called the "pair of tongs."

(2) When, while engaged in congress, she turns like a wheel, it is called the "top." This is learnt by practise only.

(3) When, on such an occasion, the man lifts up the middle part of the body, and the woman turns round her middle part, it is called the "swing."

When the woman is tired, she should place her forehead on that of her lover, and should thus take rest without disturbing the union of the organs, and when the woman has rested herself she should turn round and begin the congress again.

There are also some verses on the subject as follows:

"Though a woman is reserved, and keeps her feelings concealed, yet when she gets on top of a man, she then shows all her love and desire. A man should gather from the actions of the woman of what disposition she is, and in what way she likes to be enjoyed. A woman during her monthly courses, a woman who has lately been confined, and a fat woman, should not be made to act the part of a man."

Treating of External Enjoyments

[From *The Ananga-Ranga* or *The Hindu Art of Love*]

————•••————

By "external enjoyments" are meant the processes which should always precede internal enjoyment or coition. The wise have said that before congress, we must develope the desire of the weaker sex through certain preliminaries, which are many and various; such as the various embraces and kisses; the Nakhadana, or unguiculations; the Dashanas, or morsications; the Kesha-grahanas, or manipulating the hair, and other amorous blandishments. These affect the senses and divert the mind from coyness and coldness. After which tricks and toyings, the lover will proceed to take possession of the place.

There are eight Alinganas, or modes of embracing, which will here be enumerated and carefully described.

1. Vrikshadhirudha is the embrace which simulates the climbing of a tree, and it is done as follows: When the husband stands up the wife should place one foot upon his foot, and raise the other leg to the height of his thigh, against which she presses it. Then encircling his waist with her arms, even as a man prepares to swarm up a palm-trunk, she holds and presses him forcibly, bends her body over his, and kisses him as if sucking the water of life.

2. Tila-Tandula, the embrace which represents the mixture of sesamum-seed with husked rice (Tandul). The

man and woman, standing in front of each other, should fold each other to the bosom by closely encircling the waist. Then taking care to remain still, and by no means to move, they should approach the Linga to the Yoni, both being veiled by the dress, and avoid interrupting the contact for some time.

3. Lalatika, so called because forehead (lalata) touches forehead. In this position great endearment is shown by the close pressure of arms round the waist, both still standing upright, and by the contact of brow, cheek, and eyes, of mouth, breasts, and stomach.

4. Jaghan-alingana, meaning, "hips, loins and thighs." In this embrace the husband sits upon the carpet and the wife upon his thighs, embracing and kissing him with fond affection. In returning her fondling, her Lungaden, or petticoats, are raised, so that her Lungi, or undergarments, may come in contact with his clothes, and her hair is thrown into the dishevelled state symbolizing passion; or the husband, for variety's sake, may sit upon the wife's lap.

5. Viddhaka, when the nipples touch the opposite body. The husband sits still, closing his eyes, and the wife, placing herself close to him, should pass her right arm over his shoulder and apply her bosom to his, pressing him forcibly, whilst he returns her embrace with equal warmth.

6. Urupagudha, so called from the use of the thighs. In this embrace both stand up, passing their arms round each other, and the husband places his wife's legs between his own so that the inside of his thighs may come in contact with the outside of hers. As in all cases, kissing must be kept up from time to time. This is a process peculiar to those who are greatly enamoured of each other.

7. Dughdanir-alingana, or the "milk and water em-

brace," also called Kshiranira, with the same signification. In this mode the husband lies upon the bed, resting on one side, right or left; the wife throws herself down near him with her face to his, and closely embraces him, the members and limbs of both touching, and entangled, as it were, with the corresponding parts of the other. And thus they should remain until desire is thoroughly aroused in both.

8. Vallari-vreshtità, or "embracing as the creeper twines about the tree," is performed as follows: Whilst both are standing upright, the wife clings to her husband's waist, and passes her leg around his thigh, kissing him repeatedly and softly until he draws in his breath like one suffering from the cold. In fact, she must endeavour to imitate the vine enfolding the tree which supports it.

Here end the embracements; they should be closely studied, followed up by proper intelligence of the various modes of kisses, which must accompany and conclude the Alinganas. And understand at once that there are seven places highly proper for osculation, in fact, where all the world kisses. These are—First, the lower lip. Second, both the eyes. Third, both the cheeks. Fourth, the head. Fifth, the mouth. Sixth, both breasts; and seventh, the shoulders. It is true that the people of certain countries have other places, which they think proper to kiss: for instance, the voluptuaries of Sata-desha have adopted the following formula:

from Arm-pit

to Navel

to Yoni

But this is far from being customary with the men of our country or of the world in general.

Furthermore, there are ten different kinds of kisses, each

of which has its own and proper name, and these will be described in due order.

1. Milita-kissing, which means "mishrita," mixing or reconciling. If the wife be angry, no matter however little, she will not kiss the face of her husband; the latter then should forcibly fix his lips upon hers and keep both mouths united till her ill-temper passes away.

2. Sphurita-kissing, which is connected with twitching and vellication. The wife should approach her mouth to that of her husband, who then kisses her lower lip, whilst she draws it away, jerking, as it were, without any return of osculation.

3. Ghatika, or neck-nape kissing, a term frequently used by the poets. This is done by the wife, who, excited with passion, covers her husband's eyes with her hands, and closing her own eyes, thrusts her tongue into his mouth, moving it to and fro with a motion so pleasant and slow that it at once suggests another and a higher form of enjoyment.

4. Tiryak, or oblique kissing. In this form the husband, standing behind or at the side of his wife, places his hand beneath her chin, catches hold of it and raises it, until he has made her face look up to the sky; then he takes her lower lip beneath his teeth, gently biting and chewing it.

5. Uttaroshtha, or "upper-lip kissing." When the wife is full of desire, she should take her husband's lower lip between her teeth, chewing and biting it gently; whilst he does the same to her upper lip. In this way both excite themselves to the height of passion.

6. Pindita, or "lump-kissing." The wife takes hold of her husband's lips with her fingers, passes her tongue over them and bites them.

7. Samputa, or "casket-kissing." In this form the hus-

band kisses the inside mouth of his wife, whilst she does the same to him.

8. Hanuvatra-kissing. In this mode the kiss should not be given at once, but begin with moving the lips towards one another in an irritating way, with freaks, pranks, and frolics. After toying together for some time, the mouths should be advanced, and the kiss exchanged.

9. Pratibodha, or "awakening kiss." When the husband, who has been absent for some time, returns home and finds his wife sleeping upon the carpet in a solitary bedroom, he fixes his lips upon hers, gradually increasing the pressure until such time as she awakes. This is by far the most agreeable form of osculation, and it leaves the most pleasant of memories.

10. Samaushtha-kissing. This is done by the wife taking the mouth and lips of the husband into hers, pressing them with her tongue, and dancing about him as she does so.

The Metamorphoses of Venus

[from *Manual of Classical Erotology*
by Friedrich Karl Forberg]

———•———

[In this work of searching scholarship, Friederick Karl
Forberg, a German philologist and collaborator with the
philosopher Fichte, combed the literary sources of classical
antiquity to learn in detail the methods man used in satisfying the sexual instinct. In the chapter below entitled
"On Copulation," which might be called a precursor of
the modern marriage manual, he drew heavily upon *The
Dialogues of Aloysia Sigaea,* a book vividly written in
Spanish by a sixteenth-century girl prodigy who was
versed in Latin, Greek, Hebrew, Syriac and Arabic; later
it was adapted by Nicolas Chorier, a French scholar of law
and letters. The remainder of Forberg's carefully docu-
mented book deals with every variety of sexual outlet,
other than heterosexual intercourse, that was known to
Greco-Roman times.]

On Copulation

And first of all let us consider what is accomplished by
means of the mentula introduced into the vulva. This is,
properly speaking, to effect copulation; but there are vari-

ous ways of doing it. As a matter of fact copulation can be effected: the man face downwards with the woman on her back, the man on his back with the woman face down, the man on his back with the woman turning her face towards him, sitting with the woman turning her back to him; the man standing or kneeling with the woman turning her face towards him, standing or kneeling with the woman turning her back to him. Let us examine each of these methods separately.

Coition with the man face down on the woman who lies on her back is the ordinary method, and the most natural.

Aloysia Sigaea says:

"For my own part I like the usual custom and the ordinary method best: the man should lie upon the woman, who is on her back, breast to breast, stomach to stomach, pubis to pubis, piercing her tender cleft with his rigid spear. Indeed what can be imagined sweeter than for the woman to lie extended on her back, bearing the welcome weight of her lover's body, and exciting him to the tender transports of a restless but delicious voluptuousness? What more pleasant than to feast on her lover's face, his kisses, his sighs, and the fire of his wanton eyes? What better than to press the loved one in her arms and so awake new fires of desire, to participate in amorous sensations unblunted by any taint of age or infirmity? What more favorable to the delight and enjoyment of both than such lascivious movements given and received? What more opportune at the instant of dying a voluptuous death than to recover again under the revivifying vigour of burning kisses? He who plies Venus on the reverse side, satisfies but one of his senses, he who does the same face to face satisfies them all" (Dialogue VI).

Ovid, the Master of Loves' Mysteries, invites pretty women to take this posture by preference:

"See you reckon up each of your charms, and take your posture according to your beauty. One and the same mode does not become every woman. You are especially attractive of face; then lie on your back" (*Art of Love*, III, 771–773).

This posture is by no means limited to one mode. The woman lying on her back, the rider may clasp her between his legs, or she may receive him between hers. Yet another position may be adopted, according as the woman lie back with legs stretched wide apart or with the knees raised.

It is this position—lying on her back with legs wide apart—that Caviceo asks Olympia to assume for making love:

"I do not wish you," he says, "to work your buttocks, or to respond with corresponding movements to my efforts. Neither do I wish you to lift your legs up, whether both at once, or one after the other, when I have mounted you. What I do wish you to do is this: First stretch your thighs as far apart, open them as wide as a woman well can. Offer your vulva to the member which is going to pierce it, and without altering this position, let *me* complete the work. . . . Count my thrusts one by one, and see you make no mistake in the total" (Aloysia Sigaea, Dialogue V).

The other position, in which the woman is lying with her knees raised, is the one which Callias makes Tullia take:

"After I am lying upon your dear body," he says, "press me fast in your arms, and hold me thus embraced. Draw your legs back as far as you can, so that your pretty feet touch your buttocks, smooth as marble" (Aloysia Sigaea, Dialogue VI).

If you would enter the woman lying on her back with her legs in the air, it may be done in yet another way than Tullia's mode, and one perhaps still more delicious, by placing your mistress so that she rests her legs crossed over the loins of her rider. A representation of this very pleasant posture, which would rouse the numbed tool of a Hippolytus, is to be found in part IV of the "Felicia" mentioned above. There is another similar plate in chap. XXI, not without charm. Doris, in the epigram of Sosipater, vol. I of the *Analecta* of Brunck (p. 584), seems to have made a trial of this figure:

"When I stretched Doris with the rosy buttocks on the bed, I felt immortal in my youthful vigour; for she clipped me round the middle with her strong legs, and unswervingly rode out the long-course of Love."

Doris did not bestride him; the expression, "When I stretched" shows this; she was lying on her back, and with her feet lifted up clasped her rider.

But again the feet of the woman lying on her back may also be held up by others. In this way Aloysio enjoyed Tullia with the help of Fabrizio, in the VI Dialogue of Aloysia Sigaea, where Tullia expresses herself as follows:

"Aloysio and Fabrizio come running towards me. Lift up your legs, says Aloysio to me, threatening me with his cutlass. I lifted them up. Then down he lies on my bosom, and plunges his cutlass in my ever open wound. Fabrizio raised my two legs in the air, and slipping a hand under each of my hams, moves my loins for me without any trouble on my part. What a singular and pleasant mode of making you move! I declared I was on fire, but before I could end my sentence, the overflowing foam of Venus quenched the fire."

So too was it with feet in air, whether of her own accord or seconded by another, that Leda gave herself, with her husband's consent, to the doctors who had been called in, as Martial describes the scene:

"To her old spouse Leda had declared herself to be hysterical, and complains she must needs be f...cked; yet with tears and groans avers she will not buy health at such a price, and swears she had rather die. The husband beseeches her to live, not to die in her youth and beauty; and permits others to do what he cannot effect himself. Straightway the doctors arrive, the matrons retire; and up go the wife's legs in air; oh! medicine grave and stern!" (XI, 72.)

Face downwards to her the man may do the woman's business, while she is half reclining, either obliquely in bed, or on a chair, or lying sideways.

The latter position is recommended by Ovid to the woman with rounded thighs and faultless figure:

"She that has young rounded thigh and flawless bosom, should ever lie reclined sideways on the couch" (*Art of Love*, II, v, 781, 782).

Copulation face to face with the woman sitting obliquely is described by Aloysia Sigaea with her usual elegance and vivacity:

"Caviceo came on, blithe and joyous (it is Olympia speaking). He despoils me of my chemise, and his libertine hand touches my parts. He tells me to sit down again as I was seated before, and places a chair under either foot in a way that my legs were lifted high in air, and the gate of my garden was wide open to the assaults I was expecting. He then slides his right hand under my buttocks and draws me a little closer to him. With his left he supported the weight of his spear. Then he laid himself down on me ... put his battering-ram to my gate, inserted the head of his member into the outermost fissure, opening the lips of it with his fingers. But there he stopped, and for awhile made no further attack. 'Olympia, sweetest,' he says, 'clasp me tightly, raise your right thigh and rest it on my side.' 'I do not know what you want,' I said. Hearing this he lifted my thigh with his own hand, and guided it round his loin, as he wished; finally he forced his arrow into the target of Venus. In the beginning he pushes in with gentle blows, then quicker, and at last with such force I could not doubt that I was in great danger. His member was hard as horn, and he forced it in so cruelly, that I cried out, 'You will tear me to pieces.' He stopped a moment from his work. 'I implore you to be quiet, my dear,' he said, 'it can only be done this way; endure it without flinching.' Again his hand slid under my buttocks, drawing me nearer, for I had made a feint to draw back, and without more delay plied me with such fast and furious blows that I was near fainting away. With a violent effort he forced his spear right in, and the point fixed itself in the depths of the wound. I cry out . . . Caviceo spurted out his venerean exudation, and I felt irrigated by a burning rain. . . . Just as Caviceo slackened, I experienced a sort of voluptuous itch as though I were making water; involuntarily I draw my buttocks back a little, and in an instant I felt with supreme pleasure something flowing from me which tickled me deliciously. My eyes failed me, my breath came thick, my face was on fire, and I felt my whole body melting. "Ah! ah! ah! my Caviceo, I shall faint away," I cried; "hold my soul—it is escaping from my body" (Dialogue V).

Finally the conjunction with the woman lying on her side, particularly on her right side, is deemed by Ovid the most simple, calling for the least effort:

"A thousand modes of Love are there; the simplest and least laborious of all is when the woman lies reclined on her right side" (*Art of Love,* III, 787, 88).

Above all this position is the most convenient for tall women:

"Let her press the bed with her knees, with the neck slightly bowed, she whose chief beauty is her long, shapely flank" (*Art of Love,* III, v. 779, 80).

It seems that the Phyllis of Martial allowed herself to be done in that way:

"Two arrived in the morning, who wanted to lie with Phyllis, and each was fain to be first to hold her naked body in his arms; Phyllis promised to satisfy them both together, and she did it; one lifted her leg, the other her tunic" (X, 81).

She was lying on her side; the f... lifted her leg; the pederast her tunic.

We now come to the manner in which the man lying on his back has connection with the woman face downwards. The parts are interchanged; the woman plays the rider and the man the horse. This figure was called the horse of Hector.

Martial says:

"Behind the doors the Phrygian slaves would be masturbating, every time Andromache mounted her Hector horse fashion" (XI, 105).

Ovid, however, with much sagacity denies that this posture could have pleased Andromache; her figure was too tall, for this to have been agreeable or even possible for her. It is for little women, that it is pleasant to be thus placed:

"A little woman may very well get astride on her horse;

but tall and majestic as she was, the Theban bride never mounted the Hectorean horse" (*Art of Love*, III, v. 777, 778).

It is no business of ours to decide the question.

At any rate Sempronia takes this posture with Crisogono.

"He could wait no longer: 'Are you undressed,' says Crisogono. 'Now, my Sempronia, take the position which gives me so much pleasure, you know which.' He stretches himself down on his back, she gets upon him astride, with her face towards him, and with her own hand guides his burning arrow between her thighs" (Aloysia Sigaea, Dial. VII).

This is the same attitude which in Horace is imposed by the slave upon the little harlot, who:

". . . naked in the light of the lantern, plied with wanton wiles and moving buttocks the horse beneath her" (Sat. II. vii, v. 50).

As to the matron spoken of v. 64 of the same satire as "never having sinned above," no doubt this posture did not suit her. Women have not all the same taste.

Evidently, it was as little to the taste of the girl whom Xanthias in Aristophanes' *Wasps* (v. 499) asked to ride him; for she asks him indignantly, and playing on the double meaning of the word (Hippias and ——, a horse), if he was for re-establishing Hippias' tyranny: "Irritated she asked me if I wanted to revive the tyranny of Hippias."

Again in his *Lysistrata* (v. 678) this master of wanton wit points to the same thing, declaring the female sex to be very good at riding and fond of driving: "Woman loves to get on horseback and to stick there."

Aristophanes mocks similarly those of whom he says, in verse 60 of the same play, that "They are aboard their

barks." "They are mounted on their chargers." For ——
signifies both a ship and a horse. Plango in Asclepiades,
Brunck's *Analecta*, vol. 1, 217, affects the same figure.

"When she in horsemanship vanquished the ardent
Philaenis, whilst her Hesperian coursers foamed under her
reins."

Yet more expert in this kind of amorous riding than
Philaenis herself, this ardent votary of pleasure thanks
Venus in this epigram, that she has been able so to exhaust
certain Hesperian gallants, whom she had mounted, that
they had left her with wanton members all drooping, and
feeling no desire left in them. To bestride men was also
the favourite pastime of Lysidice, who was never tired in
the service of Venus, of whom the following epigram of
Asclepiades treats:

"Many a horse has she ridden beneath her, yet never
galled her thigh with all her nimble movements."

Courtesans consecrated to Venus a whip, a bit, a spur,
in order to signify that with their clients they liked best
to pose themselves in that way, and that they preferred
riding themselves to being ridden—nothing more.

It is the same when in Apuleius, Fotis satiated her Lu-
cius with the pleasures of the undulating Venus:

"Saying this she leaped upon the couch and, seated
upon me backwards, plying her hips, vibrating her lithe
spine lasciviously, she satiated me with the delights of the
undulating Venus, till both of us exhausted, powerless and
with useless limbs, sunk down, exhaling our souls in mutual embraces" (*Metamorph.*, II, ch. II).

The next figure—the man lying supine and the woman
turning her back to him, is executed by Rangoni with
Ottavia, under the direction of Tullia:

RANGONI: Look how stiff I stand! But I want to try the bliss in a new way.

TULLIA: In a new way? No! I swear by my wanton soul you shall not. You shall not take a new way.

RANGONI: It was a slip of the tongue; I meant to say a new posture.

TULLIA: And what sort of one? I have an idea . . . what they call the horse of Hector. Lie down on your back, Rangoni; let your puissant spear stand firm to the enemy, who is to be pierced. Well done!

OTTAVIA: What must I do, Tullia?

TULLIA: Clip Rangoni between your thighs, mounting him astraddle. His cutlass as he lies should meet your sheath poised over it. Why! you've taken the position admirably. Excellent!

RANGONI: Oh! what a back, worthy of Venus! Oh! the ivory sides! Oh! the inviting buttocks!

TULLIA: No naughty words! He who praises the buttocks, slanders the vulva! You know better, Ottavia! Her greedy vulva has swallowed your bristling member whole, Rangoni.

OTTAVIA: Quick, Rangoni, it is coming! . . . quick, quick, help me!

RANGONI: I am coming, Ottavia—I am come! Are you? —Are you, darling!

TULLIA: How now? Are you so quickly done up, you two? (Aloysia Sigaea, Dial. VI.)

The pygiacic mysteries, to which Eumolpus in Petronius (Satires, ch. CXL) invites a young girl, refer to the posture practiced by the man lying on his back, with the woman upon him, her back turned towards him.

"Eumolpus did not hesitate to invite the young girl to

the pygiacic mysteries, but begged of her to seat herself upon the goodness known to her (that being himself, to whose goodness the mother had recommended her daughter), and ordered Corax to get on his stomach under the bed on which he was, so that with his hands pressed against the floor, he might assist with his movements those of his master. Corax obeyed, beginning with slow undulations responding to those of the young girl. When the crisis was approaching, Eumolpus exhorted Corax with a loud voice to quicken up his movements. Thus placed between his servant and his mistress, the old man took his pleasure as in a swing."

Would it be surprising, if in these posterior mysteries, Eumolpus' member had perchance gone wrong, and taken by mistake one orifice for the other?

You will find this figure represented in a copper-plate engraving in the very elegant book of d'Hancarville, *Monuments du culte secret des dames romaines,* ch. XXV, and you will be glad to know the note with which the learned annotator accompanies the same.

"This attitude is to the taste of many men, and even the ladies find an increase of pleasure in practising it. It is supposed, that Priapus penetrates farther in, and that the fair one by her movements procures for herself a more voluptuous delight, and a more abundant libation."

Is it possible for the man, conveniently, to manage the business while turning his back to the woman lying on her back? Experts must decide. Aloysia Sigaea says with good common sense:

"There are many postures it is impossible to execute, even supposing the joints and loins of the candidates for the sacred joys of Venus more flexible than can be believed. By dint of pondering and reflection more ideas occur to the fancy than it is practicable to realize: Nothing is inconceivable to the longings of an unbridled will; nothing difficult to a furious and unregulated imagination. Love will find out a way; and an ardent fancy levels mountains. Only the body is unable to comply with everything the mind, good or bad, suggests."

In another work of d'Hancarville's, *Monuments de la vie privée des douze Césars*, plate XXVII, you find represented men seated and copulating with women, who are facing them; plate XV, in the same book, presents to your curiosity a man sitting and working a woman, who turns her back on him. Augustus is seated: he is attacking backwards, with true imperial audacity, Terentia, the wife of Maecenas, after drawing her onto his lap; Maecenas is present, asleep—asleep of course only for the Emperor. You may see a similar posture in the *Contes et Nouvelles en vers* by Jean de la Fontaine: it is on the plate appended to the tale, called "Le Tableau," p. 223, vol. II, Amsterdam, 1762.

Nothing is more frequent than conjunction whilst standing, the woman with her back to the man; it is indeed very easy to do it that way in any place, as you have only to lift up the fair one's petticoats, and out with your weapon; it is, therefore, the best manner for those who have to make instantaneous use of an opportunity, when it is important to be sharp about it, as may happen, when you take your pleasure in secret. Thus Priapus complains of the wives and daughters of his neighbours, who came incessantly to him burning with ticklish desires.

"Cut off my genital member, which every night and all night long my neighbours' wives and daughters, for ever and for ever in heat, more wanton than sparrows in springtide, tire to death—or I shall burst!" (Priapeia, XXV.)

I remember a medical man of our time, one of the most celebrated professors (I had nearly uttered his name), who to emphasize this, called his daughter, and pointing to the blushing girl, while his hearers could not help smiling, said: This girl I fabricated standing. A representation of this position is to be found in the *Monuments de la vie privée des douze Césars,* pl. XLVI, and another in the *Monuments du culte secret des dames romaines,* pl. XIII. But further, a man may join himself to a woman standing face to face by supporting her in such a way that her whole body is lifted up, her thighs resting on the man's hips, or else by lifting up the lower part of her body, whilst the upper part is resting on a couch. Will you feast your eyes with a representation of this not ungraceful position? If so you will not omit to look at plate XXIV of the *Monuments du culte secret des dames romaines,* and plate XL of the *Monuments de la vie privée des douze Césars;* Ovid, if I am not mistaken, had his eyes on one or the other of these figures:

"Milanion was supporting Atalanta's legs on his shoulders; if they are fine legs this is how they should be held" (*Art of Love,* III, vv. 775, 776). The former of these modes is no doubt that described by Aloysia Sigaea, Past Mistress of these naughtinesses, and with a vivacity, a grace, and elegance that leaves nothing to be desired:

"La Tour came forward instantly . . . I had thrown myself on the foot of the bed" (Tullia is speaking) . . . "I was naked; his member was erect. Without more ado he grasps in either hand one of my breasts, and brandishing his hard and inflamed lance between my thighs, exclaims, 'Look, Madam, how this weapon is darting at you, not to kill you, but to give you the greatest possible pleasure. Pray, guide this blind applicant into the dark recess,

so that it may not miss its destination; I will not remove
my hands from where they are, I would not deprive them
of the bliss they enjoy.' I do as he wishes, I introduce myself the flaming dart into the burning centre; he feels it,
drives in, pushes home. . . . After one or two strokes I felt
myself melting away with incredible titillation, and my
knees all but gave way: 'Stop,' I cried, 'stop my soul, it is
escaping!' 'I know,' he replied, laughing, 'from where. No
doubt your soul wants to escape through this lower orifice, of which I have possession; but I keep it well stop-
pered.' Whilst speaking he endeavoured, by holding his
breath, still further to increase the already enormous size
of his swollen member. 'I am going to thrust back your
escaping soul,' he added, poking me more and more violently. His sword pierced yet deeper into the quick. Re-
doubling his delicious blows, he filled me with transports
of pleasure—working so forcefully that, albeit he could
not get his whole body into me, he impregnated me with
all his passion, all his lascivious desires, his very thoughts,
his whole delirious soul by his voluptuous embraces. At
last feeling the approach of the ecstasy and the boiling
over of the liquid, he slips his hands under my buttocks,
and lifts me up bodily. I do my part; I twine my arms
closely round his form, my thighs and legs being at the
same time intertwisted and entangled with his, so that I
found myself suspended on his neck in the air, lifted clean
off the ground; I was thus hanging, as it were, fixed on a
peg. I had not the patience to wait for him, as he was
going on, and again I swooned with pleasure. In the most
violent raptures I could not help crying out 'I feel all . . .
I feel all the delights of Juno lying with Jupiter. I am in
heaven.' At this moment, La Tour, pushed by Venus and

Cupido to the acme of voluptuousness, poured a plenteous flood of his well into the genial hold, burning like fire. The creeper does not cling more closely round the walnut tree than I hold fast to La Tour with my arms and legs" (Dial. VI).

As to the last manner by means of which copulation may be achieved, the man standing with the woman half lifted up, Conrad practices it with slight modifications.

(Tullia speaking) "He opened my thighs—I do not dislike Conrad, though I am not particularly partial to him. I neither consented, nor refused. As to him, he fancied a novel posture, and not at all a bad one. I was lying on my back; he raised my right thigh on his shoulder, and in this position he transfixed me, while I was awaiting the event, without greatly desiring it. He had at the same time extended my left thigh along his right thigh. His tool plunged into the root, he began to push and poke, quicker and quicker. What need to say more? Picture the conclusion for yourself" (Dial. VI).

Last of all, a man can get into a woman turning her back to him after the manner of the quadrupeds, who can have no connection with their females otherwise than by mounting upon them from behind. Some authorities have held that a woman conceives easier while on all fours. Lucretius says:

". . . Women are said to conceive more readily when down after the manner of beasts, as the organs can absorb the seed best so, when the bosom is depressed and the loins lifted" (*Of the Nature of Things,* IV, vv. 1259–1262).

Also Aloysia Sigaea:

"Some people pretend that the fashion to make love indicated by Nature is that one where the woman offers herself for copulation after the manner of the animals, bent down with the hips raised; the virile ploughshare penetrates thus more conveniently into the female furrow, and the seminal flow waters the field of love. . . . The doctors, however, are against this posture; they say it is incompatible with the conformation of the parts destined for generation" (Dial. VI).

However this may be, it happens frequently that women cannot be managed in any other way. Given an obese man and a woman likewise obese or with child, how are they to do the thing otherwise? This is the reason why, so they say, Augustus having married Livia Drusilla, divorced wife of Tiberius Nero and already six months gone in pregnancy, had connection with her after the manner of animals. Plate VII of the *Monuments de la vie privée des douze Césars* will give you an idea of the posture assumed by both of them. But why should we not give you the annotations whereby the learned editor has elucidated the plate? Here they are:

"This Drusilla was the famous Livia, the wife of Tiberius Nero, who had been one of Anthony's friends. Augustus fell violently in love with her, and Tiberius gave her up to him, although she was at the time six months with child. A good many jokes were made about the eagerness of the Emperor, and one day, while they were all at table, and Livia was reclining by Augustus, one of those naked children, whom matrons used to educate for their pleasures, going up to Livia said: 'What are you doing here? yonder is your husband,' pointing to Nero, 'there he is.' Soon afterwards Livia was confined, and the Romans said openly, that lucky people get children three months after being married, which passed into a proverb.

One historian says that Augustus was obliged to caress his wife 'after the manner of beasts' on account of her pregnancy, and it was to this luxurious attitude that the cameo of Apollonius, the celebrated gem-cutter of the time of Augustus, makes allusion. True that the state in which Livia was may have made this posture necessary: but it seems that it was at all times to the taste of the Ancients, either because they considered this attitude favourable for procreation, as Lucretius maintains, or because they found it to be a refinement of voluptuousness. The most extraordinary and least natural postures have always appeared to rakes as enhancing the pleasure of the conjunction. But it must be admitted that imagination still outruns actual possibilities."

A singular reason for the necessity of encountering a woman backwards is given by Aloysia Sigaea, with her usual sagacity:

"For pleasure, one likes a vulva which is not placed too far back, so as to be entirely hidden by the thighs; it should not be more than nine or ten inches from the navel. With the greater number of girls the pubis goes so far down, that it may easily be taken as the other way of pleasure. With such coition is difficult. Theodora Aspilqueta could not be deflowered, till she placed herself prone on her stomach, with her knees drawn up to her sides. Vainly had her husband tried to manage her, while lying on her back, he only lost his oil" (Dial. VII).

Ovid recommends this way with women who begin to be wrinkled:

"Likewise you, whose stomach Lucina has marked with wrinkles, mount from behind, like the flying Parthian with his steed" (*Art of Love*, III, v. 785, 786).

The same advice also seems to be given by him a little before:
"Let them be seen from behind whose backs are sightly"
(v. 774).

But besides necessity, it is a fact that women are worked in this way out of mere caprice, variety offering the greatest pleasure. It is simply for this reason that Tullia suffers Fabrizio to do her that way, in Aloysia Sigaea:

"As Aloysio got up," (Tullia speaks) "Fabrizio makes ready for another attack. His member is swollen up, red and threatening. 'I beg of you, Madam,' he says, 'turn over on your face.' I did as he wished. When he saw my buttocks, whiter than ivory and snow, 'How beautiful you are!' he cried. 'But raise yourself on your knees and bend your head down.' I bow my head and bosom, and lift my buttocks. He thrust his swift-moving and fiery dart to the bottom of my vulva, and took one of my nipples in either hand. Then he began to work in and out, and soon sent a sweet rivulet into the cavity of Venus. I also felt unspeakable delight, and had nearly fainted with lust. A surprising quantity of seed secreted by Fabrizio's loins filled and delighted me; a similar flow of my own exhausted my forces. In that single assault I lost more vigour than in the three preceding ones" (Dial. VI).

This copulation from the back is practicable in another very pleasant fashion, an excellent reproduction of which can be seen in the *Monument du culte secret des dames romaines,* plate XXVIII. A woman is represented with her hands placed on the ground, while the lower part of the body is lifted up and suspended by cords; she is turning her back to the man who stands. This seems to be much the same position as was taken up by the wife of the artisan Apuleius speaks of in his *Metamorphoses* (book IX), whom "bending over her, the lover planed with his adze, while she leant forward over a cask." An engraving showing this ingenious attitude is appended to the story of *The Tub* in the *Contes et Nouvelles en vers* of Jean de la Fontaine, vol. II, p. 215.

Book of Exposition

[Authorship Disputed]

———•———

The Mother's Marriage Advice

[from the Arabic]

It is related—and Allah is All-knowing, All-wise—that a mother was about to marry her daughter, a girl famous amongst all the tribes of the Arabs for her surpassing beauty—her face was oval-shaped, her form upright and perfect; her buttocks swung from side to side, as she walked, like the balancing of a poplar-tree trembling in the evening-breeze; her eyes were coal-black, and the light of a virgin's desire shone from beneath her half-closed lids; firm as a rock on a billowy sea-shore her breasts stood out bold and prominent above her navel—may Allah have mercy on her, the fairest of his creatures, fashioned in the likeness of the peerless Houris, reserved for true Believers —and underneath it, down below, nestling between two ivory-columned thighs, hid Something wonderful and of astonishing stoutness, puffed-up proudly, looking out from behind her flowing skirts like the head of a patient calf awaiting pasturage—And the mother spake to her daughter counselling her this counsel—quoth she to her:

"O daughter mine! ward off from thyself all affliction of misfortune and hearken to my saying, and in thus wise act with the men who shall lie with thee and love thee. For I counsel thee, O my dear Daughter! a counsel; in thy heart therefore treasure it up, and to remember it well be careful, and, on every night that thou liest with man, of its diligent practice be wareful. Surpassing shall it make thee above all other women of similar rank and station, and spread abroad 'mong men, like a sweet perfume, the glory of thy reputation."

Thereupon, the girl exclaimed to her mother, her curiosity roused to the highest pitch:

"By God! out and tell me what this counsel is that thou speakest of."

Said she then to her: "O daughter mine, listen to what I say. When thy husband shall draw near to thee, and be stretched out along by thy side, then move with gracefulness, changing and turning about with decency and becomingness, and to him manifest only innocent unguardedness, and fatigue-weariness, and sweet love-sighing of abandoned languidness. So will his heart be inclined towards thee and his love flame forth. When thou seest this, increase thy playfulness with him before his lance doth enter thee or give over its upswelling, until strongswollen, stiff and warm 'tween him and thee breaks forth in might the fierceness of the storm." Then she recited, saying:

O Daughter mine! thy Wooers long to leave thee never durst
So that thou manifest them nor repulsion and disgust,
And when thy lover comes to thee fired mad with passion's thirst,
Soften him thy heart for fear he may depart or tire to thrust;

Discover him thy bosom and twin high-swelling breasts,
Until thy Bower of bliss be seen, and thy buttocks are
   undrest,
Then sigh thy full and give forth cries of love-joyed
   tenderness
So shall men seek no other fire than that of thy recess;
And when they hear the happy cries of thy love-gentleness
Upon Allah will they call that she who bore thee may be
   blessed.

And the mother counselled her daughter further:
"When thy lord shall have come between thy legs then
prevent him not from passing through the rosy portals of
thy vulva, and redouble for his delight thy amorous groaning and happy crying and soft caressing. For know, my
Dear! that man's dormant prizzle puts on tougher gristle,
and starts up excitedly at woman's half-refusal. So show
him thy teeth and make pretence to bite him, then tighten
thy close-hold upon him, and wind arms and legs more
securely about him, thus wilt thou find that his yard will
rise stronger and stronger against thee; and 'tis here thou
must exclaim, 'Oh dear! Oh dear! what is this!,' doing
with him in the same wise that he shall do with thee, and
failing not to let him see thy gentle love-panting and
delicious heaving and lost condition, whilst with regular
rub and repetition thou workest underneath him the
come-and-go swift motion of soft-limbed oscillation. Thou
must not omit either to lift up towards him thy middle
portion, and direct his hand upon thy slit, and when thou
feelest approach the time of enjoyment and thou per-
ceivest that he is played out, then seize hold of him afresh
with both thy hands, and press him close against thee, and,

giving him a fiery kiss, lay hold upon his weapon and stroke and slip it up and down, then wipe it, and stir up anew mutual passion-desire, lest his yard fall asleep or diminish its fire, and thus shall pleasure's storm wage high and yet higher."

How the Pretty Maid of Portillon Convinced Her Judge

by Honoré de Balzac

The maid of Portillon, who became, as every one knows, La Tascherette, was, before she became a dyer, a laundress at the said place of Portillon, from where she took her name. If any there be who do not know Tours, it may be as well to state that Portillon is down the Loire, on the same side as St. Cyr, about as far from the bridge which leads to the Cathedral of Tours as the said bridge is distant from Marmoutier, since the bridge is in the center of the embankment between Portillon and Marmoutier. Do you thoroughly understand?

Yes? Good! Now the maid had there her washhouse, from which she ran to the Loire with her washing in a second, and took the ferry-boat to get to St. Martin which was on the other side of the river, for she had to deliver the greatest part of her work in Chateauneuf and other places. About Midsummer day, seven years before marrying old Taschereau, she had just reached the right age to be loved. As she was a merry girl she allowed herself to be loved, without making a choice from any of the lads who pursued her with their intentions. Although there

used to come to the bench under her window the son of
Rabelais, who had seven boats on the Loire, Jehan's
eldest, Marchandeau the tailor, and Peccard the ecclesiasti-
cal goldsmith, she made fun of them all because she wished
to be taken to Church before burthening herself with a
man, which proves that she was an honest woman until she
was wheedled out of her virtue. She was one of those girls
who take great care not to be contaminated, but who, if
by chance they get deceived, let things take their course,
thinking that for one stain or fifty a good polishing up is
necessary. These characters demand our indulgence.

A young noble of the court perceived her one day when
she was crossing the water in the glare of the noonday sun,
which lit up her ample charms, and seeing her, asked who
she was. An old man, who was working on the banks, told
him she was called the Pretty Maid of Portillon, a laundress, celebrated for her merry ways and her virtue. This
young man, besides ruffles to starch, had many precious
linen draperies and things; he resolved to give the custom
of his house to this girl, whom he stopped on the road. He
was thanked by her and heartily, because he was the Sire
du Fou, the king's chamberlain. This encounter made her
so joyful that her mouth was full of his name. She talked
about it a great deal to the people of St. Martin, and when
she got back to her washhouse was still full of it, and on
the morrow at her work her tongue went nineteen to the
dozen, and all on the same subject so that as much was
said concerning my Lord du Fou in Portillon as of God
in a sermon; that is, a great deal too much.

"If she works like that in cold water, what will she do in
warm?" said an old washerwoman. "She wants du Fou;
he'll give her du Fou!"

The first time this giddy wench, with her head full of

Monsieur du Fou, had to deliver the linen in his hotel, the chamberlain wished to see her, and was very profuse in praises and compliments concerning her charms, and wound up by telling her that she was not at all silly to be beautiful, and therefore he would give her more than she expected. The deed followed the word, for the moment his people were out of the room, he began to caress the maid, who thinking he was about to take out the money from his purse, dared not look at the purse, but said, like a girl ashamed to take her wages, "It will be for the first time."

"It will be soon," said he.

Some people say that he had great difficulty in forcing her to accept what he offered her, and hardly forced her at all; others that he forced her badly, because she came out, like an army flagging on the route, crying and groaning, and came to the judge. It happened that the judge was out. La Portillone awaited his return in his room, weeping and saying to the servant that she had been robbed, because Monseigneur du Fou had given her nothing but his mischief; whilst a canon of the chapter used to give her large sums for that which M. du Fou wanted for nothing. If she loved a man she would think it wise to do things for him for nothing, because it would be a pleasure to her; but the chamberlain had treated her roughly, and not kindly and gently, as he should have done, and that therefore he owed her the thousand crowns of the canon. The judge came in, saw the wench, and wished to kiss her, but she put herself on guard, and said she had come to make a complaint. The judge replied that certainly she could have the offender hanged if she liked, because he was most anxious to serve her. The injured maiden replied that she did not wish the death of her man, but that he should pay her a thousand gold crowns, because she had been robbed against her will.

"Ha! ha!" said the judge, "what he took was more than that."

"For the thousand crowns I'll cry quits, because I shall be able to live without washing."

"He who has robbed you, is he well off?"

"Oh, yes."

"Then he shall dearly pay for it. Who is it?"

"Monseigneur du Fou."

"Oh, that alters the case," said the judge.

"But justice?" said she.

"I said the case, not the justice of it," replied the judge. "I must know how the affair occurred."

Then the girl related naively how she was arranging the young lord's ruffles in his wardrobe, when he began to play with her skirts, and she turned round, saying—

"Go on with you!"

"You have no case," said the judge, "for by that speech he thought that you gave him leave to go on. Ha! ha!"

Then she declared that she had defended herself, weeping and crying out, and that constitutes an assault.

"A wench's antics to incite him," said the judge.

Finally, La Portillone declared that against her will she had been taken around the waist and thrown, although she kicked and cried and struggled, but that seeing no help at hand, she had lost courage.

"Good! good!" said the judge. "Did you take pleasure in the affair?"

"No," said she, "My anguish can only be paid for with a thousand crowns."

"My dear," said the judge, "I cannot receive your complaint, because I believe that no girl can be thus treated against her will."

"Hi! hi! hi! Ask your servant," said the little laundress, sobbing, "and hear what she'll tell you."

The servant affirmed that there were pleasant assaults and unpleasant ones; that if La Portillone had received neither amusement nor money, either one or the other was due her. This wise counsel threw the judge into a state of great perplexity.

"Jacqueline," said he, "before I sup I'll get to the bottom of this. Now go and fetch my needle and the red thread that I sew the legal paper bags with."

Jacqueline came back with a big needle, pierced with a pretty little hole, and a big red thread, such as the judges use. Then she remained standing to see the question decided, very much disturbed, as was also the complainant at these mysterious preparations.

"My dear," said the judge, "I am going to hold the bodkin, of which the eye is sufficiently large, to put this thread into it without trouble. If you do put it in, I will take up your case, and will make Monseigneur offer you a compromise."

"What's that?" said she. "I will not allow it."

"It is a word used in justice to signify an agreement."

"A compromise is then agreeable with justice?" said La Portillone.

"My dear, this violence has also opened your mind. Are you ready?"

"Yes," said she.

The waggish judge gave the poor nymph fair play, holding the eye steady for her; but when she wished to slip in the thread that she had twisted to make straight, he moved a little, and the thread went on the other side. She suspected the judge's argument, wetted the thread, stretched it, and came back again. The judge moved, twisted about, and wriggled like a bashful maiden; still the cursed thread would not enter. The girl kept trying at the eye, and the judge kept fidgeting. The marriage of the thread could not be consummated, the bodkin remained virgin, and the servant began to laugh, saying to La Portillone that she knew better how to endure than to perform. Then the roguish judge laughed too, and the fair Portillone cried for her golden crowns.

"If you don't keep still," cried she, losing patience; "if you keep moving about I shall never be able to put the thread in."

"Then, my dear, if you had done the same, Monseigneur would have been unsuccessful too. Think, too, how easy is the one affair, and how difficult the other."

The pretty wench, who declared she had been forced, remained thoughtful, and sought to find a means to convince the judge by showing how she had been compelled to yield, since the honor of all poor girls liable to violence was at stake.

"Monseigneur, in order that the bet may be fair, I must do exactly as the young lord did. If I had only had to move I should be moving still, but he went through other performances."

"Let us hear them," replied the judge.

Then La Portillone straightens the thread; and rubs it in the wax of the candle, to make it firm and straight; then she looks towards the eye of the bodkin, held by the judge, slipping always to the right or to the left. Then she began making endearing little speeches, such as, "Ah, the pretty little bodkin! what a pretty mark to aim at! Never did I see such a little jewel! What a pretty little eye! Let me put this little thread into it! Keep still! Come, my love of a judge, judge of my love! Won't the thread go nicely into this iron gate, which makes good use of the thread, for it comes out very much out of order?" Then she burst out laughing, for she was better up in this game than the judge, who laughed too, so saucy and comical and arch was she, pushing the thread backwards and forwards. She kept the poor judge with the case in his hand until seven o'clock, keeping on fidgeting and moving about like a schoolboy let loose; but as La Portillone kept on trying to put the thread in, he could not help it. As, however, his joint was burning, and his wrist was tired, he was obliged to rest himself for a minute on the side of the table; then very dexterously the fair maid of Portillon slipped the thread in, saying—

"That's how the thing occurred."

"But my joint was burning."

"So was mine," said she.

The judge, convinced, told La Portillone that he would speak to Monseigneur du Fou, and would himself carry the affair through, since it was certain the young lord had embraced her against her will, but that for valid reasons he would keep the affair dark. On the morrow the judge went to the Court and saw the Monseigneur du Fou, to whom he recounted the young woman's complaint, and how she had set forth her case. This complaint lodged in Court, tickled the king immensely. Young du Fou having said that there was some truth in it, the king asked if he had much difficulty, and as he replied, innocently, "No," the king declared the girl was quite worth a hundred gold crowns, and the chamberlain gave them to the judge, in order not to be taxed with stinginess, and said that starch would be a good income to La Portillone. The judge came back to La Portillone, and said, smiling, that he had raised a hundred gold crowns for her. But if she desired the balance of the thousand, there were at that moment in the king's apartments certain lords who, knowing the case, had offered to make up the sum for her with her consent. The little hussy did not refuse this offer, saying, that in order to do no more washing in the future she did not mind doing a little hard work now. She gratefully acknowledged the trouble the good judge had taken, and gained her thousand crowns in a month. From this came the falsehoods and jokes concerning her because out of these ten lords jealousy made a hundred, whilst, differently from young men, La Portillone settled down to a virtuous life directly she had her thousand crowns. Even a duke, who would have counted out five hundred crowns, would have found this girl rebellious, which proves she was niggardly with her property. It is true that the king caused her to be sent for to his retreat of Rue Quinquangrogne, on the mall of Chardonneret, found her extremely pretty, exceedingly affectionate, enjoyed her society and forbade the sergeants to interfere with her in any way whatever. Seeing she was so beautiful, Nicole Beaupertuis, the king's mistress, gave her a hundred gold crowns to go to Orléans, in order to see if the colour of the Loire was the same there as at Portillon. She went there, and the more willingly because she did not care very much for the king. When the good man came who confessed the king in his last hours, and was afterwards canonized, La Portillone went to him to polish up her conscience, did penance, and founded a bed in the leper-house of St. Lazare-les-Tours. Many ladies whom you know have been assaulted by more than two lords, and have founded no other beds than those of their own houses. It is well to relate this fact in order to cleanse the reputation of this honest girl, who herself once washed dirty things, and who afterwards became famous for her clever tricks and her wit. She gave a proof of her merit in marrying Taschereau, whom she cuckolded right merrily, as has been related in the story of The Reproach. This proves to us most satisfactorily that with strength and patience justice itself can be violated.

Indiscretion

by Guy De Maupassant

They had loved each other before marriage with a pure and lofty love. They had just met on the sea-shore. He had thought this young girl charming, as she passed by with her light-colored parasol and her dainty dress amid the marine landscape against the horizon. He had loved her, blond and slender, in these surroundings of blue ocean and spacious sky. He could not distinguish the tenderness which this budding woman awoke in him from the vague and powerful emotion which the fresh salt air and the grand scenery of surf and sunshine and waves aroused in his soul.

She, on the other hand, had loved him because he courted her, because he was young, rich, kind, and attentive. She had loved him because it is natural for young girls to love men who whisper sweet nothings to them. So, for three months, they had lived side by side, and hand in hand. The greetings which they exchanged in the morning, or in the evening on the sand, under the stars, in the warmth of a calm night, whispered low, very low, already had the flavor of kisses, though their lips had never met.

Each dreamed of the other at night, each thought of the other on awakening, and, without yet having voiced their sentiments, each longed for the other, body and soul.

After marriage their love descended to earth. It was at
first a tireless, sensuous passion, then exalted tenderness
composed of tangible poetry, more refined caresses, and
new and foolish inventions. Every glance and gesture was
an expression of passion.

But, little by little, without even noticing it, they began
to get tired of each other. Love was still strong, but they
had nothing more to reveal to each other, nothing more
to learn from each other, no new tale of endearment, no
unexpected outburst, no new way of expressing the well-
known, oft-repeated verb.

They tried, however, to rekindle the dwindling flame
of the first love. Every day they tried some new trick or
desperate attempt to bring back to their hearts the un-
cooled ardor of their first days of married life. They tried
moonlight walks under the trees, in the sweet warmth of
the summer evenings: the poetry of mist-covered beaches;
the excitement of public festivals.

One morning Henriette said to Paul:

"Will you take me to a café for dinner?"

"Certainly, dear."

"To some well-known café?"

"Of course!"

He looked at her with a questioning glance, seeing that
she was thinking of something which she did not wish to
tell.

She went on:

"You know, one of those cafés—oh, how can I explain
myself?—a sporty café!"

He smiled: "Of course, I understand—you mean in one
of the cafés which are commonly called bohemian."

"Yes, that's it. But take me to one of the big places, one
where you are known, one where you have already supped

—no—dined—well, you know—I-I-oh! I will never dare say it!"

"Go ahead, dear. Little secrets should no longer exist between us."

"No, I dare not."

"Go on; don't be prudish. Tell me."

"Well, I-I-I want to be taken for your sweetheart—there! and I want the boys, who do not know that you are married, to take me for such; and you too—I want you to think that I am your sweetheart for one hour, in that place which must hold so many memories for you. There! And I will play that I am your sweetheart. It's awful, I know —I am abominably ashamed, I am as red as a peony. Don't look at me!"

He laughed, greatly amused, and answered:

"All right, we will go tonight to a very swell place where I am well known."

Toward seven o'clock they went up the stairs of one of the big cafés on the Boulevard, he smiling, with the look of a conqueror, she, timid, veiled, delighted. They were immediately shown to one of the luxurious private dining-rooms, furnished with four large armchairs and a red plush couch. The head waiter entered and brought them the menu. Paul handed it to his wife.

"What do you want to eat?"

"I don't care; order whatever is good."

After handing his coat to the waiter, he ordered dinner and champagne.

The waiter looked at the young woman and smiled. He took the order and murmured:

"Will Monsieur Paul have his champagne sweet or dry?"

"Dry, very dry."

Henriette was pleased to hear that this man knew her husband's name. They sat on the divan, side by side, and began to eat.

Ten candles lighted the room and were reflected in the mirrors all around them, which seemed to increase the brilliancy a thousand-fold.

Henriette drank glass after glass in order to keep up her courage, although she felt dizzy after the first few glasses. Paul, excited by the memories which returned to him, kept kissing his wife's hands. His eyes were sparkling.

She was feeling strangely excited in this new place, restless, pleased, a little guilty, but full of life. Two waiters, serious, silent, accustomed to seeing and forgetting everything, to entering the room only when it was necessary and to leaving it when they felt they were intruding, were silently flitting hither and thither.

Toward the middle of the dinner, Henriette was well under the influence of champagne. She was prattling along fearlessly, her cheeks flushed, her eyes glistening.

"Come, Paul; tell me everything."

"What, sweetheart?"

"I don't dare tell you."

"Go on!"

"Have you loved many women before me?"

He hesitated, a little perplexed, not knowing whether he should hide his adventures or boast of them.

She continued:

"Oh, please tell me. How many have you loved?"

"A few."

"How many?"

"I don't know. How do you expect me to know such things?"

"Haven't you counted them?"

"Of course not."

"Then you must have loved a good many!"

"Perhaps."

"About how many? Just tell me about how many."

"But I don't know, dearest. Some years a good many, and some years only a few."

"How many a year, did you say?"

"Sometimes twenty or thirty, sometimes only four or five."

"Oh! That makes more than a hundred in all!"

"Yes, just about."

"Oh! I think that is dreadful!"

"Why dreadful?"

"Because it's dreadful when you think of it—all those women—and always—always the same thing. Oh! it's dreadful, just the same—more than a hundred women!"

He was surprised that she should think that dreadful, and answered, with the air of superiority which men take with women when they wish to make them understand that they have said something foolish:

"That's funny! If it is dreadful to have a hundred women, it's dreadful to have one."

"Oh, no, not at all!"

"Why not?"

"Because with one woman you have a real bond of love which attaches you to her, while with a hundred women it's not the same at all. There is no real love. I don't understand how a man can associate with such women."

"But they are all right."

"No, they can't be!"

"Yes, they are!"

"Oh, stop; you disgust me!"

"But then, why did you ask me how many sweethearts I had had?"

"Because—"

"That's no reason!"

"What were they—actresses, little shop-girls, or society women?"

"A few of each."

"It must have been rather monotonous toward the last."

"Oh, no; it's amusing to change."

She remained thoughtful, staring at her champagne glass. It was full—she drank it in one gulp; then putting it back on the table, she threw her arms around her husband's neck and murmured in his ear:

"Oh, how I love you, sweetheart! how I love you!"

He threw his arms about her in a passionate embrace. A waiter, who was just entering, backed out, closing the door discreetly. In about five minutes the head waiter came back, solemn and dignified, bringing the fruit for dessert. She was once more holding between her fingers a full glass, and gazing into the amber liquid as though seeing unknown things. She murmured in a dreamy voice:

"Yes, it must be fun!"

Venetia Stanley

[As quoted from Sir Kenelm Digby's Memoirs in
"The New Spirit" by Havelock Ellis]

For the classic vision of Nature, listen to that fantastic
and gigantic Englishman, Sir Kenelm Digby, whose "Memoirs," whose whole personality, embodied the final efflor-
escence of the pagan English Renaissance. He has been
admitted by her maids to the bed-chamber of Venetia
Stanley, the famous beauty who afterwards became his
wife; she is still sleeping and he cannot resist the temptation to undress and lie gently and reverently beside her, as
half disturbed in her slumber she rolled on to her side
from beneath the clothes; "and her smock was so twisted
about her fair body that all her legs and the best part of
her thighs were naked, which lay so one over the other that
they made a deep shadow where the never-satisfied eyes
wished for the greatest light. A natural ruddiness did shine
through the skin, as the sunbeams do through crystal or
water, and ascertained him that it was flesh that he gazed
upon, which yet he durst not touch for fear of melting it,
so like snow it looked. Her belly was covered with her
smock, which it raised up with a gentle swelling, and
expressed the perfect figure of it through the folds of that
discourteous veil. Her paps were like two globes—wherein
the glories of the heaven and the earth were designed, and

the azure veins seemed to divide constellations and king-
doms—between both which began the milky way which
leadeth lovers to their Paradise, somewhat shadowed by the
yielding downwards of the uppermost of them as she lay
upon her side, and out of that darkness did glisten a few
drops of sweat like diamond sparks, and a more fragrant
odor than the violets or primroses, whose season was nearly
passed, to give way to the warmer sun and the longest day."